PSYCHOLOGY FOR WBCS

ENGLISH VERSION

PAYAL BANERJEE

This book is dedicated to my parents who have taught me to have a positive attitude towards life. Thanks to them, who have always motivated me, and support me, so that I can face any negative situation in the life. Without their guidance and support, I would not be able to reach here, where I am.

Also, I am thankful to my teachers for empowering their love and guidance upon me.

Also, thanks to all my friends and students who have always inspire me to excel in life. They have always act as my support system.

And at last, I would like to thank, the Almighty God, to shower blessings on me, so that I can always walk in the right path.

Contents

Preface

This book provides the complete guidance to the students who are preparing for West Bengal Civil Service Examination, and has opted for Psychology as their optional subject. In this book, detailed notes are provided to the students, mostly in question answer pattern, so that the students do not have to depend upon any other external source for making their notes. As optional paper in WBCS exam is a descriptive one, so the answer writing pattern is very important. Generally, the students face difficulty in writing and formation of answer, this book is a solution to that. Since, there are two papers in optional subject. This book deals with the syllabus of paper 1, as well as paper 2 of Psychology. Each and every chapter with complete explanation is given in this book. Also, the students face difficulty in buying a number of books, as no single book covers the complete syllabus. This problem is also solved, as this single book will cover the complete notes regarding paper 1 and paper 2 of Psychology as optional paper.

Chapter 1-14 deals with paper 1 and chapter 15-24 deals with paper 2.

Acknowledgements

I am grateful to my students for their consistent love and support. Also, I am grateful to my teachers who have taught me everything I know about the subject- Psychology.

ONE

INTRODUCTION TO PSYCHOLOGY

Q1. Define psychology. What are the branches of psychology?

Ans: The concept of psychology is very rich that makes researchers hard to define it more precisely. There are lot of disagreement among the authors about what psychology is, what the goal of psychology should be, and what method should be used in psychology to understand human nature. It is the fact to understand that psychology aims at comprehensives account of human activity and psychology is a science which adheres to common scientific method that emphasizes strict definition, clearly defined procedures and reproducible results. Behavioral components are studied in its parts so that it can easily be measured and related with other parts. In history psychology has been defined as the study of behavior of human beings and animals. Here, the definition of psychology will be incorporated under different headings.

(1) Psychology as science of soul: Earlier the concept of psychology was defined in philosophy term, Psychology as the study of soul as it is derived from two Greek words psyche, meaning soul and logos, signifying a rational course of study. Hence, the soul was considered as the subject matter of psychology. The method of studying subject matter was suggested to be introspection. The definition of psychology as the study of soul was denied because philosophers found it difficult to reach on any conclusion about the nature of soul. It was believed that the soul has no existence which cannot be seen and heard. Studying psychology makes it more of religion than of science. Also, soul makes psychology a speculative science as it is not open to observation and experimentation and therefore not given to verification.

(2) Psychology as a science of mind: About 400 years ago the term psyche was translated as mind, psychology was then defined as the study of mind. Mind is something in the body or heart which thinks, feels and acts. So, it was considered as a combination of some total of a mental process and it stands for personal internal experiences of a man. To understand mind better, some of its characteristics can be numerated below:

(1) Continuity (Mind work continuously. There is constant low of mental processes one after another.)

(2) Unity (Mind does not work as a number of separate processes such as thinking, reasoning and imagining. It is the one and same mind which thinks, reason and remember.)

(3) Active (All the time mind is engaged in constant activity)

(4) Immaterial (Mind is not made of flesh or other matter like brain)

(5) Private (Except individual himself, no one else can observe any one's thoughts and wishes.)

To understand mind three kinds of mental activities, that needs to understand: (1) cognitive, (means knowing which includes thinking, reasoning and imagining.) (2) conative (means doing which includes do walking, swimming and dancing) (3) Affective (Means feeling, which include feeling happy, sad and angry.)

This definition of psychology as mind discarded because of its complexities in defining its nature and methods of its study, like mind is subjective, it can't be seen or touched, unity and continuity of mind is lacking in abnormal people and animals.

(3) Psychology as science of consciousness:

Consciousness means those aspects of human experiences and personality of which the person himself is aware. According to William James (1890) "The definition of psychology may be best given as description and explanation of states of consciousness as such." There are three states of consciousness are explained: (1) Consciousness: Awareness of processes that are going inside or outside our bodies, The conscious mind can contain only a limited amount of thought. Perceptions, and memories at any given time. (2) Sub conscious: some thoughts and memory exist on the fringe of awareness which can be pulled back into consciousness fairly earlier (3) Unconscious: Certain ideas, feeling and memories are repressed to unconscious because they are too painful or traumatic to deal with of conscious level. According to Wundt (1892) psychology has to investigate internal experience our thoughts, feelings and sensations. Titchener also defined psychology as a science of conscious experience. This definition of psychology too was not accepted due to the following limitations. (1) Psychology does not believe in consciousness but in its process. (2) Some believe that consciousness in a substance but others take it as a process (3) It does not talk about the subconscious and unconscious activities of mind which constitute 9/10th part of mind. (4) We can be conscious only of our mental activities. We can't know the consciousness of others.

(4) Psychology as science of behavior: Science is systematic knowledge acquired through scientific method. Behavior means those acts of organism that can be observed, recorded and studied behavior can be external (eating, sleeping, drinking which can be observed by naked eye) and internal (Blood pressure, brain waves which can be studied by instruments only. Some goal directed behavior like seeking food, sex avoiding pain etc. are also grouped under behavior. Processes like thinking, reasoning emotion etc. are also called behavior. According to Watson (1878 - 1958) behavior consisted of learned responses to external stimuli that are perceived by senses. Stimulus any energy change which excites a receptor, employed loosely of any object or event which has such an effect if a stimulus is normal stimulus for a receptor, it is described as adequate, if it is not and yet effective, it is described inadequate. Response The activity, muscular, or glandular, of an organism with reference to a situation with which it is faced, or as a result of stimulation. First man to defined psychology as science of behavior was Willam Mc Dougall (1908). According to him "Psychology is a science which aims to given is better understanding and control of the behavior of organism as a whole." J.B. Watson (1913) defined psychology as "the science of behavior taking into account the human as well as animal behavior"

Skinner defined "Psychology is science of behavior and experiences. According to Woodworth "psychology can be defined as the science of the activities of the individual in relation to environment."

When we look at all the definition of psychology, we find there is no agreement over universal definition of psychology, yet definition may generally be viewed to central around a common pivot of behavior. Consequently, it may be concluded that psychology is a science of behavior or scientific study of behavioral activities and experiences.

Branches of Psychology

Psychology studies many aspects of behavior and also it compares and find out general principles useful in the understanding and control of behavior. Psychologist, Wundt founded the first psychology laboratory at

Leipzig in 1879. In 1979 Psychology completed its first century with great pride.

Psychologists try to look at human behavior from a range of different angle. Where there is behavior, one finds the scope of psychology. Behavior of normal, abnormal, the young and the old belonging to all spheres of life are studied by psychology. Its scope is not confined to human behavior but encompasses the behavior of animals too.

The branches of psychology can be categorized under specifies; (1) Research specialties and (2) Applied specialties. All the branches of psychology covered in these two criteria's:

(1) Research Specialties:

(I) Experimental psychology: This branch aims of understanding the fundamental causes of behavior under laboratory condition. The domain of study generally covers sensation, perception, learning, memories, problem solving, emotion, motivation etc. The variables are determined, and the experimentation is done on animal adopting scientific procedure under controlled condition.

(2) Physiological Psychology (Neuropsychology): This Branch of psychology deals with the connection between the nervous endocrine system and behavior. The research is conducted on how the brain regulates the motivations such as hunger and thirst. Also, the effect of hormonal imbalances, brain injury, circulation of blood on behavior are studied.

(3) Developmental psychology: Psychology changes throughout life are studied in this brand of psychology. All psychological domains – learning, memory, motivation, perception, personality and thinking and so on are examined in terms of changes over a life time. Under this umbrella term child development, adolescent psychology, adult psychology and Geriatric or psychology of aging are flourishing as almost separate and independent field.

(4) Personality Psychology: This branch of psychology is also known as differential psychology. It is the study of individual differences in behavior, the sources and consequences of such differences, and the degree of consistency of characteristics within the individual across situation and over time.

(5) Cognitive psychology: It investigates all aspects of cognition, memory, thinking, reasoning, decision making and so on.

(6) Animal psychology: This branch of psychology is also called comparative psychology. In this branch of psychology, the study is

performed on animals like rats. Cats, dogs, monkeys and chimpanzees who love similar heeds like the human being and perform similar activities like human. Human psychology is generally compared with animal psychology.

(7) Psychometrics psychology: This branch is concerned with the development of the tests and inventories for the measurement of human capacities and abilities. The study is also done on already existing tests and inventories, and develop statistical method for the use in the measurement of human abilities.

(8) Social Psychology: In this branch thoughts, feelings and behavior are studied in social context. The domains covered in this branch for study are, prejudice, attitude, aggression, social conflicts, leadership, love, marriage and relationship etc.

Applied specialties': There are a variety of other specialties in which research is important component but which are by nature very strongly involved in the delivery of psychological services in the applied field.

(1) Educational Psychology: This applied branch of psychology examines and evaluates learning emotional and motivational aspects of students and teachers Research is generally based on gender differences in mathematical ability, teacher's effect on student, identification of gifted children and attention problems in learning disabled children.

(2) School Psychology: The approach of this branch of psychology is concerned with testing children in elementary and secondary schools and devising programs to train teachers and parents to help students with emotional and learning problems. Personality, intelligence, achievement and motivation are generally assessed in the students to help them perform better in academic as well in social life.

(3) Industrial and organizational Psychology: Generally, relation between people and their job are studied in this branch of psychology. Psychologist generally perform task related to selection, training, placement and efficiency of workers. Employers' morale, job related stress qualities that the authority possess, Job enrichment and working liars are studied so as to enrich productivity. Industrial problems like strike, lock out and industrial accidents too generally taker up by the psychologist to solve.

(4) Clinical Psychology: This branch of psychology studies mild to severe mental and adjustment problems and apply therapeutic procedure for the treatment of disorders such as juvenile delinquency, alcoholism anxiety disorder schizophrenia etc. Clinical psychology in considered as an objective science in which problems disorders are treated by adopting

biopsychosocial approach.

(5) Forensic/Criminal Psychology: This branch of psychology deals with the theories and principles that apply to low enforcement and court procedures. Forensic psychologist generally provides services in academic settings, researching the psychological implication of eyewitness, expert testimony, jury selection and their decision making, and criminal correction and rehabilitation.

(6) Guidance and counseling Psychology: This field or branch of psychology is also considered as sub-branch of clinical psychology that deals with comparatively less severe behavioral issues and emotional problem. Vocational guidance and counseling are provided to generally young students to help them choose their careers according to their interest and ability counseling services to people having mental health issues like anxiety stress, depression, conflict, aggression, frustration is provided based on the counseling psychology related theories and principles.

Q2. What are the different methods used in psychology? Explain with merits and demerits.

Ans. Psychology is understood as a science, it is emphasized that the discovery of new knowledge about – behavior is based on experiment and observation. All scientists (Whether they are physicists, Chemists, biologist, sociologist, or psychologists) are engaged in the basic processes of collecting date and drawing conclusions about those date. The methods used by scientists have developed over many years and provide a common framework for developing, organizing, and sharing information. The scientific method is the set of assumptions, rules, and procedures scientists use to research.

INTROSPECTION METHOD:

Introspection is one of the most important methods of psychology introspection is internal perception. In its person himself observes his internal activities and processes. This method is indispensable in the description of individual experience e.g., if a man geos to see a movie film and returns after seeing it, it is through introspection that he can tell others how he feels about its introspection can best be defined as the inner observation of mental events by the man himself at the time occurrence. When observation of mental states or activities is careful and detailed, it is called introspection e.g. If the doctor asks you, how do you fell? and you say that you feel tired, you are making a report on your mental state and it is subjective observation. The word “introspection” is made up two Latin words, intro words, intro meaning "within" or "inward", and spire, meaning to "look". Hence, introspection means looking within or looking inward. In introspection, then, one is required to get inside one's own mind. It is a sort of self-observation in which one perceives, analyses and reports one's own feeling and in fact, everything that takes place in one's mind during the course of a mental act. For example, when in a state of anxiety, fear or anger, one way be asked to determine by one's own observation what one sensed, thought or felt at the time of experiencing that emotion.

MERITS

Introspection- the observation and reporting of one's own mental process-is considered important on account of its unique nature. It is a simple and readily available method. One's mental processes are always present and can be introspected at any time. Introspection is, therefore, able to give us a direct and immediate insight into one's own mental process without involving any extra expenditure of material or apparatus. Moreover, introspection provides adequate knowledge of the inner or covert experiences and thus the inner behaviour of an individual in the form of thought or feeling can be revealed through introspection.

LIMITATIONS

1. Introspection is not easy because one needs to observe one's mental processes carefully in the form of thoughts, feeling and sensations. But the state of one's mental processes is constantly changing and moreover we cannot at the same time be angry and yet look and watch ourselves carefully why we are angry. Introspection has to observe experiences going on in our minds, but the more successfully we introspect, the more readily the thing we want to introspect is missed. By concentrating on the mental process, we withdraw it from the object of the process we withdraw it form the object of the process and so arrest the process itself. Introspection, can remedy the above given defect by retrospection i.e., by recalling the process in memory when it has passed.
2. Introspection is unscientific i.e.; individual investigators differ in their results due to ambiguity of the correct information and personal bias.
3. Another difficulty is that introspection is purely an individual, subjective matter. It doesn't cater to universal mind thus, finding on an individual's introspective cannot be generalized.
4. The method of introspection would require a very keen power of abstraction because we are dealing not with things but mental process

which are difficult to grasp and explain.

5. The results lack reliable communicability and repeatability because we have no means for the objective observation of the introspection phenomenon.
6. Finally, the scope of introspection as a method of studying behaviour is rather limited. It can only be applied satisfactorily in the case of adult normal human beings. The behaviour of children, abnormal human beings. The behaviour of children, abnormal humans, animals etc., cannot be studied by this method.

In addition to requiring science be empirical, the scientific method demands that the procedures used be objective, or free from the personal bias or emotions of the scientist. The scientific method prescribes how scientists collect and analyze date, how they drew conclusions from date and how they share date with others. These rules increase objectivity by placing data under the Scrutiny of other scientists and even the public at large. Because date is reported objectively, other scientists know exactly how the scientist. Collected and analyzed the data. Most new research is designed to replicate that is to repeat add to, or modify – previous research findings. The scientific method therefore results in an accumulation of scientific knowledge through the reporting of research and the addition to and modifications of these reported findings by other scientists.

Thus, in psychology a number of methods are used to carry out scientific studies. These methods are discussed below.

(1) Experimental methods: The basic idea behind the experimental method is straight forward. Having formulated a testable hypothesis in terms of observable events, the experimenter (1) changes or varies the events which are hypothesized to have an effect, (2) Keeps other conditions constant, and (3) Looks for an effect of the change or variation on the system under observation. The psychologist looks for an effect of the experimental changes on behavior. There is a concept of variables in experimental method, which implies, an event or condition which can have different values. In other words, variables can be understood as an event or condition which can be measured and which varies quantitatively. Variables may be either independent or dependent. An independent variable is a condition set or selected by as experimenter too see whether it will have an effect on behavior. The independent variable is so called because this is the variable that is independently chosen and directly manipulated by the experimenter.

The dependent variable is the behavior of the person or animal in the experiment. A dependent variable might be the response of a person to a stimulus. The dependent variable is so called because its value depends, or may depend, on the value of the independent variable.

In doing experiments, hypotheses are formulated about the effect of one thing on another, the independent variable is the one expected to produce changes in the dependent variable.

In graphing the results to as experiment, it is conventional in psychology to plot the values of the independent variable on the horizontal axis, or x axis, and the values of the dependent variable on the vertical axis, or ordinate. With the graphical representation of results, we can see at a glance how the dependent variable of behavior in related to the values of the independent variable.

Very important characteristics in experimental method is 'control'. While conducting experiment it is important that only the specified independent variable be allowed to charge. Factors other than the independent variable which might affect the dependent variable must be held constant. If those factors not controlled the result might be misleading. It is said that an experiment is no better than its control.

Two main strategies, or experimental designs, are used to control extraneous factors. One strategy employs control groups. In the other, measures of behavior are made before the independent variable is introduced in order to establish a behavioral baseline against which to compare behavior after the independent variable has been presented, the subjects are said to serve as their own control in this before and after, or within subjects, type of experiment.

* Control group-design – Experiments generally involve one or more experimental groups and one or more control groups. An experimental group is a group in which members of the group are exposed to the independent variable manipulation. The control group is a group called comparison group that is treated in every way like the experimental group except that the manipulated variable is absent in it, when a control group design in used, the groups should be equivalent in every way except for the independent variable. We therefore match subjects is the experimental are control groups. The matching is done considering factors like general intelligence, gender, are age.

It is very difficult to match subjects in control and experimental groups on all the factors that might conceivably affect their performance in such case Randomization is done. Randomization in a method that ensure that people have an equal chance of being included in any of the groups. If in one group the experimenter includes only males and in the other group females, the results obtained in the study, could be due to the differences in gender rather than due to experimental manipulation.

* Baselines: If is assumed the better control can be achieved with the before and after, or with in subject, design in which subject serve as their own controls, in this method, a baseline (normal level) of behavior is established before the independent variable is induced. The behavior after the addition of the independent variable can then be compared with the baseline behavior. The before and after method gives good control over individual differences among the subjects which might affect the outcome of the experiment because such individual differences are present both before and after the independent variable is introduced. If the individual differences factor is hold constant, changes in behavior must be due to the independent variable.

To make sure that the independent variable produced the change in the behavior, it is good idea to see what happens when the independent variable is removed after it has been introduced. The behavior should go back to baseline levels if the independent variable did, in fact produced the observed changes. This is called an A-B-A within subjects' experimental design; the first A is the baseline condition without the independent variable, B is the condition with the independent variable, and the last A refers to the final test of the behavior without the independent variable. This design is a good one to use when the independent variable does not have a long-lasting effect. Some independent variables, though produce stable, long term changes in behavior.

* Replication: It is important that experiments can be repeated, or, in other works, replicated. We can show that recitation is an aid to memory by having two groups study something. One with recitation and other without, and then measuring the difference in memory. If this experiment is performed under the proper conditions, it will show that recitation helps memory. This finding too, has been repeated, or replicated, many, many times.

The advantages and importance of replication are obvious. If we get the same results over and over again under the same conditions, we can be sure of their accuracy beyond all reasonable doubt. Replication or "check-up-ability" as it has been called, is an essential part of the experimental method.

The strength of well-designed experiment is that it can provide relatively, a convincing evidence of a cause effect relationship. Between two or more variables.

ADAVANTAGES:

Experiment method is scientific as it uses scientific method. The main advantage of experimental method is better control of extraneous variable. In the ideal experiment no factors (variables) expect the one being studied are permitted to influence the outcome. Experiments are performed to test theories and to provide the theories and to provide the data base for explanations of behaviour. Merits of experimental method are as under:

1. **Economy:** Using the method of naturalistic observation requires that scientist wait patiently until the condonations of interest occur. In experimental method an experimenter controls the situation by creating the conditions of interest, thus obtaining data quickly and effectively.
2. **Experimental Method is based on facts:** Here experimenter studies facts with an objective attitude. We can generalize data after observation and recording. These generalizations are sometimes known as universal laws which can be verified.
3. **Result of Experimental Method are valid and Reliable:** Experimental method is most reliable, most valid and most systematic, more precise and most objective method of Psychology. Its results are more reliable than other methods of Psychology.
4. **Experimental Method can be repeated:** Objective measurement helps ensure that other researchers can repeat an experimental that is of interest to them. Such REPLICATION of studies is essential in science. The more often a research finding can be replicated, the more confidence we can have in it. Replication means repetition of a scientific study, if its finding is accurate, any study should be able to be repeated.
5. **Experimental Method involves Objectivity:** Minute and detailed observation is needed in experimental method. The accuracy of the instruments is ascertained. Observation and recording of data are objective in experimental method.
6. **Experimental Method uses control:** Experimental method is superior to observation method because it controls independent and dependent variables. Exercising adequate experimental control is essential in experimental planning. In performing all such experiments, we try to establish certain cause and effect relationship through the objective

observations of actions performed and subsequent changes produced under pre-arranged or rigidly controlled conditions.

7. **Experiment explains cause and effect Relationship:** It is through experimental method that we know the cause-and-effect relationship of variables. It explains and describes the existing relationship between the two variables (0independent and dependent.)
8. **Experimental method** has a Provision of Quantitate Measurement: It has introduced quantitative measurement in psychology.
9. **Experimental method** can predict human Behaviour: By following scientific method and discovering cause and effect relationship psychology can make predictions which are generally correct.
10. **Experimental method has wide applications:** It can be applied on children, adult and animals as well. It has wide applications in all branches of psychology especially in intelligence, personality, attitude, -aptitude learning, memory, attention transfer, sensation, perception, motivation etc.

Limitations of experimental method: Experimental method in conducted in a highly controlled laboratory situation, it this sense they only stimulate situations that exist in the outside world. This is because this method in criticized. The result obtained from experimental method may not have the potential to generalize to real situation. Another limitation of experimental method is that if in not always feasible to study a particular problem experimentally. For e.g., the effect of nutritional deficiency on intelligence level of children cannot be conducted as it would be ethically wrong to starve anyone. One more limitation of this method is that it is difficult to know and control all the relevant variables.

(2) Observation method: Observation, is a method of enquiry is often understood as a systematic registering of events without any deliberate attempt to interfere with variables operating in the event which is being studied, this method is used in natural as well as laboratory settings. When it is used to study the events happening in natural environment it is called naturalistic observation such as observing the behavior of children on playground. In this case the observer (Psychologist) has no control on the extraneous variables. They simply record the entire activities and then analyze them. On the contrary in the case of laboratory observation the event under study is controlled by the psychologist observer. For e.g., studying the effect of induced stress on task performance.

Observation is also divided into participant and non-participant types depending on the role of observer. In the participant observation the researcher mites up with the event under study and carry out study. In the non-participation part observation, the researcher maintains an optimum distance and has little impact on the event under study.

The most important advantages of observation are that it studies the range of behaviors in the form in which they are happening. The limitation of this method is that, this requires more time and effort. Also, there are changes of observe biasness that effect the result of the observation.

MERIT OF OBSERVATION:

Observation method occupies a leading role in the study of human behaviour.

1. It is economical, nature as well as flexible
2. It is objective and scientific.
3. It is reliable and valid. Its results can be verified and relied upon.
4. Behaviour of children, abnormal and animals can also be studied. Particularly in studying the developmental characteristics of individuals the naturalistic observation method proves quite suitable.
5. Similarly, a clinical psychologist may be able to collect the required data about abnormal behaviour of an individual by observing him in day-to-day life under natural conditions.

(3) The clinical Method: This method is ordinarily used only when people came to psychologists with personal problems. Not all clinical problems require through study. But when they do, the psychologist usually begins by getting a detailed account of the person's history. Including this family relations. All the information psychologist collects by interviewing the person and his associates. Sometimes the psychologists have; a specially trained social worker study the persons social background and environment. The psychologist may administer tests of various kinds intelligence test, interest test, tests of emotional maturity, personality tests etc. Form these tests and biographic information gathered previously, the psychologist will try to diagnose the problem and treat or remedy, the distress. All the method of collecting information will vary from case to case. Clinical method in considered as a tool of science. As a method, it combines features of clinical observation, experiment and systematic observation.

CLINICAL METHOD:

Clinical psychology is one of the major fields of psychology and is concerned mainly with the diagnosis, treatment and prevention of mental disorders at the individual level. When the clinician wants to treat the patient so that he may be restored to normality he has to probe deeper into the genesis of his problem to find out the causes of the disorder. A clinical psychologist usually does this by constructing a detailed case history of his patient. Such a case history may often begin with the birth of the patient and may contain detailed information about the ways in which he was bought up, his relationship to his parents, friends, relatives, his likes, dislikes, worries, fears, conflict the incidents which led to his present symptoms; his behaviour in various situations in life, and many other related things. By utilising this information, a clinician may get some insight into his patient's problem. Such information is also useful in suggesting the treatment for the patient. (Ghorpade, 1977)

Clinical psychologists probe deeper into an individual's life because his experiential background often determines his peculiar symptoms which provides for the clinical psychologist, an insight into the causation of the disorder. By utilising this method, clinical psychologist is often able to construct their own theories of mental disorders and also the methods or techniques or treatment.

Clinical psychologists are trained to diagnose and treat problems ranging from the everyday crises of life such as grief due to death of a loved one to more extreme conditions, such as loss of touch with reality. Some clinical psychologists also conduct research, investigating issues, that range from identifying the early signs of psychological disturbance to studying the relationship between how family members communicate with one another and the psychological disorder.

The main strength of this method to that it suggests fruitful ideas which can be interrogated more rigorously by experimental and systematic observation methods.

The limitation of the clinical method is that the clinical observation does not often provide much scientific information. It to casually subjective, causal, uncontrolled, and lacking in precise measurement. What appear to be cause and effect in one case may not be in another. Even in single case it is difficult to assign cause and effect relationship significantly.

SURVEY METHOD

A Survey is a way of obtaining descriptions of human behaviour drawn from more people than direct observation usually allows. Survey researchers ask subjects carefully prepared sets of questions about their attitudes, beliefs and characteristic ways of acting. A survey or it is sone times called a questionnaire (a printed from with questions) allows, researcher to gather a large amount of information from a large number of people in a relatively short time. In writing these questions, the researchers try to avoid vague or biased wording. Vaguely worded questions can cause confusion about what is being asked, and biased questions can invalidate answers by prompting subjects to respond as the researchers want them to. Surveys depend on direct contact with those persons, or a sample of those persons whose characteristics, behaviours, or attitude are relevant for a specific investigation. It is used when information cannot be collected by any other method. Survey's supply "How many" and "How much" information e.g. How many people are aggressive? Or how many uses library?

Survey, are used to obtain information or political opinions, consumer preferences, health care needs and many other topics. E.g., Gallop Poll, U.S. census, opinion polls.

LIMITATIONS OF SURVEY METHOD:

1. It is based on sample which is subject to sampling error.
2. It depends on voluntary co-operation of respondents.
3. There are limits to the number of topics that can be covered in a survey.
4. Long questions are required for establishing rapport with the subject but in questionnaire there is limitation of length for example in survey on personal maladjustment we need long questions.
5. Historical studies cannot be done by this method.

TYPES OF SURVEY

These are the alternatives forms which the survey researcher may choose in deciding how to conduct interview.

1. **Mail Survey:** Mail surveys represent the most common means of distributing self-administered questionnaires. A principal advantage of mail surveys is that they can be done relatively quickly. Because they are self-administered, mail surveys avoid the problems of interviewer bias, Mail surveys are the best for dealing with highly personal or

embarrassing topics, especially when anonymity of respondents is preserved. It is less costly than interview. A major problem of mail survey is response bias which is a threat to representativeness of sample. The major factor leading to response bias is low response rate. Quite often people are not interested or they are too busy to return a questionnaire. Low response rates produce smaller samples.

2. **Personal Interview:** Interview is a series of open-ended questions used to gather basic detailed information about a person. Usually, subject's responses are recorded on tape or written down. Respondents are usually contacted in their homes and trained interview administer the questionnaire. Personal interview allows much greater flexibility in asking questions than does the mail survey. Here interviewer can obtain clarifications about ambiguous answer to survey. Here interviewer can obtain clarifications about ambiguous answer to open ended questions. Personal interview is offset by two disadvantages firstly the high cost and secondly the interviewer bias. Bias occurs when the interviewer tries to adjust the wording of question to 'fit' the respondent or records only selected portions of respondent's answers. It can be removed by highly motivated, well paid interviewers who are properly trained.
3. **Telephone surveys:** High travel costs and the difficulties involved in supervising interviewers have led the researcher to have telephone survey or interview. It provides a quick and speedy collection of information about the respondents. There is still a possible selection bias when respondents are limited to those people who have telephones.

FIELD STUDY METHOD:

The field study method may be described as making direct observation of a phenomenon under investigation by going to the very place in which it occurs. The observer simply geos to the place with a definite question or set of question or set of questions in his mind to find out their answers by a careful observation of the prevalent conditions. He has, obviously, little or no control over the happenings and cannot get any co-operation from his subject. In fact, some field studies are most successful when the subjects are not aware that they are being observed. One of the greatest advantages of this method is that once the possible causes of a phenomenon are ascertained by direct and systematic observation, it often becomes easier to study the same conditions in a laboratory by introducing appropriate controls of conditions. It is in this sense that the field study method may be required as sort of a preliminary preparation for experimentation. Actually, many of the experiments in psychology are suggested by field observations.

The method of field study is often very useful in psychology and can be applied with great case in studies of public opinion, the effects of advertisements and other mass communication systems on consumer preferences and a host of social problems, and even in determining the role of such factors as heredity and environment.

CASE HISTORY/CASE STUDY METHOD:

Case history method is particularly used by clinical psychologists for the diagnosis and treatment at behaviour disorders. Uniqueness of case history method lies in observing and interviewing the parents, teacher and guardians of the case under observation.

Case Study: A carefully drawn biography that may be obtained through interviews, questionnaires, and psychological tests. Our own informal ideas about human nature tends to be based on case studies, or information we collect about individuals and small groups. But most of us gather our information haphazardly. Often, we see what we want to see. Unscientific accounts of people's behaviour are referred to as anecdotes. Psychologists attempt to gather information about individuals more carefully.

The case study is also used in psychological consultation. Psychologist learn whatever they can about individuals, agencies, and business firms so that they can suggest ways in which these clients can more effectively meet their challenges. Psychologists base their suggestions on laboratory research whenever possible, but psychological practice is also sometimes an art in which psychologist and client agree that a suggestion or a treatment has been helpful on the basis of the client's self- report.

One chief disadvantage is that case studies usually do not allow form inferences to be made about what causes what. Typically, all one can do is describe the course of events. Case study method is highly subjective unless trained and competent investigators conduct the interview or collect case history it may lead to erratic and erroneous findings. Subjectivity can be reduced by using a particular format as a guideline to the person who is collecting the information.

PSYCHOPHYSICAL METHODS (Moshsin, S.M.)

For a study of the relationship between the physical and the psychological dimensions, the psychophysicists developed three different methods of collection and treatment of data. A brief description of each one is given below:

1. **The Method of Mean or Average Error, also called the Method of Adjustment or the Method of Reproduction:** As the name suggests, the method is used to determine the average magnitude of error in one's perception of the value of a stimulus. In using this method, the experimenter repeatedly presents to the subject a stimulus of a fixed or constant value called the standard stimulus, together with a variable stimulus, that is a stimulus whose value can be changed, also called the comparison stimulus. The subject can increase or decrease the magnitude of the variable stimulus until it appears to him to be equal to the standard stimulus; the subject I required to adjust the variable stimulus to equality to the standard stimulus. The difference between the value of the standard stimulus and the value of the variable stimulus which S makes equal to the standard stimulus gives an estimate of the magnitude of the error S makes in perceiving the standard stimulus. The Mean of the differences obtained from several observations provides the Average Error of mean Error in perception. Since S adjusts the variable stimulus to equality to the standard stimulus, the method I s also called the Method of Adjustment. Sometimes, the constant stimulus is alone presented to S and he is asked to reproduce the stimulus. For example, he may be shown a line of fixed length and he may be required to draw other lines of the same length. A comparison of the length of the lines drawn by S gives an estimate of S's error of perception of the constant line. Hence the other name of method, namely, the Method of Reproduction.

1. **The Method of limits, also Called the Method of just Noticeable Stimulus Difference, or the Method of Minimal Change, Or the Method of Successive or Serial Exploration:** This method has been principally used for the determination of the RL or the DL. RL is the lower or upper limit of a stimulus value that can be barely noticed, the just noticeable values of the stimulus, or that value of the stimulus which produces a change in the S's response. Similarly, DL is the limit of the difference between two values of a stimulus that can be noticed the just noticeable difference, or the minimal difference, or the minimal difference that can produce a change in the perception of the stimulus. The procedure for determining the RL or the Dl by this method involves the presentation of the variable stimulus in a successive or serial order, that is, by gradually increasing or decreasing its amount. Hence the other name, i.e., the method of successive or serial exploration.

3. **The Method of constant Stimuli or the Method of Frequency:** The chief purpose of this method too is to determine the RL or DL. This method is very similar to the method of limits. Here also Different values of a stimulus are presented to S. Each time, for determining RL, S has to report whether he notices the stimulus or fails to notice it. To determine DL, S has to report whether a particular value of the stimulus is the same or different from a standard stimulus which is kept constant. The two methods differ only in the mode of presentation of the variable stimulus. In the method of limits E presents the variable in a regular increasing or decreasing order; in the constant stimuli method, E changes the value of the variable stimulus in an irregular or chance order; a large value of the stimulus may be abruptly followed by a very small value, a small larger value, or by one of medium size. It is just a matter of chance which value of the variable stimulus follows or precedes which other value. The S cannot anticipate whether he would get a large or a smaller value at the next instant. However, through different values of the variable: stimulus is presented in chance order, the same values are presented throughout the entire sets of observations E decides to take in the experiment. That is why it is called the method of constant stimuli.

THE CORRELATIONAL METHOD:

Sometimes researchers want to explore how various factors are related to one another- that is, whether or not these factors are correlated. Is major surgery correlated with the onset of depression? Is being a first-born child correlated with high academic achievement?

Correlational Research: Investigates such possible relationships. It determines whether certain factors occur together at a rate significantly higher than would be expected to happen by chance.

Correlational research often deals with variables that are beyond a researcher's power to control. Examples are age, gender, and race. This method is also useful for studying that cannot ethically be imposed on people just for the sake of science (drug addiction, for instance, or emotional abuse). Instead, researchers find naturally occurring instances of such factors and explore what other phenomena regularly accompany them. Are drug addicts usually young, and are they more likely to be male than female?

In correlational research, the degree of relationship between two variables is statistically calculated and called the **correlation coefficient**. A correlation coefficient is expressed by a number ranging from -1 to +1.

Sometimes it is possible to gain insights into causality by conducting what is called a longitudinal study. In a **longitudinal study**, the same group of people is followed over time. A researcher might select a sample of married couples, for example, and assess their economic situations, their marital satisfaction, and their emotional health over, say, ten years. If the incidence of both divorce and emotional problems increases whenever economic conditions decline, there is reason to believe that financial hardship is a third variable contributing to a link between divorce and emotional disorders.

Q3. What are schools of psychology? Explain in brief.

Ans: Psychology become distinct from philosophy when researcher began to use the scientific method to study behavior and mental processes. By 1920s, the field's earliest researchers had laid the foundation of the major schools of thought and psychological perspectives that exist in psychology today. There were quite different, views among the psychologist about the nature of mind and behavior, and the best way to study it. During the same time, fundamental questions were raised about what should be studied in psychology: Should psychology be the study of mind, should it study behavior, or both mind and behavior be included? Different influential psychologists of the time told quite different views on the nature of mind and the proper subject matter of psychology. School of thought formed around these leaders as their students adopted their ideas. These school of thought are known as the school of psychology; they set the direction for much of the research on min and behavior in the early years of this century. The following are some of the major schools of thought that have influenced our knowledge and understanding of psychology.

(1) **Structuralism:** Wilhelm Wundt (1832-1920) who is generally thought of as the "father" of psychology. Wundt's vision for the discipline of psychology Wundt's vision for the discipline of psychology included studies of social and cultural influences on human thought (Benjafield, 1996). Wundt established a psychological laboratory at the university of Leipzig in Germany in 1879, an event considered to mark the birth of psychology as a formal academic discipline. Using a method called introspection, Wundt and his associates studied the perception of variety of visual, tactile, and auditory stimuli, including the rhythm patterns produced by metronomes set of different speeds.

Wundt's student Titchener (1867-1927) set up a psychological laboratory at Cornell University. He gave the name structuralism this first formal school of thought in psychology, which aimed at analyzing the basic elements, or the structure, of conscious mental experience. They thought that as in chemistry, a first step in the study of mind should be a description of the basic, or elementary, units of sensation, image, and emotion which compose it. The main method used by Titchener too, to discover these elementary units of mind was introspection. Subjects were trained to report as objectively as possible what they experienced in connection with a certain stimulus, disregarding the meaning they had come to associate with that stimulus.

(2) **Gestalt Psychology:** This school of psychology made its appearance in Germany in 1912 by Max Wertheimer (1880-1943) and his colleagues Kurt Koffka (1846-1942) and Wolfgarg Kohler (1887-1967). These psychologists felt that structuralists were wrong in thinking of the mind as being made up of elements. They maintained that the mind is not made up of a combination of simple elements. The German word Gestalt roughly means "whole, form or pattern". It was believed that the mind should be thought of as resulting from the whole pattern of sensory activity and the relationships and organizations within this pattern. For instance, we recognize a tune when it is transposed to another key; the elements have changed but the pattern of relationship has stayed the same.

(3) Functionalism: Functionalists, such as john Dewey (1873-1954), James R. Angell (1869-1949) and Harvey Carr (1873-1954) at the University of Chicago proposed that psychology should study "what mind and behavior do". It was concocted not with the structure of consciousness but with how mental processes function that is, how humans and animals use mental processes in adapting to their environment. The functionalists did experiments on the ways in which learning, memory, problem solving, and motivation help people and animals adapt to their environments.

(4) **Behaviorism:** This school of psychology originated with john B. Watson (1879-1958) who looked at the study of psychology as defined by the structuralists and functionalists and disliked virtually everything he saw. In his article "Psychology as the behaviorist. View it" (1913), Watson proposed a radically hew approach to psychology. This new school redefined psychology as the science of Behavior". Termed behaviorism by Watson, this school of psychology confines itself to the study of behavior because behavior is observable and measurable and therefore, objective and scientific. Behaviorism also emphasizes that behavior in determined primarily by factors in the environment. There are three important

characteristics of behaviorism: (I) an emphasis on conditioned responses (conditioned response can be described loosely as a relatively simple learned response to a stimulus) as the elements, or building blocks of behavior. (II) Its emphasis on learned, rather than unlearned, behavior. It denied the existence of inborn, or innate behavioral tendencies. (III) third characteristics of behaviorism was its focus on animal behavior. Watson held that there are no essential differences between human and animal behavior and that we can learn about our own behavior from the study of what animal do.

(5) **Psychoanalysis:** Strictly speaking, psychoanalysis is not a school of psychology, but it has had great impact on the thinking and theorizing of many psychologists (Morgan et. al., 2011). Psychoanalysis was developed in Vienna, Austria by the psychiatrist Sigmund Freud (1856-1938) based largely on case studies of his patients. Freud maintains that human mental life is like an iceberg. The smallest visible part of the iceberg represents the conscious mental experience of the individual. But underwater, hidden from view, floats a vast store of unconscious impulses, wishes, and desires. It was emphasized that individual do not consciously control their thoughts, feelings and behavior, these are instead determined by unconscious forces. Freud also gave large emphasis on sexual and aggressive impulses, that caused much controversy both inside and outside the field of psychology. The most notable of Freud's famous students – Carl Jung. Alfred Adler, and Karen Horney – broke away from their mentor and developed their own theories to personality they are often collectively referred as neo-Freudians.

The new perspectives which have arisen in the last 50 years or so give psychologists a rich variety of viewpoints to choose from in their task of describing and understanding behavior. Examples of these newer viewpoints include the biological, cognitive, developmental, humanistic and social perspectives.

The perspective taken depends partly on the basic of the individual psychologist and partly on what aspect of behavior is under study. Certain perspectives are more appropriate for some behaviors than others.

(1) **The behavioral perspective:** This perspective confines itself to the study of behavior because behavior is observable and measurable, and therefore, objective and scientific. Also, behavioral perspective emphasizes that behavior is determined primarily by factors in the environment. Individual learn to behave in certain way because the behavior paid off in the past. So the behavioral psychologist fours on a precise description of the

changes in an individual's behavior.

(2) **The Biological Perspective:** Biological perspective emphasizes on the link between specific behaviors and partial biological factors that often help explain individual differences. They study the structure of the brain and central nervous system, the functioning of neurons, the delicate balance of neurotransmitters and hormones, and the effect of heredity to look for links between these biological factors and behavior.

(3) **The cognitive perspective:** This perspective sees human not as passive recipients who are pushed and pulled by environmental forces but as active recipients who seek out experiences, and who use mental processes to transform information in the course of their own cognitive development. It studies mental processes such as memory, problem solving, reasoning, decision making, perception, language, and other forms of cognition.

(4) **The social perspective:** This perspective emphasizes social and cultural influences on human behavior and stresses the importance of understanding those influences when interpreting the behavior of others. Social and cultural influences on behavior are often studied within the broader context of a systems perspective. The primary idea behind the systems approach is that multiple factors work together holistically; that is their combined, interactive influences on behavior are greater than the sum of the individual factors that make up the system. A good example of the systems approach may be found in a theory propose by psychologist Gerald Patterson and his colleagues that explains how variables interact to predispose some teenagers to antisocial behavior (Granic Patterson, 2006).

(5) **The Developmental perspective:** The developmental perspective is concerned with characteristic changes that occur in people as they mature – changes in the way they think. This approach assumes that development is an ongoing process over a person's lifetime. Changes occurs as children and adulates develop as a result of inherited factors (genetics) or environmental factors. The three goals of developmental psychology are to describe, explain and to optimize development (Baltes, Reese and Lipsitt, 1980) Do describe development it is necessary to focus both on typical patterns of change (normative development) and individual variations in patterns of change (i.e. ideographic development). Although there are typical pathways of development that most people will follow, no two people are exactly alike.

(6) **The Humanistic perspective:** This perspective focuses on the uniqueness of human beings and their capacity for choice, growth, and psychological health. This approach emphasizes a much more positive view

of human Nature. Abraham Maslow and other early humanists, such as Carl Rogers (1902-1987), Pointed out that Freud based his theory primarily on date from his disturbed patients. They maintain that people are innately good and that they possess free will. The humanists believed that people are capable of making conscious, rational choices, which can lead to personal growth and psychological health.

(7) **The Psychoanalytic Perspective**: This perspective is part of the broader perspective called psychodynamic – A perspective that focuses on the role of feelings and impulses which are thought to be unconscious. A key psychodynamic idea is that when these impulses are unacceptable, or when they make us anxious, we use defense mechanisms to reduce the anxiety. Another key idea of the psychoanalytic perspective is that slips, or accidents, often happen for a reason and they may reveal hidden motives. It is mentioned the psychoanalytic perspective digs beneath the surface of behavior, looking for hidden processes and impulses.

TWO

BIOLOGICAL BASES OF BEHAVIOR

Q1. Explain the structure and function of brain with the help of diagram.

Ans: The brain is very soft and jellylike. The considerable weight of a human brain (approximately 1400 g), along with its delicate construction, necessitates that it be protected from shock. A human brain cannot even support its own weight well, it is difficult to remove and handle a fresh brain from a recently deceased human without damaging it. The intact brain within a living human is well protected. It floats in a both of cerebrospinal fluid contained within the subarachnoid space. Because the brain is completely immersed in liquid, Because the brain is completely immersed in liquid, its het weight is reduced to approximately 80 gms thus pressure on the base of the brain is considerably diminished.

In all the animal kingdom, human is unique because of the capacities for learning and thought made possible by brain. Our brain serves several different functions that together make us both alive and human. Our brain regulates our vital bodily activities, such as breathing, circulation, and digestion. The brain produces the emotions we feel, it enables us to experience anger and shame or surprise and happiness. Our brain receives information about the outside world through our sense organs and in response issues commands to move various parts of our body. Our brain is our machinery for learning, thinking, and planning; it stores past experience and uses them to determine how to act in a given situation. Different brain regions are involved in different behaviors. For e.g., the parts of brain that enable us to see a sunset, for e.g., are not the same as those that allow us to solve a mathematical question. The brain works by integrating the activities of its many different parts, each of with controls a limited set of functions.

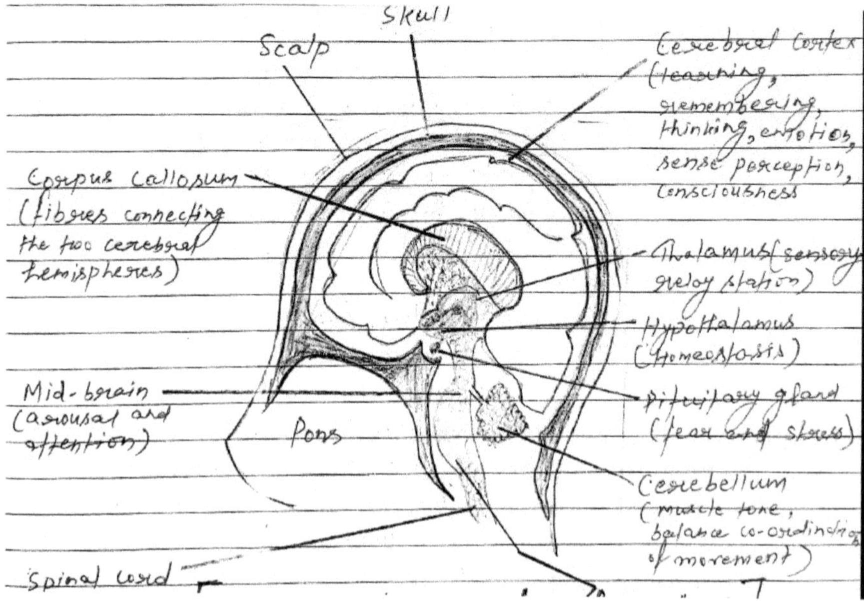

The brain is composed of two large cerebral hemispheres are on the right side and one on the left side. The exterior covering of the brain, the cortex, occupies the major portion of the cerebral hemispheres.

The cortex is two millimeters thick, and consists of several thin layers of cells that are convoluted, folded or crumpled, to accommodate a large surface area in a much smaller space.

There is a large, thick structure called the corpus callosum that connects the two cerebral hemispheres and permits the transfer of information between them.

The brain is divided into areas with special functions. Some parts are specialized for visual activities, others are involved in hearing, sleeping, breathing, or eating. Some brain activities are localized; speech and language activity, for e.g. can be pinpointed to a specific area usually in the left side of the brain. Other activities may occur at several locations; visual activity for eg. occurs in the visual cortex, which occupies both sides of the brain.

To understand the structure and functions of the brain well, it is divided into three separate sections:

(1) The Hindbrain

(2) The midbrain

(3) The fore brain

(1) The hindbrain – This consists of three main structures (I) The medulla, which is the base of the brain stem and which helps regulate many autonomous activities, such as circulation and breathing. Medulla is also involved in the control of chewing, salivation and facial movements. Within the medulla there is a lattice like network of nerve cells called the reticular formation, which controls individual's state of arousal, walking, sleeping and other body functions, damage to it can lead to come and death.

(II) The pons – It is a Latin word for "bridge", the bundle of nerves passes through it. Neural fibers from the two sides of body cross over here. The pons transmits information about body movements and it is also involved in functions related to attention. Sleep or dreaming and alertness are also regulated by pons.

(III) The cerebellum – Cerebellum lies behind the pons. In Latin cerebellum is called tittle brain. The back of the brain where the cerebellum is located. It is responsible for muscle tone, posture, movements, fine motor control and balance in the body. The cerebellum controls most of our physical activity. Although it doesn't make the decisions about what we should do. Its co-ordinates our actions and makes sure that we can do them smoothly and easily. Damage to the cerebellum can cause a lack of coordinate that resemble the movements of a person who has had too much to drink.

(2) The midbrain – This is just above be medulla, and almost a part of it. It maintains tracts between the cerebrum and the spinal cord and functions as part of the overall impulse conduction system. The midbrain is composed of a number of nuclei (collections of cell bodies) that accept afferent signals, interpret them, and either relay this information to a more complex part of the brain or cause the body to act at once. The midbrain continues the reticular formation system (RAS). The RAS is that vital function in attention, sleep and arousal. Injury to RAS may leave an animal COMATOSE. RAS seems to be for switch on large areas of the cerebral cortex, the part that involve in consciousness. It also plays part in directing attention, also midbrain controls some auditory and visual responses. Two structures of mid-brain, tegmentum and the tectum, have been identified, but there is

little evidence about what they do.

MID BRAIN HAS TWO MAJOR PARTS:

- Tectum: Structure includes superior colliculli

(part of visual system) and inferior colliculi (part of auditory system), which appear as four bumps on the dorsal surface

- Tegmentum: Controlling eye movement

(3) The forebrain – The forebrain is the largest of the three divisions of the brain, occupies the entire upper portion of the skull. This part of the brain control. Complicated patterns of behavior and are the source of those higher level – activities that differentiate human beings from other animals. The forebrain includes two parts diencephalon and telencephalon.

Diencephalon is composed of two structures the thalamus and the hypothalamus. The telencephalon, comprises three main structures: the basal ganglia, the corpus callosum, and the cortex.

(*) The thalamus is located near the center of the brain; it serves as a relay station for sensory stimulation. Nerve fibers from our sensory systems enter from below; the information carried by them is then transmitted to the cerebral cortex by way of fibers that exist from above. It also involves in controlling sleep and attention.

(*) The Hypothalamus – It lies beneath the thalamus and above the pituitary gland. It controls the autonomic nervous system and endocrine system and maintain Homeostasis in the body. It also controls hunger, thirst, and sexual drives, regulates body temperature. It plays a role in emotions as well as well as in body's responses to stress.

(*) The limbic system – This is made up of group of interconnected structures including parts of cortex, thalamus, any hypothalamus. It plays role in memory, emotions, hunger, sex and aggression. Also, it is involved in sleep, wake fullness and emotional activity.

(*) The basal ganglia – It is a series of nuclei located deep in the brain, control movement posture and the co-ordination of limbs.

(*) The corpus callosum – It is the wide band of neural fibers that connects the two hemispheres of the brain. Also, it permits the transfer of information between them.

(*) Cerebral cortex – Cortex means 'bark' cerebral cortex surrounds the cerebral hemispheres like the bark of a tree. In human the cerebral cortex is greatly convoluted. These convolutions, consisting of sulci (small grooves). Fissures (large grooves), and gyri (bulges between adjacent sulci or fissures). The presence of gyri and sulci triples the area of the cerebral cortex. The total surface area is approximately 2360 cm^2 (2.5 ft^2), and the thickness is approximately 3 mm.

The cerebral cortex mainly consists of glia and the cell bodies, dendrites and interconnected axons of neurons. Cerebral cortex RAS a grayish brown appearance i.e., called gray matter. There is a large concentration of myelin round the axons gives the tissue an opaque white appearance hence the term is white matter.

* Different regions of the cerebral cortex perform different functions.

(*) Primary visual cortex – receives visual information from specialized sensory organ, is located at the back of the brain.

(*) The primary auditory cortex, which receives auditory information from specialized sensory organ, a vertical strip of cortex just caudal to the central sulcus.

(*) The primary somatosensory cortex – different regions of it receives information from different regions of the body.

(*) The primary motor cortex – this is directly involved in controlling movement, located just in front of the primary somatosensory cortex.

The cerebral cortex is divided into four areas or lobes, named for the bones of the skull that cover them.

(1) Frontal lobe (The front) includes everything in front of the central sulcus. Frontal lobe consists of motor cortex, the area which control body movements. Damage to this area results in loss of in fine movements, especially in the finger. The association area of the frontal lobe plays important role in decision making, problem solving planning and foal setting.

(2) The parietal lobe – Across the central fissure from the frontal lobe is the parietal lobe. This contains the somatosensory cortex, to which information from the skin senses touch, temperature, and so on. Discrete damage to this area produces variety of effects, depending in part of whether injury occur to the left or right cerebral hemisphere.

(3) The Occipital lobe – This is located near the back of the head. Its primary role is to control vision, and it contains a sensory area that receives input from the eyes. Injury to the occipital lobe may produce contrasting

effects depending upon which cerebral hemisphere is affected.

(4) The temporal lobe – This lobe is located along the side of each hemisphere. This lobe is primarily concerned with hearing and contains a sensory area that receives input from the ear. Damage to this lobe can result in intriguing symptoms.

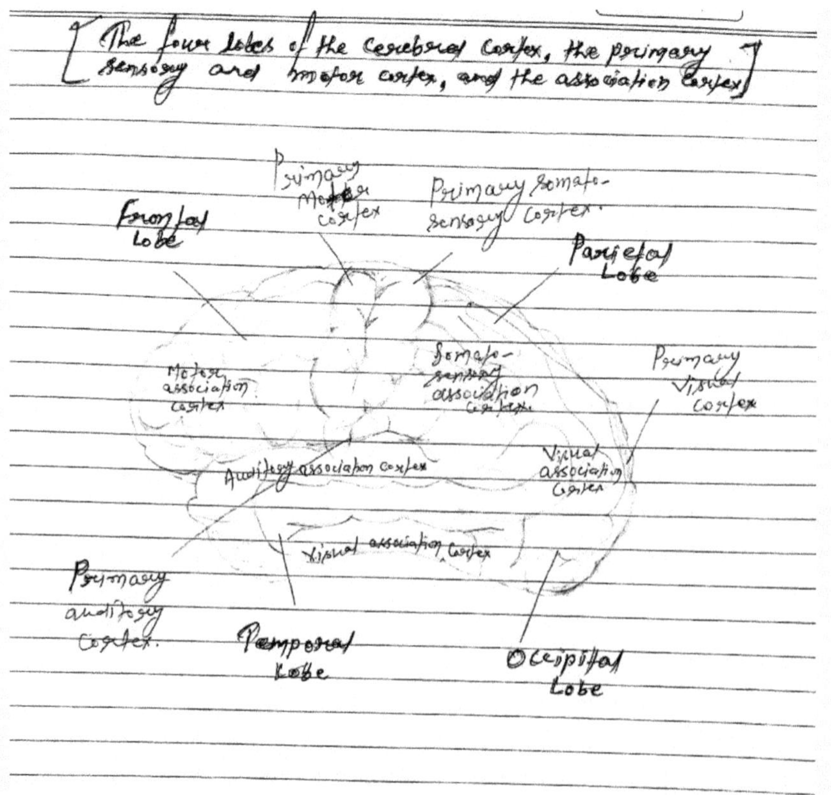

Q2. Explain the structure and function of neuron and spinal cord with the help of diagram?

Ans: Neuron – The neuron (nerve call) is the information processing and information transmitting element of the nervous system. Neurons come in many shapes and varieties, according to the specialized jobs they perform.

Most neurons have, in one form or another, have following four structures:

a) Cell body

b) Dendrites

c) Axon
d) Terminal Buttons

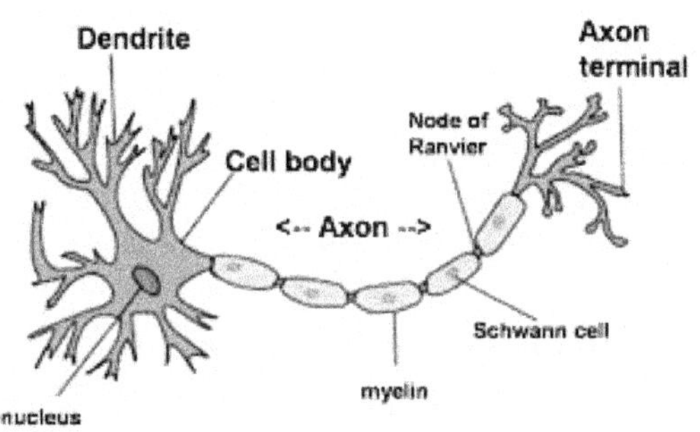

a) Cell body (Soma): The some (Cell body) contains the nucleus and much of machinery that provides for the life processes of the cell. The membrane defines the boundary of cell consisting of double layer of lipid. Embedded in membrane, variety of proteins that detect substance outside the cell and pass information to inside of cell. The cell is filled with cytoplasm a felly like substance that contains specialized structures called as organelles like mitochondria which break down nutrients such as glucose and provide the cell energy in the form of ATP (Adenosine triphosphate) that can be used as energy source. Deep inside cell is nucleus. The nucleus contains chromosomes consisting of long strands called DNA (deoxyribonucleic acid (DNA)) Golgi bodies, Endoplasmic reticulum and microtubules are also present

b) Dendrites – Dendron is the Greek work for tree, as the dendrites look very much like trees. Neurons 'converse' with one another, and dendrites serve as important recipients of these messages. The message that passes from one neuron to neuron are transmitted across the synapse, a function between terminal button of sending cell and a portion of the somatic or dendritic membered of receiving cell Communication at a synapse proceeds in one direction from terminal button to the membered of the other cell.

(c) Axon: The axon is a long, slender tube often covered by a myelin sheath. The axon carries information from the cell body to the terminal buttons. The basic message it carries called and action potential like dendrites, axons and their branches come in different shapes. Three principal types of neurons are classified according to the way in which their axons and dendrites leave the soma.

- Multipolar neuron – The somatic membrane give rise to one axon but to the trunks of many dendritic trees.
- Bipolar neuron – Gives rise to one axon and one dendritic tree, at opposite end of the soma.
- Unipolar neuron – It has only one stalk, which leaves the soma and divided into two branches a short distance away.

d) Terminal buttons – Most axons divide and branch many times. At the ends of the twigs are found little knobs called terminal buttons. Terminal buttons have a very special function: when an action potential traveling down the axon reaches them, they secrete a chemical called neurotransmitter. This chemical inhibits or excites the receiving cell and thus helps to determine whether an action potential occurs in its axon.

Classification:

- Sensory neuron: collect messages from inside and outside the body and carry them to the spinal cord and brain
- Motor neuron: carry messages from brain and spinal cord to the muscles and glands
- Inter neurons: also known as association neurons. Carry messages from one neuron to another

Characteristics

- Resting position: inside is negatively charged ions outside is positively charged ions
- Action potential: inside is positively ions outside is negatively charged ions
- Resting state is known as state of polarisation
- If the incoming message is not strong enough, it will not cause a change in electrical potentiality
- The incoming message must be above certain threshold, to cause neural impulse
- A neuron will either be releasing the neural impulse to the extent it is being excited by the messages or impulses it receives or it will not be disturbed at all releasing no neural impulse. This principle is known as

all-or-none law

Function of Neurons

- Neurons are the most important cell of the nervous system. The function of neuron is to communicate by means of synapses, located at the end of the axons.
- Neurons contain a gratuity of clear cytoplasm, enclosed in a membrane. Embedded in the membrane are portion molecules that have specialized functions, such as the transport of particular substance into and out of the cell. The nucleus contains the genetic information the recipes for all the protons that the body can make. Endoplasmic reticulum helped in manufacturing fats. Microtubules are responsible for rapid transport of material. The Golgi bodies have function in packaging of molecules in the vesicles. Mitochondria serve or location for most of the chemical reaction through which cell extracts energy from nutrients.

When an action potential travels down an axon, the terminal buttons secrete a chemical that has either an excitatory or an inhibitory effect on the neuron with which it communicates. The interaction of circuits of neurons, with their excitatory and inhibitory synapses, are responsible for all of our perceptions, memories, thoughts and behavior.

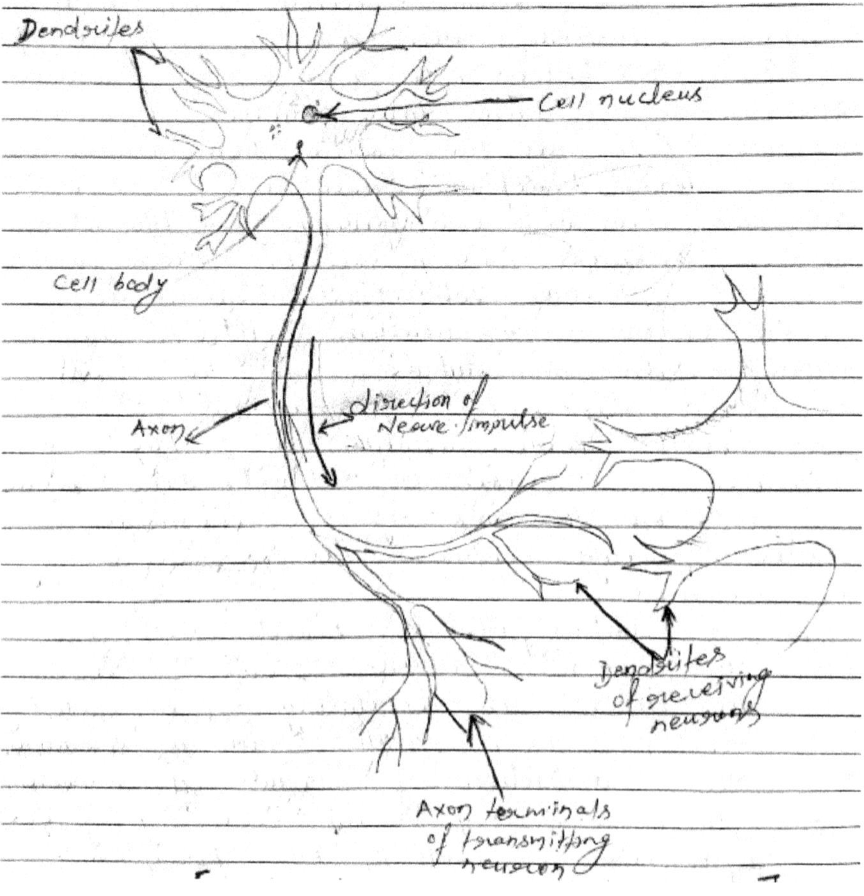

[A schematic neuron to illustrate some general features of nerve cells]

Q3. Explain the structure and function of neuron and spinal cord with the help of diagram?

Ans.

The spinal Cord

The spinal cord is a long conical structure, approximately as thick as an adult's little finger.

Structure – The spinal cord is protected by the vertebral column, which are composed of twenty-four vertebral of cervical (neck), thoracic (chest), and lumber (lower back) regions and the fused vertebrae making up the sacral and coccygeal portions of column (located in the pelvic region). The spinal cord passes through a hole in each of the vertebrae (the spinal foramens). The spinal cord is only about two- thirds as long as the vertebral column, the rest of the space is filled by a mass of spinal roots composing of cauda equine.

Early in embryological development, the vertebral column and spinal cord are of same length. As developments progresses, the vertebral column grows faster than spinal cord. Along the length of the spinal cord are the spinal nerves that branch out between pairs of vertebral. These nerves connect with various sensory organs, muscles and glands served by peripheral nervous system. The spinal nerves occur in thirty-one matched pairs, with one nerve of each pair connected to the right side of spinal cord and its counterpart connected to the left side.

The spinal cord consists of small bundles of fibers emerges from each side of the spinal cord in two straight lines along its dorsolateral and ventrolateral surfaces Groups of these bundles fuse together and become the 31 paired sets of dorsal and ventral roots, they four together and become spinal nerves. Like brain, the spinal cord consists of white matter and grey matter. Unlike brain's its white matter is on outside and gray matter is on inside.

Functions of Spinal Cord

- Spinal cord transmits messages from receptors to the brain and from the brain to muscles and glands throughout the body.
- Spinal cord is capable of some local government responses to external stimulation through spinal reflexes.

A spinal reflex is an unlearned response to a stimulus.

A reflex is controlled by the spinal cord and involves the action of three different types of nerve cells.

-- Sensory neurons – Message picked up from the skin and passed along to the spinal cord

-- Connector neuron -- When the message arrives at the spinal cord, it is picked up and passed on by a connector neuron, which make connections will several other neurons within the spinal cords.

Motor neuron -- A message travels down a motor neuron to the muscles, they 'instruct' them to contract the muscle and move your hand or leg

- The spinal cord is connected by nerves to the external parts of the body. Functions of hands and feet are controlled by it.
- It has free control on all learned activities including writing, cycling, typing, running etc.
- Spinal cord also controls variety of reflexes (responses that are automatic) that regulate posture when the body is stationary. Different parts of spinal cord control different reflexes like hand withdrawal are controlled by upper spinal cord, whereas knee jerk response is controlled by lower cord.

Thus, in short, the principal function of the spinal cord is to distribute motor fibers to the effector organs of the body (glands and muscles) and to collect somatosensory information to be passed on to the brain.

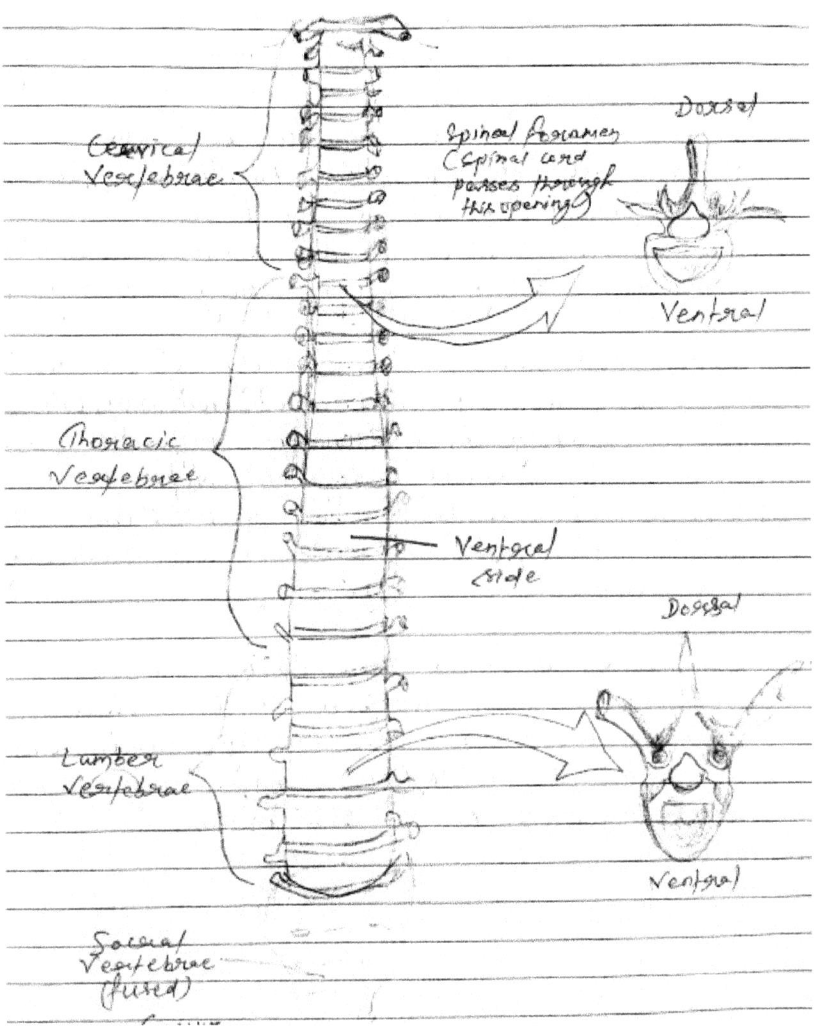

[A ventral view of the human spinal column, with details showing the anatomy of the vertebrae]

THREE
SENSATION

Q1. Define sensation. Explain nature and types of sensation.

Ans: In psychology the physical world is considered as 'stimulus' its effects on person are called 'sensation' and interpretation of the effects is called perception. Human behavior has been described as the response to the environmental stimuli. They act upon the human nervous system and arouse responses and simplest of such response is known as sensation. Sensation is the elementary form of mental activity and it arises only when a particular sense organ is stimulated. Sensation is primary knowledge of the outside world. Sensation is the first response of an organism to the stimulus. Stimuli act upon the sense organ and this impression is conducted by sensory nerves to sensory center in brain, there it is experienced as sensation; Hence the sense organs are those windows through which we look around.

There are five sense organs in our body which are related to different kind of sensation i.e., eye, ear, nose, tongue and skin. All of these sense organs produce five different kinds of senses, vision, hearing, taste, smell, and touch. Vision enables us to find out our way through crowded streets to admire beauty, hearing makes possible for us to listen two different voices. Chemical sensation is taste and smell enable us to avoid the spoiled food. Skin senses enable us to feel pain, touch cold and warmth. Thus, it is through the sense organs that we come in contact with the physical and social environment.

Each sensory system is a kind of channel, consisting of a sensitive element (the receptor), nerve fibers leading from this receptor to the brain or spinal cord, and the various relay stations and processing area within the brain. When a sensory channel is stimulated, we have a sensation that is characteristic of that channel.

In order for us to know about the world around (and within) us, physical energy must be charged into activity within the nervous system.

Transduction – This is the process of converting physical energy into nervous system activity. Transduction occurs at the receptors – cells which are specialized for the most efficient conversion of kind of energy. During the transduction process, receptor cells convert physical energy into an electric voltage, or potential, called the receptor potential. Generator potential – whether it is the receptor potential itself or some other voltage, the electrical event that triggers nerve impulses is known as the generator potential. The physical energy is changed into a code made up of a pattern of nerve firings. The environment is known as afferent codes (the word afferent in this context means "input").

Psychologists have defined sensation in different ways.

According to Jalota, "Sensation is primary cognitive experience".

According to Woodworth, "sensation is first step of our knowledge".

Eysenck (1972) - "Sensation is a psychic phenomenon incapable of further division and which is produced by external stimuli acting on sense organs, in its intensity it depends on the strength of stimuli and in its quality on the nature of sense organs"

According to Fieldman (1996), "Sensation is the process by which an organism responds to physical stimulation from the environment."

Basic Principles of sensory systems/ Attributes of Sensation/ Factors Affecting Sensation/ Characteristics of Sensation

(1) Quality: Sensation differ in quality. Tastes can be salty, bitter, sweet or sour, sounds can be varying in pitch and complexity. This suggests that a separate class of receptor cells within each system is specialized to determine each distinct quality.

(2) Quantity: Sensation differ in quantity, or intensity. Thus, tones vary in loudness, and lights vary in brightness. A sensation's quantity seems to be signaled primarily by rate of firing system's receptor's cells.

(3) Timing: Sensation differ in timing; each starts at a particular moment and continues for a measurable period.

(4) Location: Some sensations carry information about location, they tell where in space the signal come from.

Nature of sensation

(1) It is relatively passive state – Sensation in relatively passive state because the sense organ receives sensation or stimulation passively.

(2) Sensation is party subjective and partly objective:

Sensations form a part of individual's personal experiences which are subjective to some extent, on the other hand they are objective as they are answered by an external stimulus.

(3) Difference in Quality: There are different sense organs and they produce different kinds of sensations from different stimuli.

(4) Difference in intensity or quality: It refers to the distinction in the intensity, duration and extensity. There shall be difference in sensation of hearing of locked sound as compared to hearing low sound.

(5) Related with other sensation: No sensation is complete by itself. It has relationship with often sensation, it is very much dependent upon the nature of other sensation.

(6) Difference in trait: The sensation of color has the different character than the sensation of voice.

(7) Special sensation can be distinguished: All the sensation can be easily distinguished easily.

In the production of sensation three agents are involved.

(a) An organ to receive the stimulus (Example – eyes)

(b) A sensory nerve to carry the impressions to the brain (optic nerve)

(c) The center in the brain to receive and convert the impression into the sensation (CNS).

Types of Sensation

(1) Organic sensation

(2) Special sensation

(3) Motor Sensation

(1) Organic Sensation: the term organic sensation is used to cover a variety of sensations from the internal organs, such as hunger, thirst, nausea, heart burn, suffocation the varve bodily sensations that color the emotional tone of any moment. The viscera include the stomachs, intestines, internal see structures and kidneys. Non-visceral inner structures are the throat, lungs and heart. Activities of the internal organs excite sensory fibers, sending nerve impulses into the central nervous system. Reception of these impulses in the brain underlies organic sensitivity. Many experiences, most of than rather vague, are associated with the activity of internal structures.

(2) Special Sensation: There are as many kinds of sensation as there are sense organs. Each of the specialized sensory systems – seeing, hearing, feeling, smelling, tasting – gathers information that humans must have to

get along in this would. The sensations of color, sound, smell, taste temperature and pressure are the special sensations. They are produced by the special kind of external stimuli like light waves and air waves etc. They can be easily distinguished from one another as each one is related to a special receptor. Receptor for visual sensation is eye. Ear is the receptor for auditory sensation Similarly nose, tongue and skin are the receptors for olfactory, gustatory and cutaneous sensations respectively.

(3) Kinesthetic or motor sensations: Kinesthetic sensation given us information about our body movements and position. Human being can go through life without vision, hearing or both, but cannot function without the senses that are responsible for the sensation of body movement and position. These sensations derive from sensory receptors in the muscle, skin, and joints and from central signals related to motor output. Kinesthetic sensations given information on what the body is doing, these sensations can also be used to judge some of the properties of objects with which the body interacts.

Q2.Explain the concept and methods related to psychophysics.

Psychophysics: concepts, laws and methods.

Ans. "Psychophysics is quantitative branch for the study of perception which is based on the assumption that the human perceptual system is based on the measuring instrument yielding results and experiences or responses." Psychophysics investigates the correspondence between the magnitude of stimulus properties assessed by instrument of physics and assumed by perceptual system. Psychophysics is a branch of experimental psychology which investigates the functional and quantitative relationship between physical stimuli and sensory events.

The term Psychophysics was coined by Gustav Theodore Fechner in 1860 to describe mathematically the relationship between body and mind. Fechner was German physicist and philosopher who used this in his book "Elementeder Psychophysics".

To understand Psychophysics, we need to understand that there is the external physical stimuli in the environment- what we see and touch. There is the brain activity accompanying environmental stimulation, and there is the conscious perception/ sensation.

- Stimulus continuous----------painful
- Response continuous----------don't feel.

- Physical continuous- it is measurable on physical units and be present a single change in some physical property. For example, frequency of sound, length of a line, weight etc.
- Physiological continuous could be aspects of sensing experience for e.g. pitch, apparent brightness, loudness, heaviness of lifted objects etc.

The two important concepts of Psychophysics:

1. Absolute threshold or limen(AL)- it is also known as direction threshold or point of subjective quality(PSE). The minimum amount, intensity, value or weight of the stimulus to get noticed or perceived by human sensory system. AL varies across individuals and situations. Depending upon various Psychophysical and situational factors. So to measure AL the number of trials forms the base. When the stimulus is perceived correctly in 50% of total trials than the particular intensity or value of the stimulus is referred as AL.
2. Differential threshold or limen(DL)- It is also known as just Noticeable Difference (JND) or Discrimination Threshold. The smallest difference in the values of the two stimuli that helps in detecting the difference between them. As AL, DL also measured using number of trials i.e. the minimum amount of change in the value of a stimulus which is capable enough to be detected correctly in 50% of the trials.

Methods of Psychophysics

The set of producers through which sensory thresholds are determined is known as psychophysical methods. To measure the relationship between intensity of stimulus and perception Fechner developed following three methods :

1. Method of limits
2. Method of constant stimuli
3. Method of adjustment.

1.Method of limits- this method is also known as method of just noticeable difference, method of minimal change or method of serial exploration. This method is a popular method of determining the threshold. In this method, a singe stimulus, say a single light, is changed in intensity in successive, discrete steps and the observer's response to each stimulus presentation is recorded. For computing threshold by this method, two moods of presenting stimulus are usually adopted- the increasing mode and the decreasing mode. The increasing mode is called ascending series and the decreasing mode is called the descending series. For computing difference threshold, the comparable stimulus is varied in possible small steps in the ascending and descending series and the subject is required to say in each step whether the comparable stimulus is smaller, equal to or larger than the standard stimulus. For computing absolute threshold, no standard stimulus is needed and the subject simply reports whether or not he has detected change in the stimulus presented in the ascending and descending series. In computing both the difference threshold and the absolute threshold the stimulus sequence is varied with a minimum change in its magnitude in each presentation. Hence it is called method of minimum change. The threshold is the average of the stimulus values at which there is a detection response transition from yes to no, or vice-versa. The threshold found in each series are also called transition points above which the subject changes his response in the ascending series and below which he also changes his response in the descending series. Several ascending and descending series are taken until the experimental is well satisfied with the relative uniformity of the different individual threshold. There is the chances of variability in the subject's performance due to some variable errors like changes in his motivation, interest and attention etc. Absolute limen or threshold may also be affected by constant errors- the error of habitation and the error of anticipation. A part from the constant error the data may also be affected by practice and fatigue.

In determining the differential threshold the entire range of comparison values be divided into upper part(where plus judgement dominates), lower part(where the minus judgements dominate, and the middle part where the equal judgement dominate. The middle part is the interval of uncertainty and covers two difference threshold or just noticeable differences from minus to equal and from equal to plus in the ascending series and from plus to equal and from equal to minus in the descending series. The difference threshold is half the interval of uncertainty and the interval of uncertainty is the difference between the mean of the upper threshold and the mean of the lower threshold. The midpoint of interval of uncertainty becomes the point of subjective equality. The difference between the point of subjective equality and the standard stimulus indicate the constant error which may be either positive or negative.

2.Method of constant stimuli- this method is also known as method of right and wrong cases or method of frequency. In this method a number of fixed or constant stimuli are presented to the subject several times in a random order. This method can also be employed for determining absolute threshold or difference threshold. For determining absolute threshold the different values of the stimulus are presented to the subject in a random order and he has to report each time whether he perceives or doesn't perceive the stimulus. Though the different values of stimulus are presented irregularly, the same values are presented throughout the experiment a large number of times, usually from 50 to 200 times each, in a predetermined order unknown to the subjects. The mean of the reported values of the stimulus becomes the index of absolute threshold. The procedure involved is known as the method of constant stimuli.

For calculating difference threshold, in each presentation the two stimuli, one standard stimuli and one variable stimuli are presented to the subject simultaneously or in succession. On each trial the subject is require to say whether one stimulus is greater or less than the other. In case of uncertainty, he reports, doubtful or equal in such a situation sometimes the experimenter forces him to guess in order to avoid doubtful judgements. The procedure involved is known as the method of constant stimulus differences and not the method of constant stimuli. If the standard stimulus and the comparable stimulus are to be presented in succession, for half of the trials, the standard stimulus is presented first and for the remaining half the order is reversed. This is done to control a constant error i.e. time error, which may occur if the standard stimulus is presented either before or after the comparable stimulus throughout the trials. This method is also known as method of right or wrong cases because in each case the subject has to report whether he perceives the stimulus (right) or he does not perceive the stimulus (wrong).

3.Method of Adjustment- this method is also called method of average error, method of reproduction or method of equivalent stimuli. This is considered as the oldest method of Psychophysics. In this method the subject is provided with a standard stimulus and a comparable stimulus. The comparable stimulus is either greater or lesser in intensity than the standard stimulus. He is required to adjust the comparable stimulus until it appears to him to be equivalent to the standard stimulus.

The difference between standard stimulus and comparable stimulus defines the error in each judgement. A large number of such judgements are obtained and the arithmetic mean or average of those judgements is calculated. Hence, the name, method of average error or mean error is given. The obtained mean is the value of point of subjective equality. The difference between the standard stimulus and point of subjective equality indicates the presence of the constant error. To calculate the constant error the formula- CE=PSE-ST(CV= constant error; PSE= point of subjective equality, ST= standard stimulus) may be applied. If the point of subjective equality is larger than the standard stimulus, constant error is positive and indicates overestimation of the standard stimulus. On the other hand, if the point of subjective equality is smaller than the standard stimulus, constant error is negative and indicates underestimation of the standard stimulus. There is possibility of movement error and space error which are generally minimized by counter-balancing and changing the spatial presentation of comparable stimulus and standard stimulus.

Q3. Explain Weber-Fechner Law.

Ans. The Weber's Law(E.H. Weber.(1795-1878)-

The size of the difference threshold is proportional to the intensity of the standard stimulus. This ratio is constant. The size of the difference threshold, a constant ratio of the standard stimulus, is often referred to as Weber Fraction. E.g. suppose that you can just tell the difference between 100 and 104 grams then you will be able to just distinguish between 200 and 208 grams, 400 and 416 grams and so forth. Fechner labelled it as Weber's Law which is algebraically put as DI/I =C where DI is the increment in stimulus intensity (i.e. the j.n.d.), I is the stimulus intensity (the standard stimulus), C is constant.

Many studies were conducted in the past to see whether Weber's Law holds for all of sensory modalities. It was verified in most of the cases except a few where the nervous system geared to notice relative differences rather than absolute ones.

This law allows us to compare the sensitivities of different sensory modalities. Suppose you want to know, whether eye is more sensitive than the ear. This can be seen using Weber's Law. If Weber's ratio is small, the discriminative power of the sense modality is great and vice-versa. This law helps in understanding the salient features of different sense modalities. It has been found out, using this law, that humans are keen in discriminating brightness than loudness, the Weber's fraction being 1/62 and 1/11 respectively.

Fechner's Law- Weber's Law postulates that the more intends the stimulus, the more the stimulus intensity needs to be increased before the person gets a change. Fechner, with a number of assumptions, generalized Weber's findings which indicated a broader relationship between sensory and physical intensity. Fechner's Law stated that the strength of a sensation grows as the logarithm of stimulus intensity. The formula is : S= K log I , where S is psychological (i.e. subjective) magnitude, I is stimulus intensity. K is constant. Fechner's Law makes good biological sense of our nervous system compress huge rage of sensation awareness into some manageable scope, and this is what a logarithmic transformation does for us.

FOUR

ATTENTION

Q1. Define attention. Explain the characteristics of attention, and also explain the factors affecting attention.

Ans: At any given moment, our sense organs are bombarded by multiple stimuli, yet we perceive only a few of them clearly. Attention is the term given to the perceptual processes that certain inputs for inclusion in our conscious experience, or awareness, at any given time. William James defined attention "Attention is taking possession of mind in clear, vivid form of one out of what seem several simultaneously possible objects or trains of thought." According to McBurney and Collins, attention is defined as "Capacity to respond to one stimulus at a time. But there is also division of attention where we can do many things at a time." According to Woodworth, attention is "to attend or to get ready to perceive a certain object or to perform a certain act." Solso (1998) "attention is the concentration of mental effort on sensory or mental events."

Types of Attention

- *Voluntary attention*: attention that is deliberately applied and controlled by the individual, also known as active attention
- *Involuntary attention*: also known as Spontaneous attention. Whenever attention is forced upon. Eg a high-pitched band playing near you.
- *Habitual Attention*: In some situations, reaction to a stimulus or attending to a. stimulus becomes a habit. So, the individual will automatically divert his attention towards that stimulus. talking on phone and doing other work
- *Ideational attention*: attention given to images or thoughts eg. Image of lost pen, image of iphone

Characteristics of attention

(1) Conscious process: Consciousness is the awareness of internal and external information. Consciousness is to distinguish between material of which we are immediately aware and material that might obscure. Process of attention divides the field of attention in to focus point and margin. At any moment, the field of Consciousness is centered on a particular object, called the focal point of attention.

(2) Selectivity: The fundamental fact regarding attention is that only one thing can be attended at a time, it is not possible to attend to each and everything. Only the object that attracts our attention are selected and noticed. Attention is the perceptual process that selects only certain inputs in our conscious experience that are relevant stimuli. Attention is the result of limited capacity information processing system. According to Broadbent, the word is made up of many more sensation that cannot be handled by perceptual-cognitive capabilities of the human observer. Therefore, in order to cope with the flood of available information, human selectively attend to only some of the cues.

(3) Shifting: Another fact regarding attention is that it is not possible to keep attention fixed on exactly the same object for more than a few seconds at a time. As Woodworth has pointed out "attention tends to shift quickly from one object to another, as you can tell from watching a person's eyes while he is surveying a scene. Every second or two they shift from one point to another. And attention is even more mobile than the eyes. For often while the eyes remain fixed on an object, attention will shift away from that object to some other interesting one. Even while one is lying on bed, with eyes closed attentions shifts rapidly from one thought to another."

(4) Attention is an act, a process, a function not any power or faculty.

(5) Attention is also a motivational process because our attention is selective and it depends upon our needs, interests, attitudes, and voluntary actions.

(6) Attention as perceptive attitude. It is a reaction of expectancy or anticipatory perceptual adjustment. Attention is also considered as a form of set which contributes or interferes with perceptual or motor responses.

(a) Receptor set means eyes focused on an object will see that object (b) muscular set means eyes turning towards the objects due to eye muscles. (c) mental set can be exemplified when mother hears the cry of the baby (d) postural set.

Usually set helps in attention but sometime sets interfere with attention. For example, The Stroop effect proposed by Strop in 1938 and founded by Dyer, 1973 discusses interferences in attention. It refers to description and delay in naming the colors of words printed in colored ink when the letters of the words spell the names of incongruous or nonmatching colors.

(7) Purposiveness: Every object attended to, any event concentrated upon or any work looked after has a degree of purposiveness or goal-oriented behavior. Without any purpose or goal, we don't attend. The stronger the purpose, the more intense is the attention.

(8) Attention is the mental activity involving all the three aspects of activity such as cognitive, affective and conative. Whenever we are attending to an object, we know about the thing, we feel about it and there is a will to perform or act to reach the goal.

(9) Attention involves efforts both at physical and mental level.

(10) Adjustment Attention involves a variety of adjustments which favors the concentration of attention on some objects or material. Munn points out four common adjustments involved in every act of attention. (a) Receptor adjustments: The head eyes turn toward to object to be observed and there is either a continued fixation or scanning process. (b) General postural adjustment: During reading one sits up and directs vision towards the book which is being read (c) Muscle tension – A person is aware of muscle tension or related feelings of effort, particularly when attention has to be directed for a long time. (d) The act of attention is characterized by increased clearness, in whatever may be attended to.

(11) It is possible to attend to an object without looking toward it. (Posner, 1980).

(12) Attention has a limited range. There is a span of attention to which we are referring to, which means as many stimuli a person is able to pay his attention.

(13) Attention is basically exploratory in nature, sometimes we attend to new objects. Novelty is favorable to attention because whenever we attend to a novel object, we would explore its qualities.

Factors affecting attention

Attention is determined or influenced by many external i.e., objective factors and by conditions within the individual i.e., the subjective factors.

External factor or objective factors – It included generally those characteristics outside the situations or stimuli which make the strongest bid to capture our attention.

(1) Nature of stimulus. All types of stimuli are not able to bring forth the same degree of attention for eg. Picture attracts attention more readily than words.

(2) Intensity of the stimulus – It refers to the strength of the stimulus for eg. A load noise has the advantage over a low murmur.

(3) Change in stimulus – other things being equal, we are almost always more likely to notice a changing in the stimulus in sudden and not gradual. Such change may be in the motion, quality, intensity or extensity of the stimulus.

(4) Size of the stimulus. – The larger the size of the thing, the more likely one notices it. Eg. Large building will be more readily noticeable than the small ones.

(5) Location of the stimulus – If the stimulus is too far it is likely that it may not attract attention but if it is too near, it is likely to be given more attention.

(6) Novelty of the stimulus – Novelty or newness attracts attention. Objects different from the type we are accustomed to see are readily noticed. We do not pay any attention to household furniture because they are too familiar but a new arrangement is readily noticed.

(7) Contrast in the stimulus – contrast occurs when there is difference in two stimuli and it can be of shape, size or form. A beautiful drawing amidst dirty, untidy sketches will easily be attended.

(8) Repetition of the stimulus – we may ignore a stimulus the first time, but when it is repeated several times, it captures our attention. Advertisement on television is so often repeated because it attracts attention.

(9) Movement of the stimulus – A moving stimulus catches our attention more quickly than one which is still. Most of the advertisers make use of this fact and try to capture the attention of people through moving electric lights.

(10) Meaningfulness of the stimulus – It is only that stimulus which holds some meaning or which is of some importance to us, which gains attention.

Subjective factors or internal factors. It is recognized that while one person attends to an object another person at one time, attends to it and at another time ignores it. Thus, it is not just external factors of the stimulus which determines attention but, anything in the individual himself which determines what objects will be attended.

(1) Interest – we attend to objects which interest us and do not attend to those that do not arise our interest. Interest and attention go hand in hand we are interested in that which are attended and we attend to that in which we are interested. But if we attend to a stimulus, our interest may develop.

(2) Motives and Needs – An important source of interest is man's motive, deserve and needs. A hungry person attends readily to food as a man in danger attends quickly and definitely to those features of his environment which helps in escape and self-preservation. Any object that appeals to our native urge and desire for esteem, recognition and praise will be attended.

(3) Attitude, likes and dislikes – Our interest may arise out of our attitudes too and they determine what we shall attend to. In a way we attend to those things that confirm to our attitudes. One with a hopeful approach will attend to all things bright and cheerful another with a hostile attitude attends to faults and shortcomings.

(4) Education and training – Attention is also determined by one's education. In a library a professor will attend to books on his subject. In a passing crowd, a barber will attend of hair, a tailor to the cut of the cloths, a dentist to the jaw line, and teeth of the person.

(5) The mood at the moment, the purpose in hand, our goals in life determines our interest and the objects to which we will attend. One in angry mood will attend to only those things which will feed his anger

(6) Mind set or readiness – It makes concentration better and thus takes the mind away from restlessness or deviations and direct to one object to be fully attended. A person waiting for a letter from his beloved can recognize her envelope from among a huge pile of envelopes.

FIVE
PERCEPTION

Q1. Define perception. What are the characteristics of perception?

Ans. Perception can be defined as the meaningful interpretation of information received by the senses. In other words, it is a process in which the sensory experience is organised, interpreted and made meaningful. Perception is considered as multimodal each sense reflecting a different mode of gathering information. According to Bootxin (1991), the effortless, multimodal process of perception can be defined as the brain's attempt to describe objects and events in the world, based on sensory input and knowledge. Perception is usually part of continuous of information processing by the central nervous system. The continuum begins with sensation, which blend into perception, attention, working memory, thought.

Cognitive psychologists have given three models to explain higher order processes in perception.

1.Bottom up model- information travels up from the senses to the brain, where it is passively interpreted. In bottom up processing model, the system takes in individual elements of the stimulus and then combines them into a unified perception. Our visual system operates in a bottom-up fashion as we read.

2.Top-down model- sensory information is interpreted in light of existing knowledge, concepts, ideas and expectations. This process occurs as we interpret the words and sentences constructed by the bottom-up process. Top down processing accounts for many psychological influences on perception, such as the role played by our motives, expectations, previous experiences and cultural learning.

3.Interactive models- of perception argue that perception will base bottom-up and top-down processes for a variety of senses and stimuli.

To understand perception we need to consider few more definition of perception given by different researchers.

Eysenck(1972) defines, "perception is a psychological function which enables the organism to receive and process information".

Harvey(1979)- "perception is the process by which brain constructs and internal representation of the outside world. This internal representation is what we experience as 'reality' and it follows us to behave in such a way that we survive in the world".

According to **Fantino** and **Reynolds (1975)**, "perception is the organizing process by which we interpret our sensory input."

Silverman (1979) defined "perception is an individual's awareness aspect of behaviour, for it is the way each person processes the raw data he or she receives from the environment, into meaningful patterns."

Process of perception- the concept of perception used to refer relatively complex receptor and neural processes which underlie our awareness of ourselves and our would, whether we look at perceiving from stand-point of behaviour, experiences, or the response mechanism involved, it is an extremely complex process. Receptor function play on necessary and a predominant role, but other function may also be involved.

1)Receptor Process.

2) Unification process.

3)Symbolic process.

4)Affective process.

1) Receptor Process: is the first process in perception. Different perceptions are visual, olfactory, auditory, factual or cutaneous activated, simultaneously perception is limited only to particular process. We not only see objects, but we hear, and perhaps even smell them at the same time.

2) Unification Process: this is the second step in the main process. For a perception of rose, a unification of the different sensation is necessary.

3) Symbolic process: this is the third process in perception. Sensory stimulation aroused certain neural activities which have their trace in the nervous system, these are properly known as neural traces. These traces act as symbols or substitute for original stimulus or experience. These are called images. For any perception present sensation and the past experience in the form of images are necessary. This process helps in adding meaning and knowledge to the interpretation of sensory experience.

4)Affective process: perceptual experience may have its affective aspects when we are perceiving an object along with receptor and symbolic process, these process involved to complete perception.

Natural characteristics of perception-

Some important characteristics are as follows:

1)Perception is response to some change or difference in environment-

If the world were perfectly homogenous and we were in equilibrium with it, we would experience nothing. Let some condition change suddenly, or one receptor be stimulated and another not, and sense the fact at once.

2)Perception is selective process-

We do not perceive each and every thing in the world or around us. We attend to only a part of the stimuli around us. We select only a limited range of stimuli to which we attend.

3) Perception is an active process-

Perception used both sensory data from present stimulation and the learning gained from past experience. Sensory uses and past experiences are organised to give us the most structure, and the meaningful picture of the word.

4) Perception requires sensation-

Perception is intimately related to sensation. In order for perception to occur, we must first experience some sensation.

5) Perception involves organization-

Perception is not merely a collection of present sensations and memory traces of past experiences. It is a meaningful and integrated organisation of past and present knowledge.

6) Perception fills the missing details-

Perception not only structures and interprets incoming stimulation but often fills in missing details. For e.g. when we look at a sofa, we cannot see all sides of it and perhaps cannot even see. One of legs; we see the sofa as being solid and whole, and we organise it as the sofa we saw yesterday event though the exact pattern of stimulation on the retina may be quite different.

7) Perception is preparation to response-

Perception is the first step towards the active behaviour of an organism. It is the preparatory stage that prepares an individual for action and response.

8) Perception is a personal thing-

It enables the individual to know where he stand in relation to the objects, conditions, and people in the environment and to act accordingly.

Even the relationship between one object and another are established in reference to one self. Terms such as right, left, above and below, for example, are obviously based on the individual's own position as a point of reference.

9) Perception has three main functions-

(I) Perception tells you where an object is in relation to yourself (location).

(II) It tells you whether the object is moving and in what direction. Finally

(III) It tells you what the object is (form).

Our reaction to any situation is determined by the way we perceive it. The same objective situation may be perceived in two quite different ways by two different people or even by the same people at two different times.

Q2.What is illusion? Explain the theories and types of illusion.

Ans. An illusion is a false perception in that it differs from actual state of the perceived object (crook and stein,1991). An illusion is a misinterpretation of the correct meaning of perception. It is not a dream object is not Present nor imagination (new creation of mind). Like other errors, these illusions are more than mere curiosities, since they afford clues to perceptual process. Some illusions, like the distorted images seen in carnival mirrors, are physical, that is, they result from as an actual distortion in the image projected on our retinas. Other illusions are perceptual in nature. Visual illusions have been Explored the most extensively, and it seems clear that our visual perceptions are not just copies of retinal images.

According to Geldard, illusion is a lack of one-to-one correspondence between physical stimulus of world and one's inner perception.

Morgan, King and Robinson defined, "illusion is the perception that does not agree with other perceptions. It is not trick or misperception, it is also a perception."

According to Eysenck, "illusion is an invalid perception."

Collins reported that, "illusion is a subjective perversion of the object context of sense perception in real illusion, there is discrepancy between what is perceived and the real object. But in geometrical optical illusion object is actually present but is apparently seen as different. A perfect square for example always looks higher than its breath. Illusion are generally of line."

- **Theories of illusions**

1. **The Eye Movement Theory**: - This theory in its simplest from assumes that the impression of length is obtained by moving the eye along a line from one end to the other. If vertical movements of the eye are more strenuous than horizonal, a given vertical distance calls for more effort than the horizonal distance equal there for seems longer. Again, if the out-ward lines in one port of the Muller – Lyer figure included line, whereas in other part of the figure the inward lines cause the eye to move a smaller distance, the first line will seem longer than the second. It is also possible to use the eye – movement theory in reverse if the illusion works the other way. If the lines in a figure draw the eyes beyond the end of figure, object sees that he has gone too far and may interpret the figure to be shorter than it is. Thus, an eye movement theory can explain any results that are obtained.

1. **Perspective Theory**: - Starting from the undoubted fact that a line drawing readily suggests objects in 3 dimensions, infers that apparent length of the lines is affected by the perspective read into the figure e.g., a short vertical line in a drawing may represent a relatively long horizontal extending away from the observer the horizontal line.

3. **The empathy theory of Theodor and Lipp (1897)**: - The author of this theory tried to explain the aesthetic effects of architecture. They said that even in looking at relatively simple figures the observer's emotional and reactive nature is stimulated. A vertical line resulting gravity, suggests efforts and thus appears longer than an equal horizontal line.

4. **The confusion Theory**: - To judge the lines and angles of a figure requires analysis which is difficult because the observer is engrossed in the appearance of the figure as a whole.

- **Types / Examples of Popular Illusions**

1. **Individual illusions**: - When illusion is limited to a specific person for example. All person does not perceive the rope as snake in dark
2. **Universal Illusion**: - The experiences of such illusions are same for most of individual's example; of geometric illusion.

i. **<u>Vertical Horizontal illusion</u>**: - Although the horizontal vertical lines are equal in length still, the vertical appears to be longer.

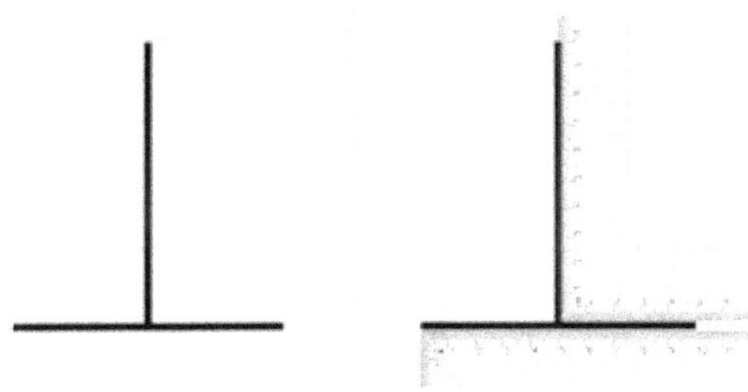

<u>ii. Zullinear Illusion</u>: - Although all the four lines are parallel but these do not look parallel because of the curved lines on them

<u>iii. Poggendorff Illusion</u>: - In this illusion there are two parallel lines which are over lapped by two separate vertical lines. But they appear to be cut through a single continued line.

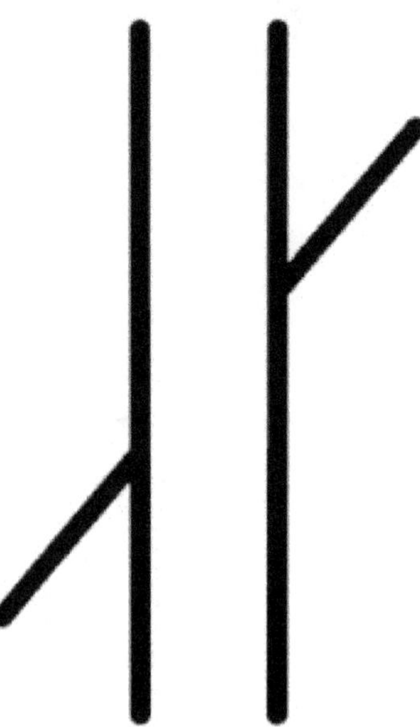

iv. Herring's Illusion (Illusion of Direction): - In this both the horizontal lines are although parallel but they appear to be curved.

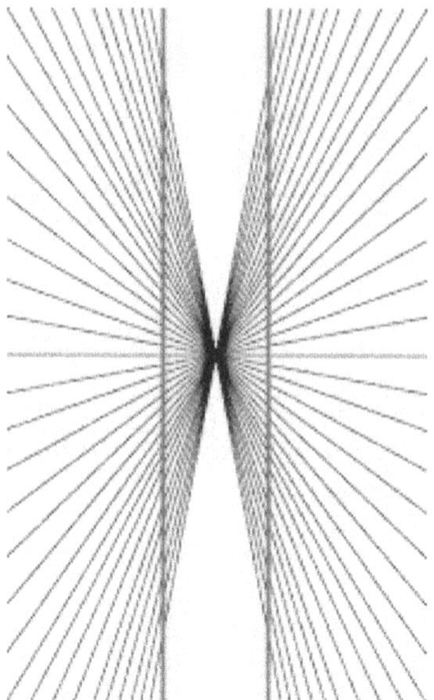

v.Illusion Of Reversible Perspective: - Reversible figures can be seen either in two ways Schroder's stair figure.

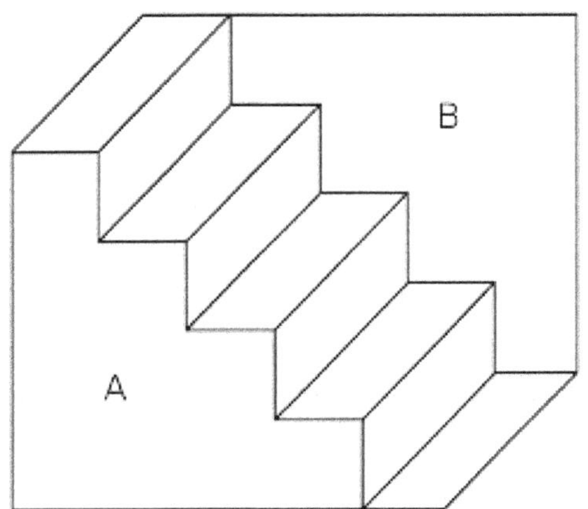

i. **vi. Illusion Of Expert or Distance Muller – Lyer Illusion**: - The two lines in the Muller – Lyer illusion are of the same length, but the line on the left, with its reversed arrow heads, looks longer.

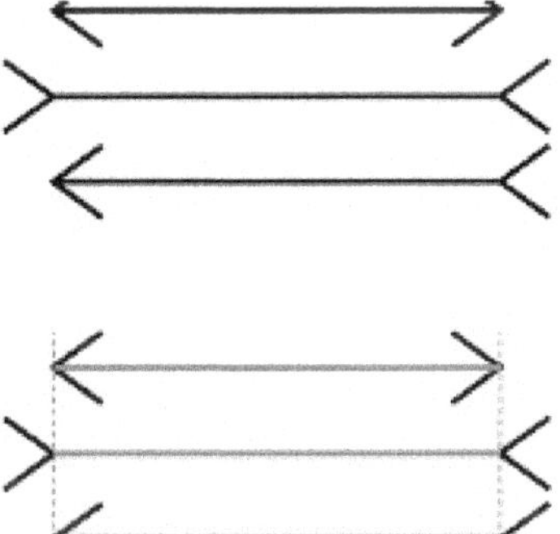

ii. **Illusion Of weight**: - Here subject is asked which of balance is heavy to us of iron and 10 kg of cottons, the subject always perceived 10 kg of cotton
iii. as heavier than iron while they had same weight.
iv. **Moon Illusion**: - moon illusion seems to result from size constancy. When the moon is low on the horizon, it appears larger than when it is overhead, yet the actual size of the mom's image on retina is the same

v. regardless of its position in the sky.

vi. **Paradoxical illusion:** - These consists of figures which seems plausible when we look at them, but which are impossible to make it in real life. The "impossible triangle" figure is a well-known example of this type of illusion

vii. **Mechanism Illusions:** - This illusion occurs as a direct consequence of the physical characteristics of the visual system. For example: - continuous sensory stimulation produces negative after – images, in which the opposite sensation is experienced after the original stimulus has ceased. So, looking at a patch of red for a long time produces a green after image when you look away, and looking of a blue one produces a yellow after image. Negative after images also occur with movement. If we look o something which is continuously moving in one direction. We experience the waterfall effect, in which it seems as though stationary objects are moving in the opposite direction. We can get this from looking at a waterfall for a long time, of course we may also get it when a train stops at a station after we have been looking out of window for a long time.

viii. Any continuous movement, as long as it only goes in one direction and carries on for long enough, will produce the waterfall effect.

Autokinetic effect occurs as a side effect of normal eye movement. This autokinetic effect is also a kind of illusion.

The phi phenomenon is an illusion in which two alternatively flashing lights are seen as having continuous movement between them.

Q3. Explain Form Perception in detail

Ans. According to Gestalt – we perceive form with the help of either by feature analysis i.e., perceiving form by analysis a scene into its parts or by immediately interpreting entire organized patterns.

ix. **Feature Analysis:** - According to feature analysis we perceive a form on the basis of a relatively small collection at feature, which can be combined, rotated and expanded to from the objects that we see in the world. For example, we perceive an alphabet, the brain notes the distinctive features, compares the with the feature stored in memory and places the alphabet in appropriate category – the feature list that

x. provides the best match with the stimulus.

xi. **The Gestalt View of From Perception:** - In Gestalt view, our perception of form is controlled by the brains organizing principles. There are organizing tendencies within an individual himself which act on sensory data to produce the world of experience. These tendencies are turned as

xii. principles or laws of organization. There are four laws of organization.

xiii. Law of figure and background.

xiv. Law of grouping.

xv. Law of Contour.

xvii. Law of Closure.

xviii. **Law of Figure And background**: - In you look out form, your window, you may see people, buildings, cars and streets, or perhaps grass, trees, birds etc. All these objects tend to perceived as figures against background of streets are easier to pick out than filled more on each other in a junk yard. Birds against the sky are more likely to be perceived thanas the saying goes, birds in the bush. The capacity to discriminate figures from background is most primitive. One of the brains organizing tendencies make figures stand out from their setting. This organizing principle is called the figure ground distinction. The figure stands out form the ground like a word on a page; it seems to be more solid and well defined and it seems to be more solid and well defined and it seems to lie in front of a uniform background. Figure has certain characteristics which are usually not to be found in the background.

Figure

Shape is clear and distinct.

It appears on the front.

It is bright.

It is meaningful.

Figure is of small size.

Background

Shape is vague, formless.

It appears behind the figure.

It is dull.

It is meaningless.

Background is of large Size.

When figure ground relationships are ambiguous, or capable of being interpreted in various ways, our perception tend to be unstable, to shift back and forth.

If your eye is drawn back and forth, so that sometimes you are perceiving light figures on a dark background then dark figure on a light background. You are experiencing figure – ground reversals.

Here, in this figure background is a meaningful as figure is used by psychologist to demonstrate figure – ground perception. There are no cues that suggest which area must be the figure. For this reason, our perception may Shift from seeing the vase as the figure and then seeing two profiles as the figure.

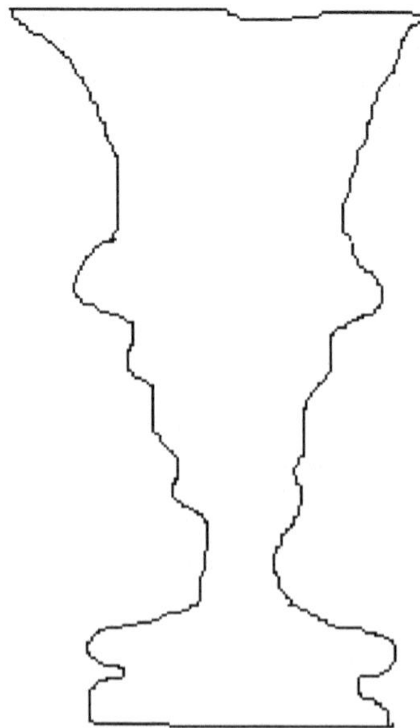

The Necker cube also provides another example of how an ambiguous drawing can lead to perceptual shifts.

- **Law of Grouping**: - According to Gestalt there is an organization in perception. Stimuli have form meaning and pattern and so they get organised in the form of perception. Perception is organized with the help of the process.

a. **Synthesis**: - All sensation is unique and taken in a whole unit.
b. **Analysis**: - Large whole and smaller units are differentiated.
c. **Law of Similarity**: - According to this principle if we look at a set of stimuli and if none of the other gestalt laws apply, then we will automatically group similar ones. The figure may be described in terms

of source or grid.

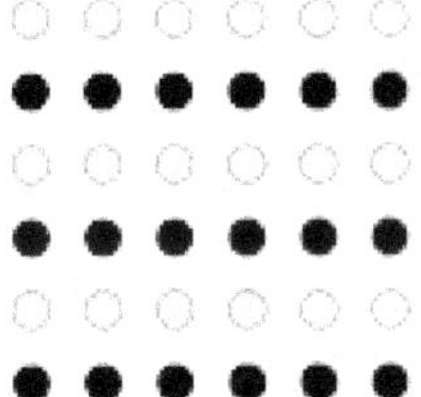

d.Law of Proximity or Contiguity: - According to this principal Stimuli, which are close to each other will be seen as forming a group, even if they are not particular similar. If we see the proximity figure and try to verbally describe the figure we will say three sets of lines, because of proximity. So, if articles of same size, colour and elements are closely together, they will be perceived as a unit.

a. **Law Of Continuity**: - See the figure naming continuity it is a circle with two lines stemming from it, or is it a (broken) line that goes through a circle? If you saw it as a single (broken) line 'you were probably organizing your perception according to the rule of continuity.' That is, we perceive a series of points or a broken line as having unity.

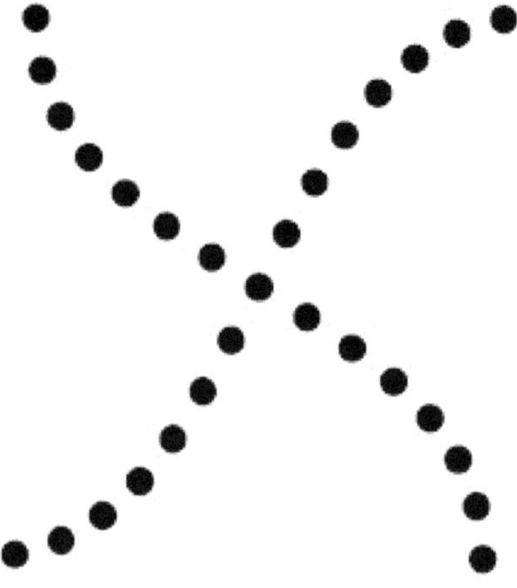

Law of Closure: - It is the Strongest Gestalt principle of perception. It is a Strong tendency to Prefer closed figure rather than fragmental or unconnected lines. Figure of Closure explains how the areas tend to be perceived as a circle (or circle with gaps rather than series of area). Law of closure makes our perceived world of form more complete, than the sensory stimulation on what is perceived.

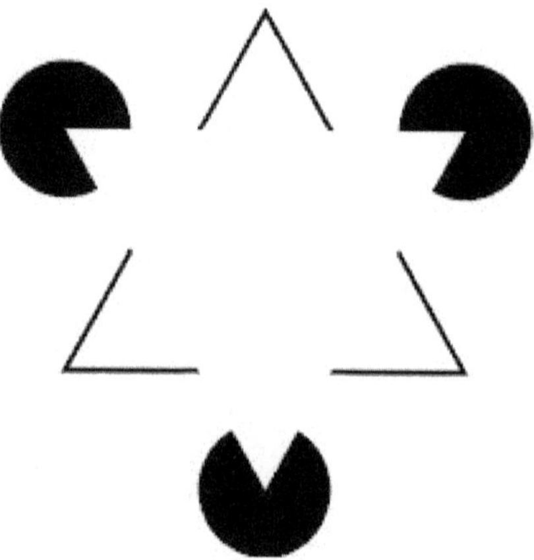

Law of Symmetry: - law of symmetry states that there is a tendency to organize things to make a balanced figure or symmetrical figure that include all parts. This effect our perception, in the form of a preference for figures which appear to be well rounded or symmetrical rather than ones than seem fragmented or messy. People identify figure with good "gestalt" much more quickly than more complex or less structured forms.

a. **Law Of Common Fate**: - Elements seem moving together are perceived as belonging together. A group of People running in some direction appear uniquid in purpose. Birds that flock together seem to be a feather.

Law of Contour: - the Separation of Objects from the general background in visual Perception is possible only Because Of the Perceptual Principle Known as contour.

If we look at a homogeneous background, unfilled with any shades or light or objects, we can see no contours. But if the same ground is filled with bright and dark lights. We can very easily see contour formation. Contour, however, are formed much more easily if there are abrupt changes in the brightness of our visual field. The major function of the principle of contours is to make off objects or regions of different degreed of illumination in our visual field. We must note, however that contours are not shapes. The fact can be clearly understood by looking at above reversible figure. In the figures, when two parts of the field are separated by a contour, the two parts may appear very different in shape, though they have some contours. In the figure, both the faces are formed by this contour, but the faces do not have the same shape.

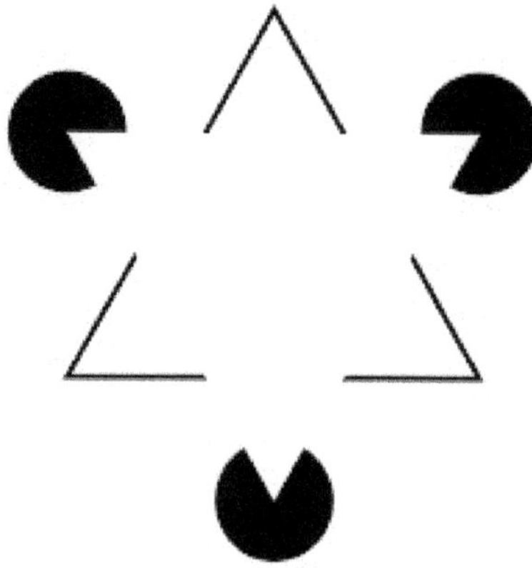

- **Principle Of Closure**: - Another powerful Principle is our inclination to perceive incomplete figure as complete, a process known as closure. A careful examination of figure Reveals that what appears to be two overlapping triangles are actually incomplete figures. Furthered more solid white triangle does not exists; it is merely an illusion we see figures because of our mental set to fill in gaps and achieve closure.

The principle of closure therefore be defined as the tendency of our perception to close the gaps in a figure so that we may see it as a whole. Brain fills the gaps in the sensory information. Brain perceives the triangle which do not exist. The lines are present perceptually, but physically they are absent.

- **Contrast**: - Contrast, like sulfation, is presumably a physiological and sentinel process which may help to explain colours constancy. We are using contrast to refer to a sensory response and not merely to a strong difference in the stimuli; As a sensory response, simultaneous contrast exaggerates the difference between two stimuli. Thus, a small gray square will look dark on a white background, light on a black background, blue on yellow, reddish on green etc.

Even if contrast effects originate in the retina, they may still be enhanced in the visual centers, or they may be seduced by the effort to perceive the true colour of objects.

Q4. Explain depth perception.

Ans. Depth perception can be defined as perception of the relative distance of objects from the observer. Depth perception is a three dimensional perception which is very often used by painters and artists to give depth to their work. With the help of depth perception we can determine either absolute or relative distance.

1. **Absolute distance:** refers to the distance between you and the object e.g. how far you are from building across the road.
2. **Relative distance:** refers to the distance between two objects or between the parts of the some object. According to Sekuler and Blake (1985), we seem to be much better to determine relative distance than we are at

judging absolute distance.

The images that are projected on retina are flat and two dimensional. Yet the world around us in three dimensional, and we perceive it that way. This is possible due to certain fine mechanisms in our eyes which is called uses of depth perception. This uses help us to perceive the world in 3D. The various uses of depth perception may broadly by divided into two groups:

(1)Monocular uses of depth perception

(2)Binocular uses of depth perception

(1) Monocular uses of depth perception- these are signals that allow us to perceive distance and depth with just one eye. Most artists and painters are aware of such uses and often make use of them to produce 3-D effects in their paintings. The following are some of the important monocular uses:

a)Size of image: the retinal image is larger for nearby than for distant objects, if the distance is to sufficiently great, so that size constancy is not involved, we perceive the object as smaller, hence as more distant, when its retinal image is smaller. But we must be acquainted with the actual size of the object.

b)Interposition: this is another monocular uses which occurs when one object obstructs our view of another object. When one object is completely visible while another is partly covered by it, the first object is perceived as being nearer.

c)Linear perspective: objects which are far away throw a relatively smaller image on the retina compared to those which are nearer. The best example of linear perspective is that of railroad track, we feel as if the two parallel track are almost merging with each other at same distance. The reason is that the image cast by the distance between the tracks becomes smaller and smaller in angle or visible angle. This supplies us with one of the most important uses for depth perception.

d)Aerial perspective: when we do not know the actual distance of objects, an important cue is provided by the clearness of perceived details. A mountain, a building, or any other object which stands out from its surroundings, seems closer on a clear day than on a smoky or foggy day.

e)Texture: when we look at a landscape, we see that the texture of the ground appears finer or denser as distance increases. Objects located in coarser ground appear closer while those on a ground of finer texture appear further away.

f)Motion parallax: the change in position of the image of an object on the retina as the head moves, providing monocular cue to distance. The relative movement of objects is sometimes important in judging distance. Other things being equal, the object which seems to move by us rapidly is judged to be closer than the which moves by slowly. If we ourselves are moving, objects nearby seem to go fast in the opposite direction to that in which we are traveling, but distance objects appear to move with us.

g)Shadows: the pattern of shadows and light is another very important cue in depth perception. Other things being equal, shadowed objects are usually judged to be farther away than lighted objects. This is true of dark colours out a great distance. Knowledge of the source of light and its direction may serve as a cue in depth perception.

(2)Binocular uses of depth perception- when both the eyes are being used in the perception of an object or distance it is called binocular perception. Experimental studies carried out in a wide variety of setting have demonstrated that binocular cues of depth perception lead to more accurate vision than the monocular cues of depth perception. The most important binocular cues of depth perception are as under:

a)Retinal disparity: the two eyes are located a little away from each other. Therefore, each eye gets a little different picture of the same object. The left eye can see a little more of the left side of the object than the right eye. This difference in view is called retinal disparity. In other words, retinal disparity is the difference in the images falling on the retina s of the two eyes. Each eye gets a little different view of the object. When the two views are compounded to form a single scene, the overlap between the two views gives us the sensation of depth.

b)Convergence: when we are looking at an object which is close to us, the eyes converge or much more toward each other. When the object is more than 20 metres away, the line of the sight of the two eyes are almost parallel. The greater the convergence, the greater the tension in the muscles of the eyes. The sensory impulses from the muscles of the eyes going to the brain gives us a cue to depth. However the value of his cue is doubled by many psychologists, specially when the objects are far away from us.

c)Accommodation: Accompanied is the adjustment of the shape of the lens of the eye in order to bring an image into focus of the retina. This adjustment is made by the ciliary muscles, which are attached to the lens and allow it to bulge when they contract, thus accommodating for near objects. The lens of the eye changes its curvature as we fixate on nearby and faraway objects.

Q5.Explain movement perception.

Ans. Movement perception is an important characteristic of our perceptual world. We are able to perceive objects in motion. The ability provides us with basic information regarding the location and the speed of a coming cars and people, watch t.v and films, the location and the path of the moving object. Perception of motion is very familiar experience but it is very complex in nature.

At first it was believed that the objects move, the retinal image caused by it also moves across the eye, feeding information of the movement to the brain. Though the movement of energy across the retina is an essential factor in the perceived motion, it is not only the factor.

There are two types of movement perception: (1) Real motion and (2) Apparent motion.

(1)Real motion: when we perceive the physical movement of objects in the world it is called as perception of real motion.

Psychologists have come forward with a number of explanations to account for real motion, most of which emphasize the role of mechanisms in the central nervous system.

(2)Apparent motion: it has interested psychologists mostly. In contrast to real motion, apparent motion is movement perceived in the absence of retinal image movement as movements of eyes, head or body. Apparent motion demonstrates, once again that there is more to the perception of motion than a moving rational image.

Types of apparent motion:

There are three types of apparent motion-a) Stroboscopic movement, b) Autokinetic movement, c) Induced movement.

A. **Stroboscopic movement** is also called the phi-phenomena such a motion occurs due to the rapid presentation of visual stimuli in rapid succession. The motion that we seen in movies is Stroboscopic. The film is simply a series of still photographs (frames), each slightly different from the preceding. The frames are projected on the screen in rapid succession, with dark intervals in between the rate at which the frames are presented is critical. In the early days of the motion pictures, the frame rate is 16 per second. This was too slow, and as a consequence, movement is these early films appear jerky and disjointed. Today, the rate is usually 24 frames per second, even at this rate the picture would appear to filcher because of the fine temporal resolution of our rival system; this perceived flicks is avoided by flashing each frame on and off three times while it is being presented.

Experiment performed on the Stroboscopic movement of this type have led psychologists to offer various explanation, none of which appears to be conclusive. The most accepted one at present outlines the brain machine mechanism involve in the movement as follows.

The brain obtains information from different parts of the retina exactly in the manner it gets it when an image of the physical object movement, across the retina. Following a physical movement, an object is first seen in one place and then in the another as the retinal image shifts. In Stroboscopic movement probably the same thing occurs, because two identical objects seen in the retina at one point appear at the other point in a few hundred mille seconds. The Stroboscopic movement, may, in point of fact, be a result of information processing by the brain which is exactly identical with the one which we find in the real movement.

A. **Autokinetic movement**- another type of apparent movement is seen when you fixate a bright spot in complete darkness. This movement is known as Autokinetic effect. Muzaffer Sherif(1936) carried out some pioneering studies on this phenomenon. For example, in a completely dark room if you concentrate on the tip of lighted 'agarbatti' or a candle, you would observe the tip of the light to be moving. It has been found that an automatic movement is considerably influenced by suggestion and the movement of the head, which stimulates the adjoining points. On the retina, thus, creating an impression of the movement of the bright spot. This mechanism involved here do not seen to be any different from those in real movement.

C. **Induced movement**- we have often seen the moon racing backward through the clouds or trees when seen through the window frame of a moving train. In fact the Moon, is stationary even then we get the illusion of movement. Induced movement occurs if a stationary spot or object is perceived as moving even it's frame or background moves.

D. ***Phi-phenomenon:*** The so-called **phi phenomenon** is an illusion of movement that arises when stationary objects—light bulbs, for example—are placed side by side and illuminated rapidly one after another. The effect is frequently used on theatre marquees to give the impression of moving lights. Eg. Diwali Lights

E. ***Motion after effect:***

The **motion aftereffect** is a powerful illusion of **motion** in the visual image caused by prior exposure to **motion** in the opposite direction. For example, when one looks at the rocks beside a waterfall they may appear to drift upwards **after** one has viewed the flowing water for a short period—perhaps 60 seconds. Or feeling of a motion after a long flight journey or train journey.

Q6. Write a short note on time perception.

Ans. The study of time perception is a branch of psychology, cognitive linguistics, and neuroscience concerned with the subjective experience, or sense, of time, as measured by one's own perception of the duration of an indefinite and ongoing series of events. Perceived duration is the perceived time gap between two consecutive occurrences. Though it is impossible to directly experience or understand another person's sense of time, it may be objectively examined and inferred through a variety of scientific studies. Some temporal illusions can assist reveal the brain processes that underpin time perception.

Kappa Effect

Due to the spatial/auditory/tactile separation between each consecutive stimuli, the Kappa effect or perceptual time dilation is a type of temporal illusion verifiable by experiment, in which the temporal duration between a sequence of consecutive stimuli is thought to be relatively longer or shorter than its actual elapsed time. When examining a travel that is divided into two halves and takes the same amount of time, the kappa effect may be seen. Even if they take the same amount of time, the travel that covers more distance may appear to take longer than the route that covers less distance.

The perceived filled duration changes according on the stimuli. Interrupted stimulation (e.g., multiple consecutive clicks) appears to endure longer than continuous stimulation, while auditory stimuli appear to last longer than visual stimuli when the interval is kept constant. As stimulus intensity (e.g., loudness) or auditory pitch rises, filled periods appear longer.

When the difference between two intervals is around 7% to 10%, one may consider one to be longer or shorter than the other (both full and empty durations). Practice lowers the relative difference threshold. These investigations also show that perceived duration stays proportionate to the interval's objectively measured length.

calculating the duration

When an interval lasts more than a few seconds, it can no longer be perceived as a whole, but its length may be approximated using the memory function. People typically determine time using indications such as the location of the sun or clocks and watches since common experience demonstrates how inaccurate these estimations are. In this case, rather than being experienced, the duration is assumed.

However, estimates are frequently made, including those of absolute time, in which an action is regarded as short or long. If you don't have a watch, you can make educated guesses based on quantitative factors like distance travelled, number of dishes done, or number of pages read.

Several important factors influence the subjects estimation of time:

Type of activity

The more a task is interrupted or split up, the longer it appears to take. As a result, a period of doing nothing looks to be longer than a similar duration of doing anything. Similarly, comparatively passive activities appear to last longer than ones that require active engagement; for example, time passes more quickly for the student who is taking notes than for the student who is quietly listening.

Level of motivation

The more one is motivated by a given task, the shorter it appears to last. Clearly, motivation and the type of activity pursued are interdependent factors. Lack of motivation tends to interrupt attention to a task; a task in which perceptual focus frequently shifts rarely corresponds to one for which there is strong motivation. The more one notices change during an interval, the longer it is judged to be. More generally, it may be said that time has subjective duration only when one notices it; *e.g.*, in awaiting the arrival of a friend (as opposed to the actual meeting) or in hoping to finish a task (in contrast to working at it).

Personality traits

Although inadequacies in quantifying personality traits and difficulties in studying estimates of time spans exceeding a few seconds have hampered scientific study, simple observation reveals marked individual differences in the ability to estimate time. Sex differences have not been reliably established, but the influence of age is well known. Experimental data indicate that children use the same criteria as do adults, but give more variable estimates of duration. One reason for this seems to be that they are less able to compensate for differences in the nature of a task or in personal motivation; also they are inexperienced in making inferences based on the volume of work they have accomplished. Elderly people tend to find time shorter, probably since they are likely to notice long-accustomed changes less frequently.

Children are as accurate as adults in reproducing various series of metronome clicks that last about two seconds or less. But estimates of longer intervals require processes for organizing experience that develop only with age, and very young children seem to depend only on limited criteria: “It lasts because it’s longer; because there’s more of it; because it goes faster.” According to Jean Piaget, estimates based on more or less explicit comparison with standard units of duration imply concrete cognitive operations that are developed only after about the age of seven or eight. Adolescents typically construct more sophisticated notions of time abstracted from such concrete experimental data.

Physiological effects: drugs

The precision with which time is perceived has not been found to be related to heart rate or to electroencephalographic data. It has been shown, however, that perception of time as in clapping or counting accelerates or decelerates with the rise and fall of body temperature.

SIX

LEARNING

Q1. Explain classical conditioning.

Ans: Conditioning is a procedure through which responses to stimuli are learned. For example, when asked to sit in a dentist's chair, because we have learned to associate the chair with driving and subsequent pain. So, a dentist's office can elicit these fear responses.

According to Bootzin (1991) the form of learning in which more than two stimuli are associated so that the first evokes the response that normally follows the second is called classical conditioning. It is also called Pavlovian conditioning. Pavlov began to study this phenomenon which he called conditioning. Therefore, he had some dogs arranged in a harness, with equipment such that he was able to measure how much saliva they produced when they were fed, and how this changed as digestion occurred. It was clear that they had learned to associate the sight of the bucket with the arrival of food.

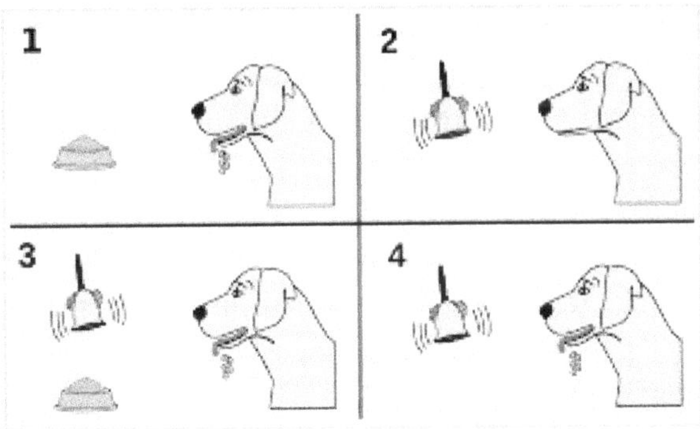

y experimenting, Pavlov discovered that if he regularly rang a bell just before he let the dogs eat, they eventually began salivating each time the bell sounded, as though they had learned to anticipate the food. In classical conditioning the organism learns to associate two specific kinds of stimuli in a temporal series in this case, first the bell, then food. Pavlov decided to investigate how the dogs learned through association to make a reflexive, involuntary response to a previously neutral stimulus, the bell. Pavlov kept a dog hungry for a few days and harnessed it in a sound proof laboratory and there was an arrangement such that as soon as a bell rang food was put in to the mouth of the dog. After a repeated pairing of the bell with food, ringing of the bell assumed a certain importance for the dog. To start with, food in the mouth, caused dog to salivate. After sometime, dog salivated on simply hearing the bell. This connection of salivation with bell was called by Pavlov as conditioning. The above experiment thus, brings into picture the four key events or elements in this experiment to classical conditioning.

(i) The Unconditional stimulus (UCS) – Food causes dog to salivate. This response occurs automatically, without learning or conditioning. A stimulus that elicits an unlearned response is called an unconditioned stimulus (UCS).

Therefore, food is a UCS.

2. The Unconditioned Response (UCR): Salivating at the presentation of food is an automatic response that does not require learning. An unlearned response is called an unconditioned Response (UCR). Thus, salivation in response to food is a UCR.

3. The Conditioned Stimulus (CS): The bell initially is a neutral stimulus it means that it does not elicit the saliva which would be a learned response. It causes salivation only when the dogs learn to associate it with the unconditional stimulus, the food. A stimulus to which an organism must learn to respond is called a learned or conditioned stimulus (CS). Therefore, the bell is a CS.

4. The conditioned Response (CR): Pavlov's dogs were taught, or conditioned, to salivate when a bell sounded. Such a learned response is called a conditioned response (CR). Thus, salivation in response to the bell is a CR.

Conditioning Process.

1.

Before conditioning

Providing meat Salivation
UCS Results In UCR
Sounding a bell But No salivation
UCS Result in UCR
2.
During Conditioning
Sounding a bell Followed by Meat Results in Salivation
3.
After conditioning
Sounding a bell Salivation
CS Results in CR
Principles of Classical conditioning
1. Acquisition

The process by which an organism learns an association in classical conditioning is known as acquisition. The conditioned stimulus (CS) and unconditioned stimulus (UCS) are paired, the experimenter waits a short time, then presents the CS – UCS paring again. Each pairing is called a trial. As the CS and the UCS are repeatedly paired, the response to the CS generally becomes stronger and quicker, as the subject's anticipation of the UCS becomes stronger.

2. Higher order conditioning

Once a conditioned stimulus has been established, it may in turn serve as an unconditioned stimulus for another neutral stimulus. A well – conditioned Stimulus can be paired with a new neutral stimulus, which eventually becomes associated with the same conditioned response (CR) as the initial CS. For example, if Pavlov's bell, to which a dog is already conditioned, is repeatedly paired with a second neutral stimulus (Say a flashing light), the second stimulus becomes associated with the first (the bell), and the new CS (the light) soon begins to elicit the CR (Salivation) by itself. This sort of chain reaction is known as second-order conditioning.

Before conditioning
Bell results in Saliva
Light No saliva
During conditioning
Light followed by Bell results saliva
(CS2) (CS1) (CR)
After conditioning
Light results in Saliva

(CS2) (CR)

3. Extinction

Once the CR has been established, it will be evoked by CS2 alone. If the animal is given occasional reinforcement that is the food and if the CS alone is presented repeatedly without any further reinforcement the animal will stop salivating to the CS, it means the disappearance of the response due to repeated non-reinforcement of the CS. If an unconditioned stimulus no longer follows the conditioned stimulus as when the dog no longer is fed after the bell rings-the organism's conditioned response gradually becomes weaker and eventually is extinguished, this process is known as extinction.

4. Spontaneous Recovery

If, an organism is returned to the experimental situation and is again exposed to the CS, the CR will reappear, though not as strongly as it once did. This reoccurrence of the CR after a lapse of time is called spontaneous recovery. For example, suppose we have extinguished Pavlov's dog's conditioned salivation by ringing the bell again, and not presenting the food, The next day, we bring the dog back into the lab and ring the bell again and present the food, the dog will salivate again.

5. Stimulus Generalization: It is the tendency for CR to be aroused by similar situation other than the stimulus aroused in training. Generalization in conditioning occurs to a certain class of stimuli rather than to a specific stimulus. For example, a dog who has learned to salivate at the sound of a bell by conditioning procedures will give the same response if the sound of a bell is substituted by that of a buzzer or by any other bell-like sound. Pavlov noticed that when the CS-CR bond has been established by conditioning, a stimulus which is similar to CS can produce the same response and this is called stimulus generalization.

6. Stimulus Differentiation:

Differentiation is the process by which an organism learns to distinguish among stimuli and to respond differently to each. A dog quickly learns to discriminate its owner's whistle (which is followed by dinner, an unconditioned stimulus) from the whistles of others who don's feed it. When its owner whistles the dog runs to its food dish, when a stranger whistle, the dog learns to ignore the sound. In discrimination training, the UCS is regularly presented after one particular stimulus but not after presentation of other, similar stimuli.

Q2. Explain operant conditioning

Ans: Operant conditioning is also known as instrumental conditioning. Organism learns to engage in certain behavior because of the effects of that behavior. In operant conditioning organisms engage in in operant behavior. Skinner developed a piece of equipment for studying learning. This is called the 'Skinner Box'. It will tend to have a metal grid floor, a food delivery chute, a lever and light. A hungry animal (usually a laboratory rat) is put into the box. Because it is hungry, it is very active and wanders around the box, exploring. There are two lights inside the box (red and green). Whenever the light blinks, the rat presses the lever, and in return gets reward or punishment. The base rule is, if the rat presses the lever on green light, he gets reward and if he presses the lever on red light, he gets punishment. As a reward, food is delivered from chute and as a punishment. He gets a little shock from the rods on which he is standing. In this way, he learns the appropriate behavior. Gradually, the rat builds up the connection between pressing the lever and getting the food as a reward.

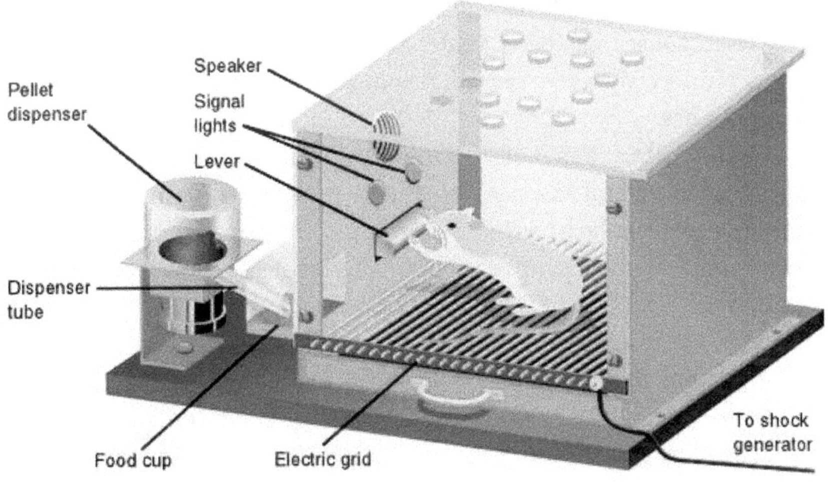

Reinforcement is something which strengthens the response. A reinforce is a stimulus if it occurs in the proper temporal relation with a response, tends to maintain or to increase the strength of a response or of a stimulus response connection.

A reinforce that when presented increases the frequency of a behavior is known as positive reinforce. They are often pleasant responses like food, drink, bonus or applause.

When a reinforce is removed to increase the frequency of an operant behavior, is known as negative reinforce.

Schedules of Reinforcement

1. Fixed Interval Schedule – In this, reinforcement becomes available after a specific period of time. An animal on this schedule tends to stop after it gets a reward, waiting until near the time that it estimates a reward is due before it responds again. A certain amount of time must pass before the rat is able to receive another reinforcement. If it presses the lever before the time is up, it does not receive any reward.

2. Variable Interval Schedule – In this, organisms are rewarded for their first response after a variable period of time has lapsed since the last reward. On such a schedule, rewards may follow the first response after 2minutes, then 30 seconds, then 6 minutes, then 10 seconds and so on. The period of time which must pass changes each time.

3. Fixed Ratio Schedule – Reinforcement is provided after a fixed number of correct responses has been made. A schedule would mean that the rat would be reinforced after every nth response, for example, after every sixth correct response.

4. Variable Ratio Schedule – Once a response has been established through frequent reinforcement, it can be maintained with progressively fewer and less regularly schedule rewards. In variable ratio, schedule, reinforcement is provided after a variable number of correct responses has been made

Principles of Instrumental Conditioning

1. Acquisition, Extinction and Recovery

When a hungry rat is placed into an operant conditioning chamber, it explores until-by chance, it presses a small switch or lever that causes a food pellet to drop into a nearby cup. The rat eats the pellet and begins to acquire an association between its lever pressing and getting food. Each time the rat presses the lever, gets a food pellet and eat it, it seems to learn a little more about the connection.

It begins to press the lever more and more often. Soon the animal is pressing and eating steadily until it is full.

Extinction occurs when reinforcements is withdrawn. It is the gradual weakening of the instrumental response because it no longer is followed by positive reinforcement.

2. Generalization and Discrimination

Generalization is also common in our own lives. A young child who has just learned to call the family dog "doggy" may generalize that name and start applying it to cats and squirrels. Apparently, the rats had learned to expect dry food to follow their lever pressing and sweet water to follow their chain pulling. When given another opportunity to press the lever and pull the chain, rats pressed the lever as often as before, but the chain – pulling declined dramatically.

ÞÞÞ

Q3. Difference between Classical conditioning and operant conditioning.

Ans.

Classical conditioning	Operant conditioning
1. Association between conditioned stimulus and unconditioned stimulus	1. Association between response and reinforcing consequence
2. Unconditioned stimulus does not depend on subject's response	2. Consequence occurs only when subject makes a critical response.
3. Response is usually involuntary	3. Response is usually voluntary
4. It was introduced by Ivan Pavlov	4. It was found by B.F. Skinner
5. Studies individual's behavior in relation to various internal or external stimuli	5. Studies behavioral patterns that take place in response to numerous rewards and outcomes.
6. Pavlov's dog experiment helped to establish the theory	6. Skinner's rat box experiment helped to prove this theory
7. Also called respondent conditioning	7. Also called instrumental conditioning
8. Focused on connection and association between UCS and CS	8. Focused on reward and punishment
9. Role of learner is passive	9. Role of learner is active.
10. Developed in Russia	10. Developed in U.S.

Q4. Explain trial and error learning.

Ans: This theory was but forward by E.L. Thorndike in 1988. He conducted a number of experiments on animals, chicks, fishes, dogs and monkeys and come to certain conclusions which he formulized in the form of theory, that both human beings and animals learn through trial and error. As the trials goes on increasing, the errors go on decreasing. Thus, we learn from mistakes and experiences. Trial and error learning consists in trying, failing, varying the procedure and gradually attaining success in a series of trials without the learner seeing clearly what the conditions of success are. Trial and error learning states that when placed in new situation individual makes random movements, those of which are unsuccessful are stamped in on fixed. This sort of hit and miss learning proceeds slowly and gradually. Thorndike viewed that animal come to learn things quite by chance rather than by anything like understanding.

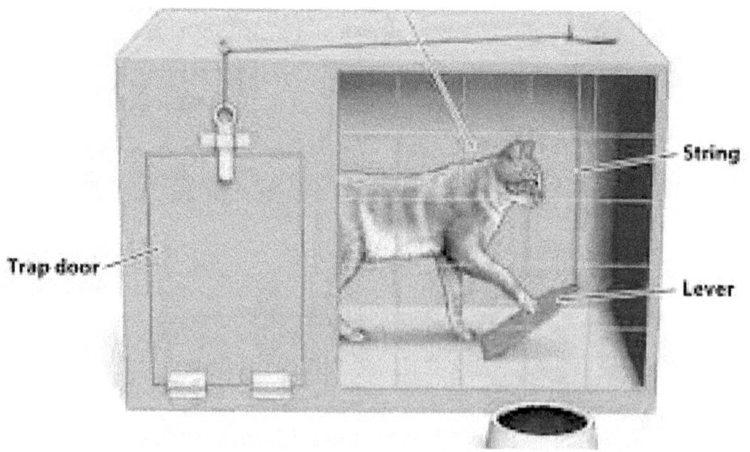

Thorndike's Experiment on CAT

A hungry cat is placed in a cage outside which there is a fish plate. The cat can come out of the cage by releasing a latch. As soon as the cat is placed inside the cage, it becomes restless. Restlessness is due to her being hungry and due to her being stimulated by the sight of fish outside the cage. Thus, to start with there is a motive and a purpose, the purpose being to get out of the cage in order to get at the fish. To attain its purpose the cat makes many random attempts. By chance the cat strikes the latch when the door gets opened and the cat comes out. On the second turn when the cat is once again placed inside the cage, the same blind fumbling starts again end continues till the door is opened. The cat continues to eliminate her errors and picks up correct moves with subsequent attempts till error reduce to zero.

Thorndike experiment on chicks

Chicks were put in a maze. There were four ways from starting point to reach out side. Food and the other chicks were placed outside which served as reinforcement. Thorndike observed their behavior and found that the chicks also learn by trial-and-error learning.

Laws of Trial-and-Error Learning

1. Law of Readiness: This law points out that we can't learn anything unless we are prepared for it. Readiness includes all those preparatory adjustments which immediately precede the activity. Psychologically 'readiness' does not concern itself only with the mood of the moment alone but also with such factors 'age', 'intelligence', 'attitude', health and previous knowledge etc.

2. Law of Exercise: This law can be divided into two parts laws of use and law of disuse.

(i) Law of use – It states that the strength of stimulus response connection is increased by exercise. In order to learn any activity best way is to repeat is again and again. In learning any skill repetition and practice is necessary. The more frequently the practice is done more prompt you become in doing the work easily and rapidly.

(ii) Law of disuse – It states that strength of stimulus response connection is decreased when it is not exercised. This attributes to forgetting due to lock of practice. Law of exercise tries to explain to effectiveness of drill in learning.

3. Law of Effect: It states that if the connection is made and accompanied or followed by an annoying state of affairs, its strength is decreased. Thus, if S-R connection is followed by reward, it is strengthened and if followed by punishment, it is weakened out.

Criticism of the theory: Trial and error does not always take place in learning an activity. It is not therefore the essential feature of learning though quite a common fact about learning process. No doubt motivation is basis of behavior but this theory lays too much emphasis on motivation. A well-fed cat will not try to came out. Also, it is a slow process of learning. It is not practical in everyday life.

But despite its limitations, it is still accepted as it explains learning of children and animals. It is the oldest theory and covers a wide range of learning, more than 50% of one's behavior is learned in childhood.

ÞÞÞ

Q5. Explain insight theory of learning.

Ans: Kohler (1925) demonstrated the importance of insight in the problem-solving behavior of chimpanzees.

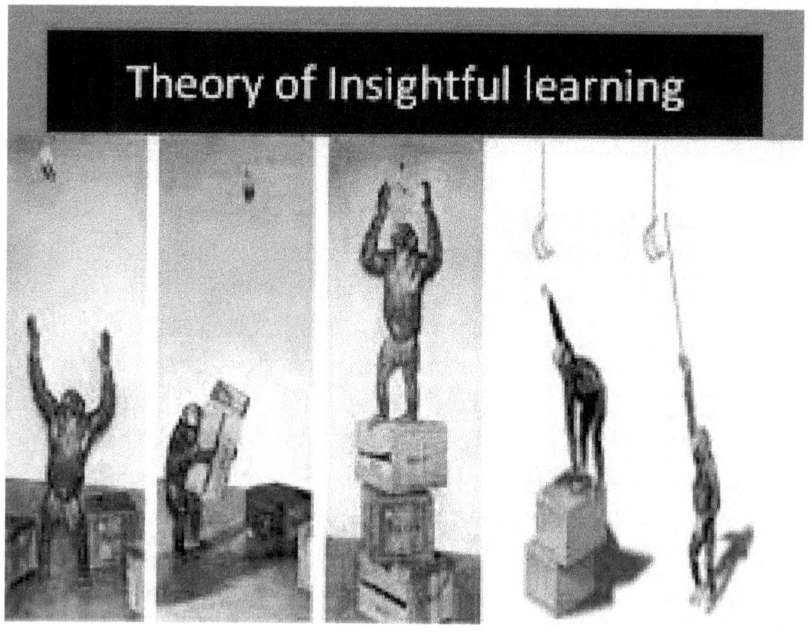

Kohler's research included two classic experiments. In one, the "box problem" a tantalizing bunch of bananas hung from the ceiling, beyond the group of a chimpanzee. No obvious tools such as sticks could be used to reach the bananas, but some wooden boxes lay on the floor. After some trial-and-error behavior, the chimp suddenly arrived at the solution. It stacked the boxes on top of each other.

In the second experiment, the "stick problem," the fruit was placed out of reach outside a chimp's cage. A short stick (too short to reach the fruit) was well within chimp's reach, a longer stick lay outside the cage. Here is Kohler's description of how one of his chimps, sultan, solved the problem sultan tries to reach the fruit with the smaller of two sticks not succeeding, he suddenly picks up the little stick, goes up to the bars directly opposite to the long stick. Form the moment his eyes fall upon the long stick, his forms one consecutive whole.

In both these problems, the solution involved more than simple trial-and-error or associative learning. Rather, after pondering the problem for same period of time, the chimpanzees suddenly seemed to perceive the important relationships among the key elements.

Gestalt psychologists believe that learning is the function of perception. For them learning is a constant change in the cognitive structure. It is continuous process of forming new Gestalts.

Gestalt psychology load stress on the principle of equilibrium in perception. According to this principle, the learner exerts himself to regain equilibrium so that tension gets released. Thus, learning can be taken as a continuous process of moving from one limiting equilibrium to the next.

Stages of Insight

1. Need: Need to learn is essential in insightful learning. The need may be biological like hunger, or social like gregariousness or personal like desire for power.

2. Preparation: Basic pre-condition for insight to start is preparation. In Kohler's experiments sultan uses the implements by making surveys and inspections.

3. Incubation: It is the stage of clearness when all overt activities are suspended. It is a period of no progress. The subject silently thinks over the problem.

4. Inspiration: in this stage, the idea for the solution of the problem comes suddenly.

5. Verification: Last stage of insightful learning in which subject makes practical application of his bright new idea.

Insight is accepted as a higher type of learning involving higher cognitive abilities. The greatest contribution of the theory of insight learning lies in the fact that it has made learning as a purposeful and goal-oriental tusk. To conclude, learning by insight may not be the only and full-fledged method of learning but it still does a good amount of justice to a big percentage of learning.

Q6. Write a short note on Programmed learning.

Ans.

Programmed learning is a method of designing a reproducible sequence of instructional events to produce a measurable and consistent effect on behaviour of each and every acceptable students- Susan Markle

Skinner and his companions had first started 'programmed learning' in 1943. This concept was used to development of self learning material or programmed learning and teaching machines.

Types of Programmed Learning :

Linear Programming: developed by Skinner and his associates. In this method the subject will be divided into very small steps each of which is called as frame. In each frame, the student has to do something. After giving the answer for the question immediately he can check whether his answer is correct or not.

Branched Programming: developed by Norman A. Crowder. Also known as intrinsic programming. Each frame is relatively bigger in size and contain two or three ideas of related sequence. Learner moves forward if correct and if wrong he is taken to a remedial frame.

Principles of Programmed Learning

Principle of small steps

The importance is given to students in this instruction. For preparing programmed instruction material, student-centered instruction sequence is more effective than any other instruction sequence. So it should be used at the beginning of preparing instructional material, then we should move further by establishing relationships with the objectives. It helps making instruction student- centered.

In programmed instruction, students are slowly moved from a chain of entering behaviour to ending behaviour through gradual progression. In gradual progression, this matter is taken care of. Student develops complex behaviour through slow response. Each fraction of the content has an arrangement that which students will gradually move up on the path of progress by relating the student's prior responses to his further responses.

A program is prepared with large number of small and easy steps. The subject matter is broken down into a sequence of small step. A learner can take a step at a time. He/she has to read a small step by being active. Learning is better when the material is presented in small steps. It also reduces the rate of committing errors and encourages further learning.

Principle of active response

Feedback is that process in which students are made aware to their weaknesses, faults and errors so that students can improve, also student's good features, good work, their quality and strengths are explained in this process so that they can display them even further into their behaviour. Reinforcement increases the possibility of response while feedback is a powerful tool for change in behaviour. Feedback methods improves the students behaviour, develop them and make desired changes in them.

Programmed instruction provides the information in the form of small steps and each step is required to be responded by the learner. Hence, the learner should be actively involved in the learning material. The learner does not remain passive because there is a need of active involvement in learning. The learner has to construct the response. It is an integral part of learning. The frames of program should also be designed logically that the learner shows interest in responding the frames.

Principle of immediate reinforcement

Reinforcement is that event which occurs after completion of a process and reinforces that process. In order words, the possibility of the occurrence of that gets increased. —Reinforcement is related to such events of the environment which increase the possibility of a response. New behaviour or change is based on such responses which are powered by the stimulus. Such events or situation of stimulus which create responses are called as reinforcement (Sharma, 1966)

Programmed instruction involves giving immediate reinforcement to the learners. When learners response to the frames, they do not know that these responses are correct or wrong. By providing immediate reinforcement or confirmation to the response, the learner gets confidence. When the learner is reinforced for a correct response, he/she becomes repetitive for further learning. The learner learns best if his/her response is confirmed immediately. The confirmation provides reinforcement to the learner.

Principle of self-pacing

Programmed instruction rests on the principle of self-pacing. It recognizes the individual differences of the learners. This principle is based on the assumption that each learner can work each step as slowly or as quickly, depending upon his/her pace. Each learner is free to move according to his/her own speed, slowly or quickly as they like. Some can learn things at a quicker speed and may skip one or more frames, whereas others can go on slowly. It satisfies every learner's need.

Principle of self evaluation

Diagnosis and Remediation refers to provide remedial instruction on students according to their needs, weaknesses and difficulties by diagnosis their difficulties and weaknesses. Student's remediation should be done on the basis of their diversity. When student makes incorrect response then his difficulty, fault or weakness gets noticed for which he get remedial instruction on wrong-page and he receives instruction from material to improve his fault.

Immediate feedback

Confirmation is also called as the third principle of programmed instruction. The feedback is immediately provided that students' response is correct due to which students move forward. Confirmation is a form of feedback due to which students attain new knowledge and also reinforcement is provided to them. Student gets the completeness of teaching material by moving forward though ordered fractions based on confirmation of his response.

The programmed instruction is based on continuous evaluation by recording the response of the learner. The learner leaves the record of his/her study for each step in response sheet. It helps to improve the quality of programmed material through checking the number of errors at each step. Also, the learner's progress can be evaluated by looking into the various types of response produced by the learner.

CHARACTERISTICS OF PROGRAMMED LEARNING MATERIAL

Following are the main characteristics of Programmed Learning Material—

1. Programmed Instruction is individual and only person learns at a time.
2. The learning material is divided into small units.
3. Then small units are sequenced.
4. In programmed material, every phase is practically logically connected to its next phase.
5. Learner has to make active responses.
6. Information is immediately provided to students that their effort is right or wrong. Thus they receive the feedback.
7. Students get the opportunity to learn at their own pace. (Principle of Self Pacing)
8. Programmed material fully verified and liable.
9. Specification of student's entering behaviour and feelings are done in it. In this behaviour, level of language understanding and simplification, level of achievement, feedback and mental level are taken into account.
10. Stimulus, Responses and Reinforcement – these elements remain active in it.
11. It has a comparatively low error rate and fault rate.
12. As feedback is provided immediately, so true responses are enforced to students which helps in effective teaching. Every response of student provides him a new knowledge.
13. While learning instructional material, students have more readiness and curiosity due to which they understand very rapidly.

14. Instruction material is evaluated through the responses of students and it is improved and modified according to that.

15. Programmed Instruction also organizes that aiding instruction to remove the weakness and difficulties of students.

16. Programmed Instruction system is based on the principles of Psychological learning.

SEVEN

MEMORY

Q1. Define memory. Explain the process of memory

Ans: Memory is one of the important cognitive functions of human beings the act of memory consists of retaining and recalling the impressions.

According to Guilford, "Memory is the retention or storage of information in any form"

According to Lefton, "Memory is the ability to recall or remember past events or previously learned information or skills".

Process of Memory

1) Perception: It is the ability to see, hear, or become aware of something through the senses.

2) Encode: Entering information into memory. Encoding is the process of receiving the sensory input and transforming it into a form or code which can be stored.

i) Visual code (which is related to eyes)

ii) Acoustic code (which is related to hearing)

iii) Semantic code (which is related to understanding the meaning of the things that one perceives)

3) Storage: It is the process of actually putting coded information into the memory. Encoded material is retained over time in our brains "Memory Banks"

4) Recall: to retrieve the material learnt or memorize earlier

Q2. What are types of memory? / Explain the stages of memory.

Ans: 1) Sensory memory

Sensory memory provides temporary storage of information brought by our senses. It is that memory which helps an individual to recall something immediately after having perceived it. In such type of memory, retention time is extremely brief, generally from a fraction of a second to several seconds. Old sensory impressions disappear as they are 'erased' by new information. It is needed when we what to remember a thing only for a very short period of time. For example, we enter the cinema hall and see the seat number given on our ticket. After occupying the seat, we forget the seat number.

It may be either Iconic (visual) memory or Echoic (Auditory) memory.

2) Short term memory

It comprises our immediate recollection of stimuli that we have just perceived. It provides a temporary resting place for information from sensory memory that we have attended to. It is our working memory. STM holds relatively small amounts of information for brief periods of time. Usually, thirty seconds or less.

This is the memory system you use when you look up a phone number and did it immediately. STM has a limited capacity. The capacity of STM is about seven items' pieces of information – which can be letters, digits, or even meaningful sentences. Chunk is a meaningful unit of STM.

3) Long Term Memory (LTM)

The third memory system is long term memory and it retains amounts of information for long periods of time. It is like a giant store house that never quite fills up with the facts, feelings, images, skills and attitudes that we keep accumulating. Long term memory allows us to do more than simply store information from past experiences. It is a vast library of facts, images and knowledge that we have stored away, for possible future use.

There are two types of LTM

1) Declarative memory: Recall of specific facts is called declarative memory. For example, memory related to names, dates, anything learned in the classroom.

It is divided into 2 types:

a) Semantic Memory

It is related to general knowledge and facts. It is our semantic memory that helps us in recalling the names of the capitals of the different countries and the various formulas of mathematics. It is based on general awareness, meaningful interpretation generalized rules, principles.

b) Episodic Memory

It is based on episodes and events, which may consist of personal events and experiences associated with one's life. For example, if an individual reads in a newspaper or becomes an eye witness to the scene of a rail accident, she may retain all her sensory impressions about this event or episode in his memory.

2) Procedural Memory

These memories are related to the skills that one performs. For example, after learning swimming we do not forget, how to swim, even if we haven't practice it for many years.

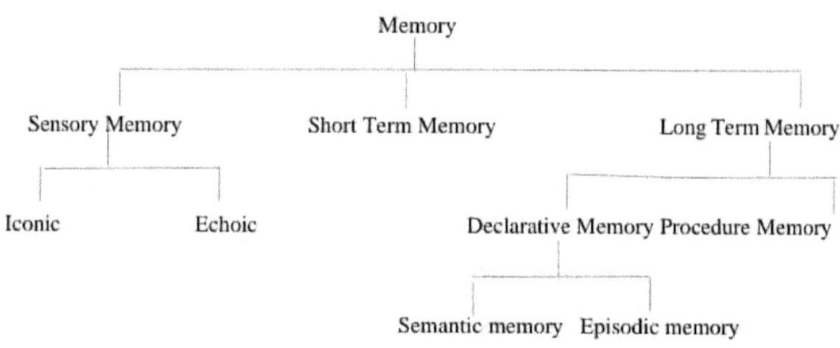

ᑭᑭᑭ

Q3. How can we measure memory?

Ans: The following methods are usually employed for the measurement of retention:

1) Method of Recall

This is to see the amount retained by the learner in his/her memory by testing his/her performance through reproduction or retrieval.

i) Free Recall Method

The learner is provided with a list of items. After such proper presentation of the list, he may then be asked to recall in any order as many items as possible from the list he has seen or been told about.

ii) Serial Recall Method

The individual is asked to recall the items in exactly the same order as presented to him previously for his learning or memorization. The serial order reproduction is quite essential in such measurement.

iii) Probed Recall Method

The individual may be provided with a cue for helping him in the process of recall. For example, in a paired associate list like music – lyrics, cat-kitty, Tom-Dog, etc. he may be asked to tell, what word appeared with cat in the list seen by him.

2) Method of Recognition

In this method, one's power of recognition is tested. The things that he has seen, the material he has studied earlier, are supposed to be present in his memory

i) Simple Recognition Type

The individual may be presented with a photograph, picture, or real item to decide whether or not he has seen it before. He may also be presented with an audio, smell or experience to decide whether the has listened, or tasted it ever before and if yes, he is asked to tell something about it through its recognition. For example, he is presented with a picture in the first phase. In the second phase, that picture is shown with some other pictures, and the person has to recognized which picture was shown earlier, in the first phase.

ii) Multiple Recognition Type

One has to recognize a particular person or item seen, heard before, out of the several pictures, items presented to him. For example, he can be presented with 10 pictures. He may be asked to recognize a particular given picture, when shown with other pictures that whether he has seen that picture earlier or not. He may be asked to recognize as may items as possible out of the given alternatives. In this, the person has two alternative answers, "yes, I have seen it," "no I haven't seen it."

3) Reconstruction Method

To begin with, the subject is presented with certain learning materials in the form of letters, words, pictures, or event. The subject is then asked to memorize it fully in the way be intends to do so. The subject is tested for his power of retention after period of considerable gap. It is assumed that he must have forgotten some things memorized earlier.

Now the subject is asked to rearrange or reconstruct the stimuli in some order as was originally learned by him. The number of items correctly rearranged is termed the retention score of the subject. For example, the subject may be asked to narrate a story using those words.

ᑭᑭᑭ

Q4. Define forgetting

Ans: Memory and forgetting are in life. If forgetting does not take place, the life will be burdened with unpleasant experiences. When we are unable to remember information that we need at a particular moment. For example, we forget the details of a movies we saw 6 months ago and what we had for dinner last night.

According to Aristotle, "forgetting is fading of original experience with passage of time. It arises due to disuse."

According to Norman and Munn, "Forgetting is failing to retain or to recall what has been acquired."

ᑭᑭᑭ

Q5. What are the causes of forgetting?

Ans: 1) Decay through Disuse

A skill that has been learnt but not used for a long time is likely to be forgotten. A mathematical formula however well it's learnt might be forgotten in course of time, it never used or retrieved meanwhile.

2) Interference

It's the idea that forgetting may occur because the information may be displaced or preceded by other similar information which interfere with its recall.

i) Proactive Interference

Proactive interference occurs when old information 'learnt earlier', blocks or disrupts the remembering of related new information 'learnt later'. For example, if information you acquired about operating an old VCR interferes with your ability to operate a new one that has very different control you are experiencing the impact of proactive inhibition.

ii) Retroactive Interference

Retroactive interference occurs when new information (learnt later) blocks or disrupts the retrieval of old information (learnt earlier). Suppose you look up a telephone number, and as you start dialing your friend distracts you by asking what time it is when you return to from your memory.

3) Motivated Forgetting

Freud (1901) believed that we forget things because we don't want to remember them. Things that we forget, he argued are either dalmatic or unpleasant for us, or could be associated with things that are traumatic or unpleasant. So, we forget them we repress the memory because in that way the unconscious mind can protect itself from harm. People often push certain kinds of memories out of conscious awareness because they are too embarrassing, frightening, painful or degrading to recall. For example, people whose child hoods were marked by sexual abuse often blot out the memory of those traumatic events.

4) Brain Damage or Disease

Amnesia may result from brain damage or disease. Amnesia can occur following a several below or wound to the head and may result in loss of memory for the events leading up to accident. Brain damage can also produce anterograde amnesia in which the individual is unable to store new memories.

5) Repression

Repression is a mental process that automatically hides emotionally threatening and anxiety producing information in the unconscious, from which repressed memories can't be recalled voluntarily, but something may; cause them to enter consciousness at a later time.

6) Psychological cause

There are some psychological causes of forgetting sometimes some psychological factors like stress, anxiety, conflicts, lack of interest, apathy, or similar emotional and psychic difficulties lead to be forgetful for some information stored before.

7) Lock of context or cues.

Contexts have shown to be an effective part of recall even mentally recreating con text has been shown to aid people to retrieve information which was previously forgotten. Memories can be enhanced by providing appropriate cues which lead to the relevant information.

8) Consumption of Drug or Alcohol

A drug marijuana appears to have a limited short-lived effect on the encoding, storage and retrieval of information. But if taken in relatively high doses, its memory effects fall short. Heavy drinking over a period of years however can result in irresistible brain damage.

Q6. Explain the theories of forgetting

Ans: 1) Decay Theory by Ebbinghaus

Ebbinghaus forgetting curve describes the decrease in ability of the brain to retain memory over time. The theory is that human start losing the memory of learned knowledge over time, in a matter of days or weeks, unless the learned knowledge is consciously reviewed time and again. The issue was hypothesized by Herman Ebbinghaus in 1885, which is why it's called Ebbinghaus forgetting curve A related concept to the forgetting curve states that the time period up to which a person can recall any memory is based on the strength of the particular memory.

Ebbinghaus conducted a series of tests on himself, which included memorization and forgetting of meaningless three letter words. Ebbinghaus memorized different nonsense words such as "WID", "ZOF" and "KAF", and then he tested himself to see if he could retain the information after different time periods. The results thus obtained were plotted in a graph, which is known as forgetting curve.

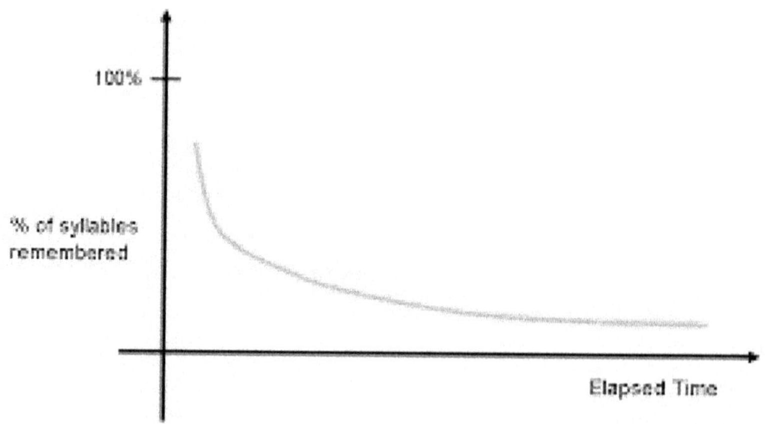

Ebbinghaus found the forgetting curve to be exponential in nature. Memory retention is 100% at the time of learning any particular piece of information. However, it drops rapidly to 40% within the first few days. After which, the declination of memory retention slows down again.

In simple words forgetting curve is exponential because memory loss is rapid and huge within the first few days of learning. But, the rate of memory loss decrease and the rate of much forgetting are much slower from then on.

Consolidation: Memory consolidation is a category of processes that stabilize a memory trace after its initial acquisition. A memory trace is a change in the nervous system caused by memorizing something. Consolidation is distinguished into two specific processes.

One is short term process where neurotransmitters are involved and the other is long term process where hippocampus is involved. In short term process, the method is really fast, and it gets stored within minutes, but in long term process, the method is slow, and it takes months and years to store in our memory as a trace.

2) Interference – Retroactive and Proactive

It's the idea that forgetting may occur because the information may be displaced or preceded by other similar information which interfere with its recall.

i) Proactive Interference

Proactive interference occurs when old information 'learnt earlier', blocks or disrupts the remembering of related new information 'learnt later'. For example, if information you acquired about operating an old VCR interferes with your ability to operate a new one that has very different control you are experiencing the impact of proactive inhibition.

ii) Retroactive Interference

Retroactive interference occurs when new information (learnt later) blocks or disrupts the retrieval of old information (learnt earlier). Suppose you look up a telephone number, and as you start dialing your friend distracts you by asking what time it is when you return to from your memory.

3) Motivated Forgetting

Freud (1901) believed that we forget things because we don't want to remember them. Things that we forget, he argued are either dalmatic or unpleasant for us, or could be associated with things that are traumatic or unpleasant. So, we forget them we repress the memory because in that way the unconscious mind can protect itself from harm. People often push certain kinds of memories out of conscious awareness because they are too embarrassing, frightening, painful or degrading to recall. For example, people whose child hoods were marked by sexual abuse often blot out the memory of those traumatic events.

Q7. Short Note on forgetting curve

Ans: Ebbinghaus forgetting curve describes the decrease in ability of the brain to retain memory over time. The theory is that human start losing the memory of learned Knowledge over time, in a matter of days or weeks, unless the learned knowledge is consciously reviewed time and again. The issue was hypothesized by Herman Ebbinghaus in 1885, which is why it's called Ebbinghaus forgetting curve A related concept to the forgetting curve states that the time period up to which a person can recall any memory is based on the strength of the particular memory.

Ebbinghaus conducted a series of tests on himself, which included memorization and forgetting of meaningless three letter words. Ebbinghaus memorized different nonsense words such as "WID", "ZOF" and "KAF", and then he tested himself to see if he could retain the information after different time periods. The results thus obtained were plotted in a graph, which is known as forgetting curve.

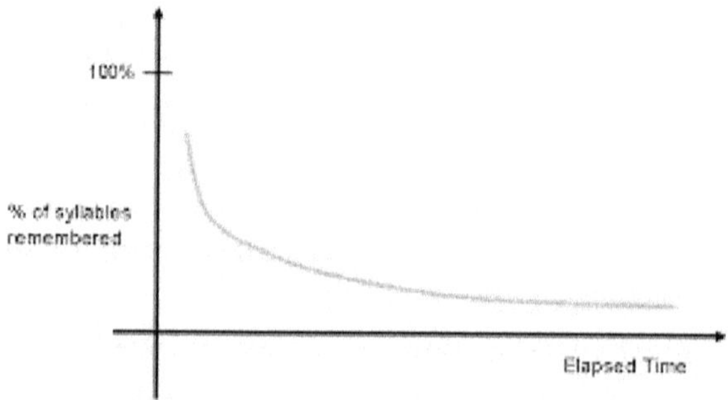

Ebbinghaus found the forgetting curve to be exponential in nature. Memory retention is 100% at the time of learning any particular piece of information. However, it drops rapidly to 40% within the first few days. After which, the declination of memory retention slows down again.

In simple words forgetting curve is exponential because memory loss is rapid and huge within the first few days of learning. But, the rate of memory loss decrease and the rate of much forgetting are much slower from then on.

Consolidation: Memory consolidation is a category of processes that stabilize a memory trace after its initial acquisition. A memory trace is a change in the nervous system caused by memorizing something. Consolidation is distinguished into two specific processes.

One is short term process where neurotransmitters are involved and the other is long term process where hippocampus is involved. In short term process, the method is really fast, and it gets stored within minutes, but in long term process, the method is slow, and it takes months and years to store in our memory as a trace.

EIGHT
MOTIVATION

Q1. Define motivation. What are the two types of motivation?

Ans: The term motivation means to move or to energize or to activate. In this sense, anything that is responsible for internal or external activity may be called motivation. So, a motive may be thought of as some internal activator that impels an organism to engage itself in a wide variety of activities of which it is capable.

According to Morgan and King, "Motivation refers to the driving and pulling forces which results in persistent behavior directed towards particular goal"

Types of Motivation

1. Intrinsic Motivation: Motivation causing people to participate in an activity for their own enjoyment not for the reward it will get them. It refers to those behavior as they are interesting, self-satisfying, fun to do even when they produce no external benefits. Hence, a person is motivated to behave not because of external rewards but due to internal, self-rewards such as happiness, satisfaction etc. It comes from within the person eg. the person enjoys playing the guitar even though no one else is around to listen.

2. Extrinsic Motivation: Motivation causing people to participate in an activity for a tangible reward. It refers to money, food, public recognition. They are energizers which guide behavior so as to obtain some external rewards. They produce satisfaction which are regulated by external event. It is when a child is motivated by a reward of a bicycle for that he works day and night to get the required marks.

Q2. Write a short note on motivational cycle.

Ans: There are three general aspects of motivation. Each may be thought as a state in a rotating cycle, for the first leads to the second and the second leads to third which finally leads to first.

a) Need: It refers to a lack or deficit within the individual. Every individual has some or the other need and the satisfaction and dissatisfaction of the needs, affects the behavior. Need or drive are sort of internal conditions whereas an incentive is an object or stimulus in external environment.

b) Instrumental behavior:

This is any behavior that is instrumental in satisfying a need or drive or motive eg. a small child cries, his crying is instrumental in getting food from his mother.

c) Goal and Incentive – Behavior is directed towards goal and when the goal is achieved the need, drive or motive is satisfied. If a person is hungry, his goal is to eat food.

d) Relief – After the goal achievement, body tissues need are fulfilled and thus relief is achieved. There is satisfaction after goal attainment, but soon another need is aroused and the circle continues.

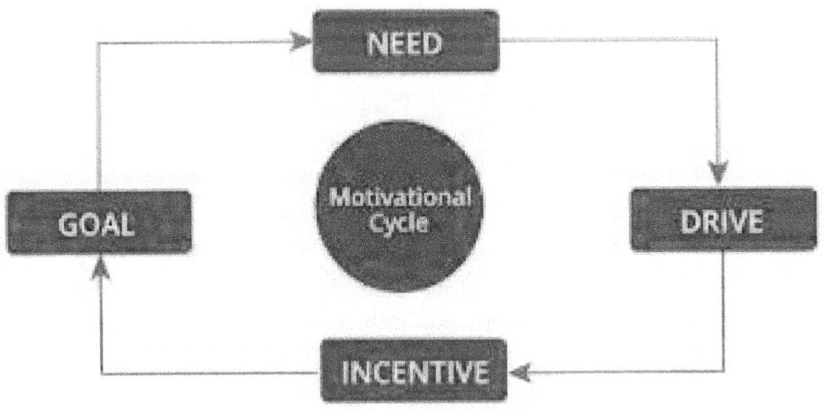

ϸϸϸ

Q3. Explain the various physiological, psychological and social motives.

Ans: Physiological Motives: They are called primary needs because they are vital to life and essential requirements for living life. They are necessary for survival. They are sometimes referred to as biological needs because they have their origin somewhere in the body of the organism.

1. Hunger: The body is always using up materials in growth, in the repair of tissues and in the storage of reserve supplies. Body needs energy and energy comes from food. Whenever there is a feeling of contraction in the stomach or when someone reports weakness or light headedness there is a need to eat food. Specific food needs arise whenever the organism need of food is not because of hunger but because of his preference of that particular food.

2. Thirst: Water is as necessary for survival. It is an essential item in body's use of food and it is constantly being lost through the lungs, skin and kidneys.

3. Sleep and Rest: Sleep is a need that must be satisfied at periodic intervals. Whenever a person works, fatigue arises which is reduced by sleep. If a person stays awake indefinitely his powers of attention and his interest and energy become less. Every person has individual and unique habits of sleep. Learned factors are important in sleep motivation.

4. Regulation of temperature: It is the biological need to avoid extremes of heat or cold. There is a need to maintain and regulate normal body temperature whenever the body temperature dips down the normal body shivers so as to produce heat and when body temperature shoots up, we perspire out producing sweat which on evaporation causes coldness lowering of temperature, bring the temperature back to normal, Hence, homeostatic is maintained.

5. Need to avoid Pain: The drive to avoid pain is one of the strongest needs for human beings and other animals. There is a need to run for safety, to avoid any injury and consequently pain. Whenever, we undergo surgery, usually anesthesia is given, the term which itself means "no sensitivity".

6. Need to respirate: Respiration refers to the intake of oxygen and release of carbon dioxide. The need for respiration is a necessary motive because of body needs and basis of survival. It is under certain circumstance urgently needed such as during accidents, mountaineering, in space, deep oceans and for breathing troubles.

7. Need to eliminate: Energy is consumed and rest is turned into waste products. They are collected in the intestine and bladder and then pressure is built in the organs to release the waste products that is to eliminate.

8. Sexual Motivation: It is the motivation to engage in various forms of sexual activity. It is necessary to understand that sex is not necessary to maintain the life of an individual, although it is necessary for survival of

the species. Sex hormone is produced by GONADS which are primary sex glands. Sex hormones such as estrogen and testosterone exert activation effects. In their absence, sexual behavior does not occur or takes place with a very low frequency.

9. Maternal love: It is necessary in the development of the child, following the birth of a new born. This is due to maternal instinct which is full of love, care, devotion and understanding of child's needs.

Psychological Motives

1. Urge to escape: Whenever there is a possibility of danger there is an urge to run for safety and shelter and to escape from any threatening situation. The natural reaction to danger is the preparation for protection against it.

2. Humor: There is a psychological need to laugh so as to deal with life's tension. This is in itself very relieving and makes us feel light and relaxed.

3. Need to fulfill one's interest: We pursue our goals and needs according to our interest and the potentiality to acquire it. Man is motivated to get those things in which they are interested.

4. Need to have a purpose: This psychological need is basic to all individuals because no man lives a purposeless life, everybody has a goal, a purpose in life to achieve and succeed. The more definite the goal, the more determined you are to overcome the obstacles and put in necessary effort.

5. Need to maintain self-esteem: The need for self-esteem is a very powerful need governing both achievement and intrinsic motivation, latest research in this area suggests that most people will go to great lengths to maintain a favorable view of themselves

Social Motives

Social Motives are the complex motive states, or needs that are learned in social groups, especially in the family as children grow up, and because they usually involve other people.

1. Achievement Motives: The desire to accomplish difficult tasks and meet standards of excellence. These are task oriented and prefer to work on tasks that are challenging and on which their performance can be evaluated in some way either by comparing it with other people's performance.

2. Power: Motivation to be in charge, have high status and exert influence over others is power motivation. The goal of power motivation is to influence, control, charm others, and the ability or capacity to produce intended effects on the behavior or emotions of another person.

3. Gregariousness: It refers to keep in contact with others. It is the tendency to live in groups. It is seen that every man needs another person's co-operation because it makes the work convenient. Alone he is afraid, but in groups he becomes bold. He gets full opportunity to show his potentialities in group.

4. Aggression: It is the most dangerous motive; it is the desire to harm on others. It has some, after results. In its occurrence of overt form of aggression, or behavior, it can get directed towards the goal of injuring another living being who wishes to avoid such treatment.

5. Imitation; It is a common knowledge that a child learns his activities, habits and behavior by imitating others, sometimes, imitating grownups without knowledge of what he is doing.

ÞÞÞ

Q4. Explain Maslow theory of Motivation

Ans; Maslow (1970) proposed an arrangement of needs from the most basic to those at the highest levels. He viewed those motives exist in a hierarchy, so that once lying near the bottom of the hierarchy must be least partially satisfied before those lying higher up can influence behavior.

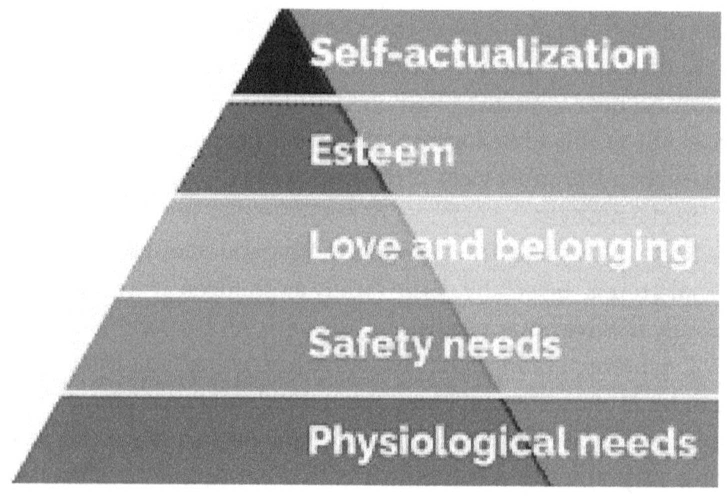

a) At the base are the most basic physiological needs for food, water, oxygen and sleep. They are the lowest level of Maslow's hierarchy of needs. A person's motivation at this level derives from their instinct to survive.

b) After these are satisfied, safety needs take precedence, including physical security and freedom from pain and fear. To find stability and security, a person must consider their physical safety. Motivation comes from protection from unpredictable and dangerous conditions.

c) The third level of Maslow's hierarchy of needs is love and belonging needs. Humans are social creatures that crave interaction with others. Human have the need to give and receive love, to feel like they belong in a group. This outlines the need for friendship, intimacy, family and love. When deprived of these needs, individuals may experience loneliness or depression.

d) The fourth level of Maslow's hierarchy of needs is esteem needs. Esteem needs are related to a person's need to gain recognition, status and feel respected. Once someone has fulfilled their love and belonging needs, they seek to fulfill their esteem needs.

e) At the top of the pyramid, Maslow, placed need for self-actualization, the motivation to live up to one's potential to be fully human. It is the desire to become all that one is capable of being.

Maslow believed that hierarchy of human motives, or needs formed a pyramid. The base of pyramid is made up of basic needs such as hunger and thirst. The intermediate level consists of psychological motives such as love and self-esteem. Motives at these two intermediate levels are also known as deficiency needs. Deficiency needs gets motivated when they are not met.

Q5. Explain McClelland's motivational need theory.

Ans: McClelland is most noted for describing three types of motivational need. These needs are found of varying degrees in all workers and managers, and motivational needs are the characteristics of a person or manager's style and behavior, both in terms of being motivated, and in are management motivating others.

1) Need for achievement

Need for achievement was one of the first social motives to be studies in detail and research still continues. They are task oriented and prefer to work on task that are challenging and on which their performance can be evaluated in some way either by comparing with other people's performance or in terms of some other standard. The expectations of McClelland is most noted for describing three types of motivational need. Parents have played a great role in the development of achievement motivation. Parents who expected their children to work hard and to strive for success will encourage them to do so and praise them for achievement directed behavior.

2) Need for Power

The goal of power motivation is to influence control, charm others and to enhance one's own reputation in the eyes of other people. The ability or capacity of a person to produce intended effects on the behavior or emotions of another person. Power motivation can be expressed in many ways, the manner of expression depends greatly on the person socio-economic status, and the degree to which the individual bears his or her down by impulsive and aggressive action or by participation in competitive sports.

3) Need for affiliation

The affiliation driver produces motivation and need to be liked and held in popular regard. These people are team players. McClelland suggested that a strong need for affiliation undermines a manager's objectivity, because of their need to be liked, and that this affects a manager's decision – making capability. A strong need for affiliation will produce a determined work ethic and commitment to the organization.

McClelland firmly believed that achievement motivated people are generally the ones who make things happen and get results, and that this extends to getting results through the organization of other people and resources, although as stated earlier, they often demand too much of their staff because they prioritize achieving the goal above the many varied interests and needs of their people.

NINE
EMOTIONS

Q1. Define emotion. Explain the theories of emotions.

Ans. The term emotion stands for a state of excitement in an organism. Emotion is a pattern of responses to an event that is relevant to the goals or needs of the organism. The responses include physiological arousal, impulses to action, thoughts and expression of all these. According to this definition, individuals who don't have needs goals or concerns can't experience emotions. According to Gates, "Emotions are episodes in which the individual is moved or exited"

The James-Lange Theory

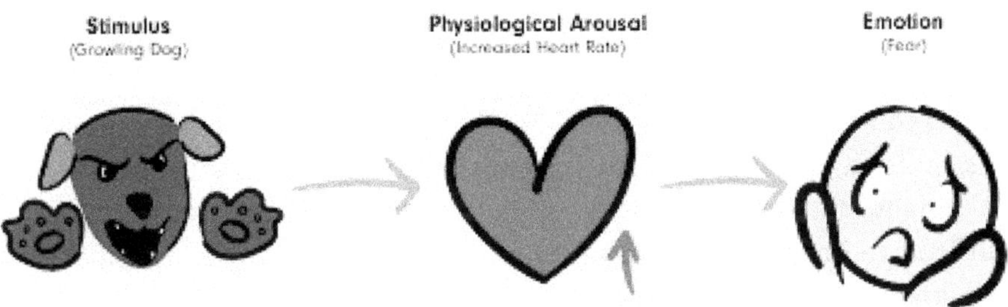

William James and Carl Lange, who were among the first researchers to explore the nature of emotions, a reaction to instinctive bodily events that occurred as a response to some situation or event in the environment. This view is summarized in James's statement, "We feel sorry because we cry, angry because we strike, afraid because we tremble"

James and Lange took the view that the instinctive response of crying at a loss leads us to feel sorrow, that striking out at someone who frustrates us results in our feeling anger; that trembling at a menacing threat causes us to feel afraid. They suggested that every major emotion has a particular psychological "gut" reaction of internal organs – called a visceral experience – attached to it, and it is this specific pattern of visceral response that leads us to label the emotional experience.

In sum, James and Lange proposed that we experience emotions as a result of physiological changes that produce specific sensations. In turn, these sensations are interpreted by the brain as particular kinds of emotional experiences. This view has come to be called the James Lange theory of emotion.

The James Lange theory has some serious drawbacks, however, in order for the theory to be correct, visceral changes would have to occur at a relatively rapid pace, since we experience some emotions – such as fear upon hearing a stranger rapidly approaching on a dark night almost instantaneously. Yet emotional experiences frequently happen even before many physiological changes have time to be set into motion. Because of the slowness with which some visceral changes take place, it is hard to see how they could be the source of immediate emotional experience.

The James Lange poses another difficulty: Physiological carousal does not invariably produce emotional experience

For example, a person who is jogging has an increased heartbeat and respiration rate, as well as many of the other physiological changes associated with certain emotions. Yet Joggers do not typically think of such changes in terms of emotions. There cannot be a one-to-one correspondence, then, between visceral changes and emotional experience. Visceral changes by themselves may not be sufficient to produce emotion.

Finally, our internal organs produce relatively limited sensations. It is difficult to imagine how the range of emotions that people are capable of experiencing could be the result of unique visceral changes. Many emotions are actually correlated with relatively similar sorts or visceral changes, a fact that contradicts the James Lange theory.

PPP

The Cannon-Bard Theory

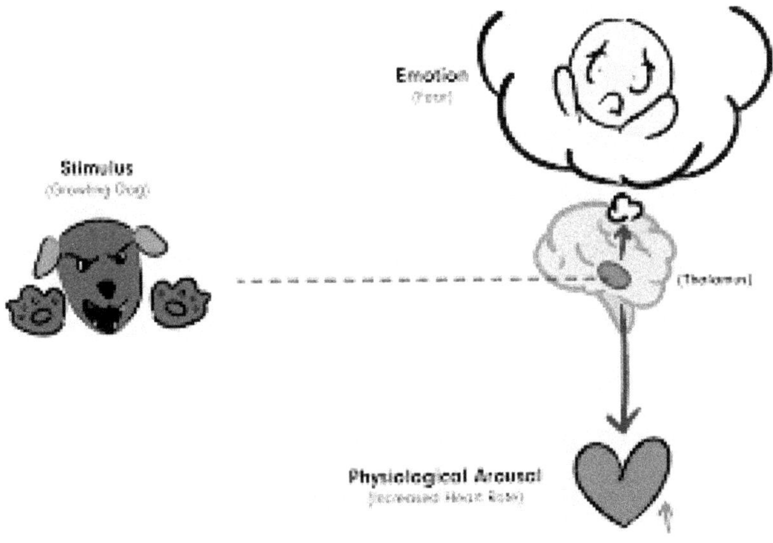

The theory assumes that both physiological arousal and the emotional experience are produced simultaneously by the same nerve impulse, which Cannon and Bard suggested emanates from the brain's thalamus.

According to the theory, after an emotion inducing stimulus is perceived, the thalamus is the initial site of the emotional response. In turn, the thalamus sends a signal to the viscera which are then activated, and at the same time communicates a message to the cerebral cortex regarding the nature of the emotion being experienced. Hence, it is not necessary for different emotions to have unique physiological patterns associated with them as long as the message sent to the cerebral cortex differs according to the specific emotion.

The Cannon – Bard theory seems to have been accurate in its rejection of the view that physiological arousal alone accounts for emotions. However, recent research has led to some important modifications to the theory, is now understood that the hypothalamus and the limbic system not the thalamus – play a major role in emotional experience. In addition, the simultaneity of the physiological and emotion responses – a fundamental assumption of the theory – has yet to be conclusively demonstrated. This ambiguity has allowed room for yet another theory of emotions known as Schachter – Singer theory.

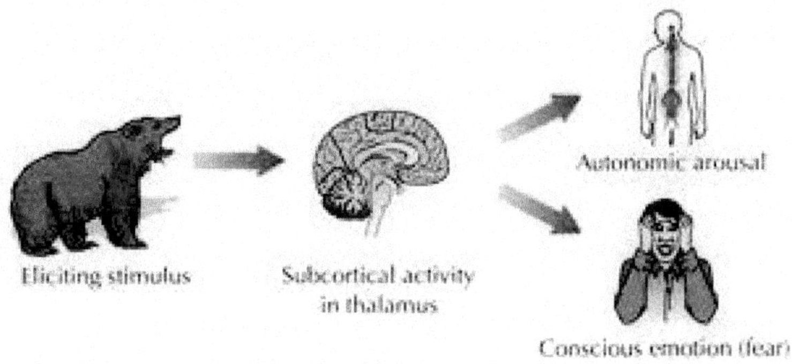

Schachter Singer two factor theory

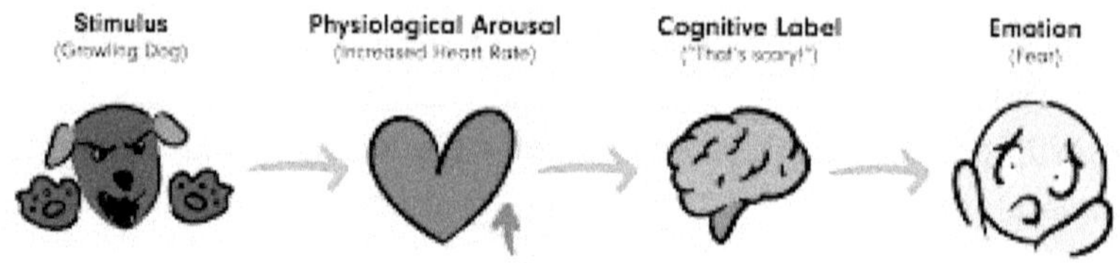

According to an explanation that focuses on the role of cognition, the Schachter Singer theory of emotion emphasizes that we identify the emotion we are experiencing by observing our environment and comparing ourselves with others.

Schachter – singer's theory of emotion suggested that emotion – provoking events produce internal arousal. Sensing this excitement, we focus our attention on the external environment in order to discover the basis for its presence. The stimuli we then observe lead us to select a label for our arousal. This, in turn, determines the precise emotion we perceive ourselves as experiencing.

For example, if we feel arousal after a near miss in traffic, we tend to label our reaction as fear. In contrast, if we experience a similar level of arousal after receiving an insult, we describe it as anger. The theory is described as a two factor view because it considers both arousal and the cognitive appraisal, we perform in attempting to identify such arousal.

Initial evidence to this theory was reported by Schachter Singer themselves in a well – known study. Participants were given injections of a drug that increased their arousal. Then they were exposed to the actions of another person, an accomplice of the researchers, who either behaved in an euphoric manner by telling jokes and shooting papers in the waste basket or demonstrated anger while filing out a questionnaire. Within each group, some participants were provided with accurate information about the effect of the drug, they were told it would raise their heart rate and produce other signs of arousal. Other were not given such information.

Schachter and singer reasoned that because they had a ready explanation for their arousal, persons given accurate information about the drug would not be affected by the accomplice's behavior. In contrast, those not given such information would use his actions as a basis for interpreting their own feelings and so would report feeling happier or angrier, depending on which behavior the accomplice showed. Results offered support for these predictions.

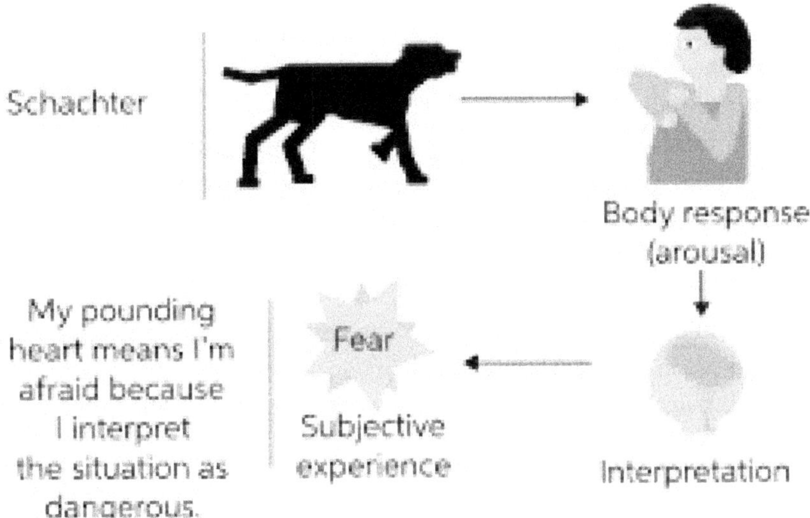

TEN

INTELLIGENCE

Q1. Define intelligence. Explain the nature of intelligence

Ans: Intelligence is considered to be a set of abilities, the ability to learn quickly, the ability to solve difficult problems, the ability to perform tasks quickly and accurately and so on. An ability allows a person to active a higher criterion of performance than someone else info lacks that ability.

According to Thorndike: The power of good responses from the point of view of truth or fact.

According to Terman: The ability to carry on abstract thinking.

Nature of Intelligence

(1) To act purpose fully we should have certain goal or purpose to do something in life. When a person has some purpose to do some work it shown his intellectual power.

(2) To think nationally – Whenever a person does certain task, first of all he thinks and then only he acts towards it. Whenever the thinking is rational, it shows the intelligence of a person. Individuals who have developed reasoning ability are among the most efficient and respected in life.

(3) To Adjust effectively: Intelligence is such an ability with which we can easily adjust in the environment.

An intellectual person has a strong power to adjustment with environment.

Q2. Discuss two factor theory of intelligence.

Ans: Two factor theory was given by Spearman in (1927). He argued that all activities share one common factor, called general intelligence, denoted as 'g'. It is defined as a basic component underlying all types of intellectual abilities and explaining correlations among all kinds of intelligence measures. However, there are several of 'specific abilities or 's' factor that may require mare or les of the g factor and which give an individual the ability to deal with specific problems. Thus, g (general intelligence) is essentially the cognitive fuel required for various specific abilities, the more fuel that is required, the greater the relation between g and s. In the diagram, quite a lot of general intelligence is required for specific ability marked S1, less for S2, and not very little for S3.

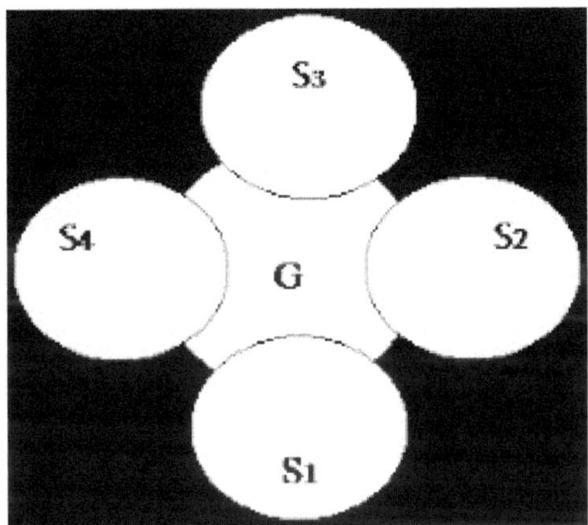

For example, an arithmetic test might tap, both G and a specific mathematical ability. Spearman's views are reflected in intelligence test e.g. Raven's Progressive Matrices, that yield a single score.

Spearman based his view on the observation that people who scored high or low on one kind of test of intelligence tended to score at a similar level on other tests too. Thus, those persons who possess more of 'g' factor and loss of 's' factor do fairly well in life.

G-Factor: It is a universal, innate ability. It is a general mental energy and remains constant in an individual. But it varies from an individual to individual. A greater g factor means a greater success in life because g-factor is used in all life activities.

S-Factor: It is learned and acquired in the environment although it is necessary that the individual has the potential to acquire it. The S-factor is essentially the mental energy which varies from task to task i.e. a person may have specific ability for mathematics and not for painting.

Spearman later on added another factor which is known as "Group factor" i.e., groups of items within a g-factor also correlated with one another such as in the factor of verbal comprehension, general knowledge, explanation of similarities and vocabulary correlate with one another. In perceptual speed as a group factor, block-puzzle solving, object assembly and digit encoding correlate with one another. Group factors are less general, widespread and homogeneous than 'g' factor and more general, wide spread and homogeneous than 's' factor.

PPP

Q3. Explain Multiple Intelligence theory given by Gardner

Ans: Gardner states that intelligence is the ability to solve problems and create products that are valued by a culture. He believes that intelligence has a biological basis. Multiple intelligence theory disapproves the idea of 'g'. Gardner does not deny the existence of a general ability, but question how useful 'g' is an explanation of human achievements. According to Gardner's theory of multiple intelligence, there are eight separate intelligences – linguistic, musical, spatial, logical mathematical, bodily kinesthetic, interpersonal, intrapersonal and naturalist.

Gardner's theory of multiple intelligence has not widely accepted. Critics states that eight intelligences are not independent, those are co-relations between the abilities.

Gardner's Intelligence:

1) Logical Mathematical: Ability to handle long chains of reasoning, sensitivity to and capacity to discern, logical and numeral patterns, skills involving problem solving and scientific thinking. Example: scientist mathematician

2) Musical Intelligence: Skills in tasks involving music, ability to produce and appreciate rhythm, pitch and timbre appreciation of the forms of musical expressiveness. Example: composer violinist

3) Linguistic Intelligence: Sensitivity to the sounds, rhythms and meanings of wards, sensitivity to the different functions of language example: poet, journalist

4) Spatial: Capacities to perceive the visual – spatial world accurately and to perform transformations on one's initial perceptions, skills involving spatial configurations. Such as those used by artists and architects.

5) Interpersonal Intelligence: Skills in interacting with others, such as sensitivity to the moods, temperaments, motivations and intensions of

others. Example therapist, sales man

6) Intrapersonal Intelligence: Knowledge of the internal aspects of oneself, access to one's feelings and emotions access to one's own feelings and the ability to discriminate among them and draw on them to guide behavior, knowledge of one's own strengths, weakness, descries and intelligence.

7) Bodily – kinesthetic: Ability to control one's body movements and to handle objects skillfully example: dancers, athlete.

8) Naturalist: Abilities to recognize plants and animals to make distinctions in the natural world, to understand systems and define categories example botanist, farmer.

ÞÞÞ

Q4. Explain in brief Thurstone – Group factor theory.

Ans: Thurstone has described intelligence in the form of groups, described as follows:

1) Verbal factor: ability of understanding ideas expressed in words.

2) word fluency: ability to speak and write with case

3) Numerical ability: ability to do numerical calculations, rapidly and accurately

4) Spatial ability: ability to mentally manipulate and visualize geometric relations.

5) Associative Memory: ability to make random paired associations that require rote memory.

6) Perceptual speed: ability to group visual details and to see differences and similarities among objects.

7) General reasoning ability: ability to find rules, for understanding and solving problems.

ÞÞÞ

Q5. Explain the structure of Intellect.

Ans: Guilford proposed a cubic model of the structure of intelligence. His model assumes that three separate factors make up any individual activity. These factors are:

i) operations: refers to what the individual des such as remembering and evaluating.

ii) Contents: refers to the material on which the individual performs these operations such as symbols or words (semantics)

iii) Products: refers to results from applying a particular operation to a particular content. The basic forms in which one can have information such as classes and implications.

Each of these parameters – operations, contents and products may be further sub-divided into some specific factors or elements. These factors were 120 in number with 5 kinds of operation, 6 kinds of products and 4 kinds of contents (5 x 6 x 4). Though his later researches Guilford (1967) expanded his cube shaped model of intellect to include 150 factors (by dividing the figural factor in contents into 2 separate categories visual and auditory). Hence there are 5 x 6 x 5 = 150 factors in all, which may constitute human intelligence. Each one of these factors in all, which may constitute human intelligence, has a trigram symbol, i.e., at least one factor from each category of the three parameters has to be present in any specific intellectual activity on mental task.

Type of information involved:

Contents:

i) Figural (visual): The properties of stimuli we can experience through the visual senses eg. color, size, shape, texture and other visual characteristics of figure.

ii) Figural (Auditory): the properties of stimuli we can experience through the auditory senses that is voice and sound.

iii) Symbolic: numbers, letters, symbols, designs

iv) semantic: the meaning of words, ideas

v) Behavioral: the actions and expressions of people

The way of processing the information – operations

i) Cognition: recognizing and discovering

ii) Memory: retaining and recalling the contents of thoughts

iii) Divergent production: Producing a variety of ideas or solutions to a problem.

iv) Convergent production: Producing a single best solution to a problem.

v) Evaluation: taking decision about the nature of the intellectual contents or gathered information whether it is positive or negative, good or bad

The results obtained through operations: Products

i) Units: Individual, pieces of information limited in size eg. a single number, letter or word.

ii) Classes: groups of units of information related to each other on the basis of some common characteristics involving a higher order concept (eg.

men + women = people)

iii) Relations: a connection between concepts

iv) Systems: an ordering or classification of relations

v) Transformation: altering or restructuring intellectual contents

vi) Implication: making inferences from separate pieces of information.

In this way, according to Guilford's model of intellect, there are 150 factors operating in one's intelligence.

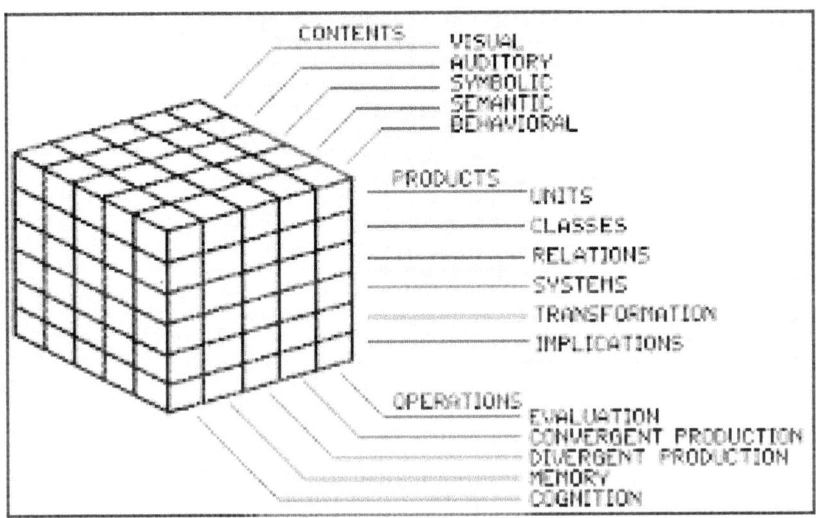

ELEVEN

GIFTED CHILDREN & INTELLECTUAL DISABILITY

Q1. What are the factors affecting intelligence?

Ans. 1) Heredity: Heredity refers to the genetic materials and codes we inherit from our parents. Evidence suggests s that heredity plays an important role in human intelligence. The IQ's of adopted children correlate more closely with those of their biological parents than with those of their adoptive parents.

2) Environment: This points out to the importance of situation that is environment e.g. family, economical level, health, facilities, etc. which influence intelligence much more than heredity does.

3) Culture: Different cultures apparently foster the development of different patterns of ability. Unfortunately, there is too little evidence on this important subject.

4) Sex differences: Early studies of differences in IQ between boys and girls wore essentially negative in that no clear differences were revealed. Most recent studies, however, using modern measuring instruments, have revealed some interesting differences.

5) Health: A good general health usually goes with high intelligence. Apparently superior heredity is a factor in both mental and physical superiority.

6) Family size: studies investigating the effects of family size on intelligence have found a low negative correlation between intelligence and number of siblings, especially is lower economic groups. Contributing to

this relationship may be the fact that among these groups people of lower intelligence tend to have more children; thus, children from larger families are likely to suffer from poor heredity as well as a poor psychological environment.

7) Education of parents: Tyler (1965) showed that children whose parents are well educated are more likely to show increases in IQ than decreases. These findings suggest that intellectual growth is greater in children of well-educated parents who provide home environment that favors intellectual development.

ÞÞÞ

Q2. Explain the concept of mental Age.

Ans. The typical intelligence level fund for people at a given chronological age.

Chronological Age: A person's physical age.

Intelligence Quotient (IQ) score: A measure of intelligence that takes into account an individual's mental and chronological ages. This term, was initiated by the German psychologist William stern and put into wide practice by Terman. It appeared to stern that if a child was 6 years old (chronologically), but could do what 8 years old normally does he would be 8/6 or 1.33 as bright as the average. And in this way, he made the ratio MA/ CA made on the basis of an IQ score.

Measure of the rate of mental development of an individual. To do away with the decimal point the ratio was again multiplied by 100 and thus the formula to calculate IQ was known as

$$IQ = \frac{\text{Mental Age (M.A.)}}{\text{chromological Age (C.A.)}} \times 100$$

ÞÞÞ

Q3. What are the uses of intelligence tests?

Ans: 1. For the purpose of selection: Intelligence tests are often used for the purpose of making selection of the suitable candidates for activities like

a) admission in a particular course of instruction

b) deciding the cases of scholarships

c) Choosing candidates for assigning some specific responsibilities

d) selecting candidates for participation in various co-curricular activities etc.

2. For the purpose of classification: Intelligence tests help the teacher to classify the student as bright, dull or average and hence make passible putting them into homogenous group in order to bring efficiency in teaching – learning process.

3. For the purpose of promotion: Intelligence tests can prove themselves alone of the useful instruments in promoting the individuals not only in educational fields but in all other occupational and social situations where one studies to go higher on the ladder.

4. For knowing once's Potentiality: Intelligence tests help in revealing the potentialities of an individual and in this way make possible the predication of one's success in a particular field. The knowledge of such potentiality helps the teacher in the following ways: giving guidance, helps in learning process and to establish a proper level of aspiration.

5. For diagnostic purpose: Exceptional children like gifted, backward and the mentally retarded children can be detected with the help of intelligence tests. Moreover, the intelligence tests help in the diagnosis of the root causes of problematic behavior of the child and like ladse suggest the possible remedy.

6. Helps in Research Work: Intelligence testing has been proved very useful in psychological, sociological and educational research. For example, in deciding the relative role of heredity and environment in the process of growth and development, research workers have made much use of Intelligence testing.

ᑭᑭᑭ

Q4. What are the misuse of Intelligence Tests?

Ans. 1) A special concern is that the sures on an IQ test easily can lead to stereotypes and expectations about students. Sweeping generalizations are too often made on the basis at an IQ score.

2) Another concern about IQ tests occurs when they are used as main or sole characteristic of competence. A high IQ is not the ultimate human value. It is important to consider not only student, intellectual competence in such areas as verbal skills but also their creative and practical skill.

3) Especially be cautious in interpreting the meaningfulness of an overall IQ score. In evaluating a child's intelligence, it is wiser to think of intelligence as consisting of a number of domains.

Q5. What are the different types of intelligence?

Ans. 1) Artificial Intelligence

Artificial Intelligence (AI) refers to computer programs capable of doing things that require intelligence when does by people. It is the intelligence of machines and the branch of computer science that aims to create it. It is the area of computer science focusing on creating machines that can engage on behaviors that humans consider intelligent. The ability to create intelligent machines has intelligent humans since ancient times, and today with the advent of the computer and 50 years of research into AI programming techniques, the dream of smart machines is becoming a reality. Researchers are creating systems which can mimic human thought, understand speech, beat the human chess player and countless other feats never before possible. For example, the military is applying AI logic to its hi-tech systems. AI may impact our lives in near future.

2) Spiritual Intelligence

Spiritual Intelligence is a term used to indicate a spiritual correlate to IQ and EQ. It is the capacity to understand and experience heightened states of consciousness, the ability to transcend the physical and material. It is the ability to sanctify every day experience. It comprises of an innate ability of thinking and understanding of spiritual phenomenon and to guide the everyday behavior by spiritual ideology. Daniel Goleman has defined spiritual Intelligence having four quadrants.

i) Higher self/Ego Self Awareness

ii) Universal Awareness

iii) Higher Self / Ego Self Mastery

iv) Spiritual Presence / social Mastery

King further proposes four core abilities or capacities of spiritual intelligence:

1. Critical Existential Thinking: The capacity to critically contemplate the nature of existence, reality, the universe, space, time and other existential / meta physical issues.

2. Personal Meaning Production: The ability to derive personal meaning and purpose from all physical and mental experiences, including the capacity to create and master a life purpose.

3. Transcend Awareness: The capacity to identify transcendent dimensions / Patterns of the self, of others, and of the physical world during normal states of consciousness.

4. Conscious state Expansion: It is the ability enter and exit higher states of consciousness, and other states of trance at one's own decision.

3) Emotional Intelligence

Emotional intelligence is the ability to identify, use, understand, and manage your emotions in positive and constructive ways. It's about recognizing your own emotional state and the emotional states of others. Emotional intelligence is also about engaging with other in ways that draw people to you. It is the ability to identify, assess, and control the emotions of oneself, of others, and of groups. The skills of emotional intelligence can be developed throughout life.

Emotional Intelligence consists of four core abilities:

i) Self-awareness – The ability to recognize your own emotions and how they affect your thoughts and behavior, know your strengths and weaknesses and have self-confidence

2) Self-management – The ability to control impulsive feelings and behaviors, manage your emotions in heathy ways, take intuitive and adapt to changing circumstances.

3) Self – awareness – The ability to understand the emotions needs and concerns of other people, pick up on emotional cues, and recognize the power dynamics in a group or organization.

4) Relationship Management – The ability to develop and maintain good relationships, communicate clearly, and influence other, and manage conflict.

ᑭᑭᑭ

Q6. Who are mentally retarded? What are the causes of this retardation?

Ans: Mental retardation is a condition of limited mental ability in which an individual has a low IQ, usually below to or a traditional intelligence, and has difficulty adapting to everyday life. There are varying degrees of intellectual disability, from mild to profound.

Causes of Mental Retardation

1) Genetic Factors: The transmission of defective genes gives rise to many disorders causing mental deficiency. Mental retardation or deficiency attributable to a dominant gene is very rare because the persons affected are generally incapable of reproduction. It is often the result of the pairing of two defective genes.

2) Infection: Mental Retardation can also be the result of many infections discases like syphilis, rubella or encephalitis which can damage brain tissue and the nervous system resulting in severe mental deficiency or retardation. If the mother suffers from one or the other of these infections' diseases, she may transmit infection to the developing fetus.

3) Intoxication: A number of toxic agents like carbon monoxide, mercury, lead and various immunological agents like arti-tetanus serum or the use of small pox, rabies and typhoid vaccines may result in brain damage during development after birth. Similarly, large doses of x-ray in radio therapy in the abdominal region of the pregnant mother, drugs administered to the mother during pregnancy, and overdose of drugs administered to the infant also lead to toxicity and brain damage.

4) Trauma: Prenatal injuries adversely affect the brain and the nervous system of the fetus. One of the main causes of such damage is asphyxia which results from oxygen deprivation and consequently causes suffocation of the tissues. Abnormal delivery and birth injuries are another cause of mental retardation. Difficulty during labor may result in damage to the infant's brain. Any abnormal delivery involves the risk of brain injuries Breech extraction use of forceps may cause hemorrhage of the brain and thus lead to mental retardation.

5) Metabolic and endocrine disorders: The chemical errors involving metabolism of fat cause the Tay –Sachs discase while disturbed protein metabolism cause PKU. Similarly, metabolic disorders like galactosemic involving an inability to metabolize galactose and maple syrup urine disease, involving chain amino acids lead to mental retardation.

6) Tumors: Mental Retardation may be caused by brain damage associated with brain tumors and other new growths. Tuberous sclerosis or epiloia is characterized by numerous nodules and tumors throughout the brain and other parts of the body.

Q7. Explain the prevention of Mental Retardation.

Ans: 1) Genetic counseling and voluntary birth control: genetic factors play a significant role in the causation of mental retardation. Chromosomal aberrations as well as pairing of defective recessive genes prove detrimental to normal train development and functioning. This knowledge may be helpful for the coring parents. There are tests to identify parents who have chromosomal abnormalities

2) Proper care of the mother and child: Adequate care of the mother and the new born infant is essential for the prevention of mental retardation. Proper care should be taken for the prevention of possible physical damage in the form of injured prior to birth, at the time of birth or immediately following birth.

3) Provision of public education: Efforts should be made to arouse the public to adopt preventive measures for controlling mental retardation. For example, by giving the right information about the correlation of the mother's age and mongolism, public opinion may be built up in favor of avoiding children after forty.

4) Provision of normal and stimulating environment after birth: For the prevention of such consequences, these is a great need for educating the parents and other responsible members of society. The children should be provided a normal, stimulating environment for the proper growth and development of their innate capabilities. Illiteracy and poverty of the parents, and poor of defective family environment should not come in the way of the satisfaction of their basic needs.

Q8. What are the different categories of Retardation?

Ans.

Mild

Moderate

Severe

Profound

Mild Mental Retardation (Educable)

Minimal retardation in sensory motor areas

Can develop social and communicative skills

Show signs of delayed development

Can walk, talk feed and toilet themselves in later years than the average

Immature behaviour

Lack judgement

Sexual behaviour is unpredictable

Needs guidance and assistance

Can learn academic skills

Moderate Mental Retardation (trainable)

Can talk and learn to communicate

Poor social awareness

Suffer from motor incoordination

Cannot acquire basic skills of reading and writing

Severe Mental Retardation (custodial)

Poor motor development

No communicative skill

Never attain an intellectual level greater than that of the average four-year-old child

Remain dependent on others throughout their lives

Profound Mental Retardation (custodial)

Needs running care

Retarded growth

Physical deformities

Severe speech disturbances

Motor incoordination

ÞÞÞ

Q9. What are characteristics of gifted children?

Ans. Characteristics:

IQ is above 130

Rapid learner

Excellent memory

Large vocabulary

Enjoys problem solving

Performs difficult mental tasks

Highly sensitive

Longer attention

Day dreamer

Very alert

Loves to read books that are one or two years in advance of the rest of the class

ÞÞÞ

Q10. What are the problems faced by gifted children?

Ans.

Habit in asking questions, but parents and teachers don't understand the urge

Adjustment problem with his classmates, becomes too conscious of his superiority

Sometimes becomes aggressive and hostile

Feels bored with the class assignment

Adjustment problems

PPP

TWELVE
THINKING

Q.1.Define thinking.

Thinking is a complex cognitive form of behaviour that occurs only at a relatively advance stage of development when simple and more direct methods of dealing with the environment have proved ineffective.

According to Garrett (1960)-“ Thinking is an implicit or hidden behavior involving symbols such as ideas and concepts and images etc.”

ϸϸϸ

Q.2.What are the tools of thinking?

Ans. 1)Images: Thinking requires use of images- Mental pictures of actual sensory experiences. Images are important to thinking, their interaction with words enables the thinker to construct- ideas. In thinking we usually manipulate the images rather than actual objects, experiences or activities.

2)Objects: We understand the word ‘ancestor’ by imagining our own grandfather. In solving geometrical problems we imagine a triangle but do not consider it as this particular imagined triangle, that means in the geometric operation you do not consider it, as obtuse, acute or any other particular kind of triangle.

3)Concepts: A very important tool for thinking is the concept. A concept is a ‘general idea’, an item in thinking that stands for a general class. The main thing to remember in this context is that thinking needs to use generalised concepts, that the concept is necessarily represented in conscious thinking but some particular item, like an image, but that the concept is never the loss more than a particular image.

4) Symbols and signs: Thinking also gains economy by making use of both symbols and signs. A symbol is a concrete particular item in thinking

that stands for something more general. For example, the sign of danger, we go to think the place must be dangerous. A traffic light, perceived or imagined, is sign. It tells what to do. They act as a signals for thinking or action, as motor response or stimuli for conscious.

5) Language: It serves to communicate ideas from one person to another. It serves to persuade or to incite others to action. It is the best medium of thinking.

ÞÞÞ

Q.3.Define problem-solving.

Ans. Problem-solving refers to an effort to develop or choose among various responses in order to attain desires goals. According to Eysneck(1972), "problem-solving is that process which starts from cognitive situation and ends in achieving desired goal. Problem-solving behavior helps in the removal or adjustment with interference and ultimately makes an individual reach the goal and satisfaction of his motives.

ÞÞÞ

Q.4.What are the strategies to solve the problem?

Ans.1) Trial and Error- a method of solving problem in which possible solutions are tried until one succeeds. It offers no guarantee that you will find a useful solution, this is the most primitive procedure to find a solution.

2) Algorithms- a second general approach to solve problems involves a rule that guarantees a solution to a specific type of problem. Algorithm involve a systematic exploration of every possible solution until the correct one is found.

3) Heuristics- Heuristics refer to a variety of rule of thumb strategies that may lead to quick solutions but are not guaranteed to produce results. They are mental shortcuts based on past experience by exploring few alternatives.

Kinds of Heuristics strategies:

1)Mean end analysis: Here over all problem is Brocken down into sub goals that can be achieved by solving smaller problems. Each sub goal you reach brings you closer to the solution of the overall problem.

2) Working backward: Some problems turn out to be easier when worked backward.

ÞÞÞ

Q.5.Define creativity.

Ans. Creativity is the power of the human mind to create new contents by transforming relations and there by generating new correlates. It is the capacity of a person to produce compositions, products or ideas which are essentially new or novel and previously unknown to the producer.

According to Stein(1974) – creativity is a process which results in novel work that accepted as enable to useful or satisfying to a group of people at some point in time".

ÞÞÞ

Q.6.What are the characteristics of creative thinkers?

Ans. 1) They are more independent in their judgements.

2) They are more self-assertive and dominant.

3) They reject suppression as a mechanism for the control of impulse.

4) They prefer complex tusk.

5) They are original, fluent and flexible in their ideas and their expression.

6) They have an investigative and curious nature, giving them a sense of adventure.

7) They exhibit diversity and divergence of thought even in convergent and stereotype situations.

8) They have the capacity to fantasize and daydream.

9) Creative people are generally high in intellectual ability as measured by standardized intelligence tests.

10) They show absence of fear, or even attraction to the unknown, mysterious and unexplained showing interest in vague and silly ideas.

ÞÞÞ

Q7.What are the stages of creative thinking?

Ans. A) Preparation: A person who develops a creative solution to an important problem generally spends long period of time immersed the problem, gathering knowledge relevant to it, and working on it.

B) Incubation: It is an interval during which the person involved stops working activity on the problem and turn to other matters. Incubation periods may provide people with an opportunity to recover from the fatigue generated by the intense preparation phase. It may occur outside the realm of consciousness, such as during sleep.

C) Illumination: At such times, individuals report that they suddenly see, perhaps only in partially developed form, they have been seeking for months or even years.

D) Evaluation: The idea must be worked out, translated into testable form, then actually tested. Only when mounting evidence indicates that it does work, is the creative solution carried to its final conclusion.

ᑭᑭᑭ

Q8.Explain Piaget's theory of cognitive development.

Ans. Jean Piaget stressed that children actively construct their own cognitive world's, information is not just power into their minds. Piaget believed that children adopt their thinking to include new ideas.

Piaget called the schema as the basic building block of intelligent behaviour. It is a way of organizing knowledge. It is also known as mental maps. Indeed, it is useful to think of schemas as "units" of knowledge, each relating to one aspect of the world, including objects, actions and abstract, concepts.

Piaget emphasized the importance of schemas in cognitive development, and described how they are develop or acquired.

Assimilation occurs when individuals incorporate new information into their existing knowledge. Accommodation occurs when individuals adjust to new information. For example, a nine years old girl is given a hammer and nails to hang a picture on the wall. She has never used a hammer, but from observation and experience she realized that a hammer is an object to be held, that is swung by the handle to hit the nail, and that is it usually swung a number of times. Recognizing each of these things, she fits her behaviour into her information she already has (assimilation). However, the hammer is heavy, so she holds it near the top. She swings too hard and the nail bends, so she adjusts pressure of her strikes. These adjustments reveal her ability to alter slightly her conception of the world (accommodation).

Equilibrium: this is the force which moves development along. Equilibrium occurs when a child's schemas can deal with most new information through assimilation. However, an unpleasant state of disequilibrium occurs when new information cannot be fitted in to existing schemas (assimilation). Equilibrium is the force which drives the learning process as we do not like to be frustrated and will seek to restore balance by mastering the new challenge (accommodation).

Stages of Development:

Each child goes through the stages in the same order, and no stage can be missed out- although some individuals may never attain the later stages.

There are individual differences in the rate at which children progress through stages. Piaget did not claim that a particular stage was reached at a certain age- although descriptions of the stages often include an indication of the age at which the average child would reach each stage.

Stages of development Key features

Sensory motor (0-2 years). Object permanence.

Pre-operational (2-7 years). Ego centrism.

Concrete operational (7-11 years). Conservation.

Formal operational (11 years to till death). Abstract Reasoning.

1)The sensory-motor stage- it costs from birth to about two years of age, is the first Piagetian stage. In this stage infants construct an understanding of the world by coordinating sensory experiences with physical, motoric actions- hence the term sensory motor. At the beginning of this stage, new borns have little more than reflexive patterns with which to work.

2)The pre-operational stage- it lasts from approximately 2 to 7 years of age, is the second Piagetian stage. In this stage, the children begin to represent the world with words, images and drawings. Symbolic though goes beyond simple connections of sensory information and physical action. In this stage, children have the tendency to focus on one detail in a situation and neglect the other important features. They have inability to consider another's viewpoint. For example, child act this stage might believe that if your pour water from a tall, thin glass into a wide-mouthed, shorter glass, you have less water.

3) Complete operational stage- in this stage, the child understand conservation. They understand, that when water is poured from a tall, thin glass into a wide-mouthed shorter glass, there is the same amount of water. They understand the concept of reversibility. They can also arrange objects according to size or wait and can divide something into its parts.

4)Formal operational stage- formal operational thinkers can handle hypothetical problems. They are able to project themselves into the future and think about long term goals. Scientific reasoning is also possible. They are capable of understanding and appreciating the symbolic abstractions of algebra. Therefore they involve in the development of logical and systematic thinking.

Criticism :

Criticism may include his underestimation of children's cognitive abilities. Studies have shown that children are capable of performing many tasks at earlier ages than Piaget predicted. Piaget paid little attention to individual differences. Some aspects of his theory may be culturally specific.

THIRTEEN

ATTITUDE, PREJUDICE & VALUES

Q1. What is attitude? How do you measure attitude? Describe any measuring scale of attitude indicating its social significance?

Ans: An attitude is an evaluation of an attitude object, ranging from extremely negative to extremely positive. An attitude can be as a positive or negative evaluation of people, objects, events activities and ideas. Psychologists define attitude as a learned tendency to evaluate things in a certain way. This can include evaluations of people, issues, objects or events. It could be concrete, abstract or just about anything in the environment. Jung defined attitude as a "readiness of the psyche to act or fact in a certain way". The components of attitudes are sometimes referred to as CAB or the ABC's of attitude.

1. Cognitive component: Thoughts and beliefs about the
2. Affective component: How the object, person, issue or event makes us feel.
3. Behavioral component: How the attitude influences our behavior.

Attitudes can also be explicit and implicit. Explicit attitude is those that we are consciously aware of and that clearly influence our behaviors and beliefs. Implicit attitudes are unconscious. But still have an effect on our beliefs and behaviors.

Attitude measurement can be divided into two basic categories:

Direct Measurement (Likert scale and semantic differential)

Indirect measurement (Projective techniques). With a view to assessing the degree of attitudes possessed by persons and to be the able to study a large member of people, the scaling technique was introduced into attitude measurement. various scales of attitude measurement have been developed.

Likert's Scale

For the Likert scale various opinion statements are collected, edited and then given to a group of subjects to rate the statements on a five-point continuant 1 = strongly agree 2 = agree, 3 = undecided 4. Disagree and 5 = strongly disagree. The subjects express the degree (one to fine) of their personal agreement or disagreement with each of the statements. Only those items which in the analysis best differentiate the high scorers and the low scorers of the sample subjects are retained and the scale is ready for use. To measure the attitude of a given group of respondents, this scale is given to then and every respondent indicates whether she strongly agrees, agrees, is undecided disagrees or strongly disagrees with each statement. The respondents attitude score is the sum of her/his ratings of all the statements. For this reason, the Likert scale is also known as the scale of summated Ratings.

In the Likert scale subject indicates her/his degree of agreement or disagreement for all the items in the scale. Further, the development of a Likert scale does not require a panel of Judges. It may also be noted that Likert did not assume equal intervals between the scale points. His scale is ordinal and therefore can only, order respondents' attitudes on a continuum, it does not indicate the magnitude of difference between respondents. By and large a great majority of researchers prefer the Likert technique. It much be noted that the typical Likert technique requires an item analysis to establish that all the items in the scale measure the same attitude no matter whether the scale has five or more points.

Advantages

Item analysis – break down into different items

Quantitative information

Easy to gather and sort out information

Find out information with direct questions (demand characteristic answering what your think is expected of you)

Disadvantages

Interpretation of undecided.

Tendency to middle answer, follow down the middle

Lie and bias results

Social desirability

Differences in individual interpretations of questions

Q2. Define prejudice. How it is formed and what are strategies that can be implied to eradicate prejudice?

Ans: Prejudice is a baseless and usually negative attitude toward members of a group. Common features of prejudice include negative feelings, stereotype beliefs and a tendency to discriminate against members of the group when people hold prejudicial attitudes toward others, they tend to view everyone who fits into a certain group as being "all the some".

Nature or Formation of prejudice

1) Prejudice is based upon ignorance:

The prejudice that exists between two different groups, parties and individuals are the outcome of ignorance or the part of both this ignorance leads to creation and adoption of different kinds of false beliefs and assumptions about other people.

2) Prejudice can both be in favor of and hosted to the existence of prejudice leads to the acceptance of one object while it also causes the rejection of some other object. So, in this way, prejudice may be in favor of some group or individual and it may be also be against the same.

3) Attitudes and Emotions are attached to prejudice

If the prejudice is favorable, the attitude attached to it is one of approval and acceptance while an unfavorable or hostile prejudice is accompanied by the attitude of disapproval or rejection.

4) Prejudice is motivated: A motive is a mental or neural set which affects the reactions of an individual towards some object, individual, group etc. A prejudice is motivated and at the base of it are superstitions and irrational judgement.

5) Wrong beliefs are included in prejudice:

Each and every individual has his own world and his own circle in which he formulates certain beliefs and convictions on the basis of what he has seen and heard. These beliefs may be good as well as bad.

6) Prejudice is hasty and leads to irrational decision:

Because of a prejudice a person reaches a decision. In other words, a prejudice fins expression in the form of a decision these decisions are reached very hastily without any reference to experience on to reason. For this reason, prejudices almost always prove to be harmful.

Strategies to reduce Prejudice

1) Training people to become more empathetic to members of other groups

2) By imaging themselves in the same situation, people are in think about how they would react and gain a greater understanding of other people's actions

3) Passing laws and regulations that require fair and equal treatment for all groups of people.

4) Gaining public support and awareness for anti-prejudice

5) Making people aware of the inconsistencies in their own beliefs.

6) Increased contact with members of other social groups.

7) Education and information for correcting stereotypical beliefs.

8) Highlighting individual identity rather than group identity

Q3. Define value. How value and attitude is related to each other?

Ans: Value can be defined as relatively permanent or relatively constant faith or concept in mind of a person. Each and every individual has got his own ideas about the things or stimulus around him.

Values are important to build up a person's moral character. Values build up person's mentality and personality and helped to project it at his matured age values helps us to maintain social unity and integrity. It is the main driving force of the society.

Value and Attitude

Attitude can be defined as a person's positive or negative preset mentality for another person or subject or object or community or anything. Attitude is a mental state where perception, feelings, emotions and actions are expressed. On the other hand, values are the sum total of attitudes which persists in an individual in a comparatively stable way values are less in number that attitudes. For example, honesty freedom etc.

But both attitude and values are changeable than values Because, values are the basement of culture.

According to Allport (1935), attitude is the preparatory expression involving neurological and psychological reaction. It is the outcome of continuous interaction between object and environment.

So, attitude is a reaction an something placed in a particular environment. Values are the meaningful or validity of such attitude. Attitude and values are interlinked and inter dependent on each other.

Q4. What are the different types of values?

Ans: 1) Theoretical value: It is related to a person's basic attitude positive and negative towards life. It is linked with truth, universal concept of honesty and dishonesty etc.

2) Economic Value: It is totally dependent on a person's economic concept or economic faith. This economic value system is generally expressed by persons' money-oriented behavior or attitude. How a person will earn money, how ambitions he/she is, how much savings will be made by the person, what would be his attitude for expenditure etc. is dependent on economic value system of that person.

3) Aesthetic value: It lies within the core trust of a person's personality, it depends upon how the person is perceiving the world, how he finds beauty in everything, how he sees and presents every part as a whole and always searches for completeness in everything.

4) Social Value: Social value is related to social behavioral pattern. When a person puts more value on social or community good or bad, then we must say the person has great social value. For a person who has great social values, things selflessly, they can sacrifice their personal objectives for the purpose of social objectives.

5) Political value: It is originated from political experience of a person. When a person is carrying out different political activities, shows different political ideas, then he must have greater political values than others. But there might be a difference between two political parties in case of projection of their political values.

6) Religions Value: This value system is dependent on religious belief and faith. Different religions values are the reason behind the existence of different religions groups.

FOURTEEN
DEVELOPMENT

Q1. Explain the difference between growth and development.

Difference between growth and development:

Growth

Development

The term growth is used in purely physical sense. It generally refers to an increase in size, length, height and weight. Changes in the quantitative aspects come into the domain of growth

1.Development implies over all changes in shape, form or structure resulting in improved working or functioning. It indicates the changes in the quality or character rather than in quantitative aspects.

Growth is one of the parts of development process. In strict sense, development in its quantitative aspects is termed as growth.

2. Development is a wider and comprehensive term. It refers to overall changes in the individual growth is one of its parts.

Growth may be referred to describe the changes, which take place in particular aspects of the body and behaviour of an organism.

3. Development describes the changes in the organism as a whole and does not list the changes in parts.

Growth does not continue through life. It stops when maturity has been attained.

4. Development is a continuous process. It goes from womb to tomb. It does not end with the attainment of maturity. The changes, however, small they may be, continue throughout the life span of an individual.

The changes produced by growth are the subject of measurement. They may be quantified and are observable in nature.

5. Development as said earlies, implies improvement in functioning and haviour and hence brings qualitative changes, which are difficult to be measured directly. They are assisted through keen observation in behavioural situations.

ᑭᑭᑭ

Q2. Explain the stages of development.

Ans.

Name of the stage

Period and Approximate Age

Pre-natal(pre-birth) stage.

From conception to birth.

Stage of infancy

From birth to two years.

Childhood stage

Early childhood

Later childhood

From 3rd to 12 years or in strict sense up the on- set of puberty

From 3rd to 5 years.

From 6 to 12 years.

Adolescent Stage

From onset of puberty to the stage of maturity (generally from 12 to 19 years).

Adulthood

From 20 years and beyond or in strict sense from the age of attaining maturity till death.

ᑭᑭᑭ

Q3. What are the different types of development?

Ans.

Aspects or dimensions in which a human child goes ahead of his complete development, can be named as follows: -

Physical development

Cognitive or mental development

Emotional development

Moral or character development

Social development

Let us see what we understand by these different aspects of development: -

Physical Development: The physical development of the individual includes the development of his internal as well as external organs.

Intellectual or Mental Development: It includes the development of intellectual powers like the powers of reasoning and thinking, imagination, concentration, creativity, sensation, perception, memory, association, discrimination, and generalization etc.

Emotional Development: Under this aspect, starting with the basic instinct, the evolution of various emotions takes place and also the emotional behaviour is developed to the paints of emotional maturity.

Moral or Character Development: Moral or character development includes the evolution of moral sense and development at character. The individual his ethical and moral codes.

Social Development: Initially the child is selfish and antisocial. Gradually he is developed into a social being by learning to behave according to the rules and norms of his society and makes adjustment to it.

Language Development: It includes the learning of the language for communication and the development or various skills and abilities for the effective use of language.

PPP

Q4. Explain the principle of growth and development.

Ans.

PRINCIPLE OF GROWTH AND DEVELOPMENT:

The changes brought about in the individual by the process of growth and development tend to follow some well-defined principles. These are known as principles of growth and development. These are known as principles of growth and development. These principles are being described below:

Principle of Continuity: Development follows continuity. It goes from womb to tomb and never ceases. An individual starting his life from a tiny cell develops his body, mind and other aspects of his personality through a continuous stream of development in these various dimensions.

Rate of Growth and Development is not Uniform: Although development follows continuity, yet the rate of growth and development is not steady and uniform at all times. It proceeds more rapidly in the early years of life but slows down int later years of instancy. Ed gain at the dawn of puberty, there is a sudden raise in the speed of growth and development but it is not maintained for long. Therefore, at no stage the rate of growth and development shows stead lines. It rather takes place by fits and starts.

Principles of Individual Differences: According to this principle there exist wide individual differences among children with respect to their growth and development in various dimensions. Each child grows at his own unique rate.

Uniformity Of Pattern: Although development does not proceed at a uniform rate and shows marked individual difference, yet it follows a definite sequence or pattern and somewhat uniform in the off-spring of human beings begin to grow from head downwards. Similarly, the motor development and language development in all children seems to follow a definite sequence.

Development Proceeds from General to Specific Responses: In all phases of child's development, general activity precedes specific activity. These responses are of a general sort before they become specific. For example, the boy waves his arms in general, random movements before he is capable at so specific response as reaching. Similarly, when a new born infants' cries, the whole of the body is involved. With growth the crying is limited to the vocal cords, eyes etc. In language development, the child learns general words before specific. He uses the word "daddy" in greeting many men and it is only afterword that he uses it for his father.

Principle of Integration: Where it is true that development proceeds from general to specific or from whole t parts, it is also seen that specific responses or part movements are combined in the later process of learning or development. "Development," as Kuppnswamy (1971) observes, "thus involves a movement from the whole to the parts and from the parts to the whole." It is the integration of whole and its part as well as of the specific and general responses that make a child develop. Satisfactory in the various dimensions of his growth and development.

Principle of Interrelation: The growth and development in various dimension like physical, mental, social etc. are interrelated and interdependent. Growth and development in any one-dimension effects the growth and development of the child in other dimensions. For example, children with above average intelligence are generally found to process above average physical and social development. The lack of growth in one dimension diminishes the bright possibility in other dimensions. That is why the child having poor physical development tend to regress in emotional, social and intellectual development.

Development is Predictable: With the help rate of growth and development of a child it is possible for us to predict the range with in which his mature developments is going to fall. For example: X-rays of the bones of the wrist of child will tell approximately, what his ultimate size will be. Similarly, the knowledge of the present mental ability of a child will help in predicting his ultimate mental development.

Principle Of Development Direction: Kuppuswamy (1971) throwing light on this principle points out two specific facts concerning the direction of the development. He says that development is "cephalic-candal as well as proximodistal." By cephalic-candal development he means, that development proceeds in the direction of the longitudinal axis (head to fact). First, the Child Gains control over his heads and arms and then on his legs so that he can stand.

According to the proximal-distal tendency of the development, it proceeds from the centre to the periphery in the beginning child exhibits its control over the large fundamental muscles but afterword's due to growth and development of smaller muscles can exhibit more movements that are refined. For example, control over fingers comes after the control over the arms and the hand.

Development Is Spiral and not Linear: The child does not proceed straight on the path of development with a constant or steady pace. Actually, he makes advancement during a particular period but takes rest in the rest next following period, to consolidate he turns back and then moves forward like a spiral.

Growth and Development is a Joint Product of Both Heredity and Environment: Child at any stage of his growth and development is a joint product of both heredity and environment. The forces of heredity and environment directly or indirectly influence his growth and environment directly or indirectly influence his growth and development in any dimension at all times.

PPP

Q5. What is the education implications of the principles of growth and development?

The above-mentioned principles of growth and development carry wide education meaning for the children, parents and the teachers. It can be explained in the following way-

Knowledge of the Principles of Growth and Development tells us that there are wide individual differences among the children with respect to their rate of growth and development. Therefore, we must pay attention to their individual pattern growth rate while planning the course for their education and development.

Its knowledge helps us to know what to expect and when to expect from an individual child with respect to his physical, mental, social development etc. at different stages of development. The correct knowledge of the growth trend of a child helps the parents and teacher not to under or over-estimate the future competency or expectancy of their child.

It helps us to know the direction as well as the general pattern of development. It guides us to locate the degree of abnormally in our children and students and to take like-wise remedial steps. The knowledge that development status from whole to parts and then from parts to whole helps us to plan the learning procedure and set the learning methods accordingly.

Principles of inter-relation and inter-dependence of the various aspects of growth and development help us to aim for the harmonious growth and development of the personality of the child and warn us not to develop a particular aspect at the cost of one or the other.

The knowledge of the uniformity of pattern with respect to growth and development makes it possible for the parents and teacher to plan ahead of time for the changes that will take place in their children. Children will also get benefited if they can be acquainted with these changes beforehand.

The knowledge that heredity and environment both play a joint role in the process of growth and development helps us to pay sufficient attention over the environmental conditions in upbringing the children.

In this way, the knowledge of the principles of growth and development helps much in the well-being of the youngsters.

❧❧❧

Q6. Explain physical development.

Ans.

It is important to know how children develop physically because physical development influences children's behaviour directly by determining what they can do and directly by influencing their attitudes towards self and others. Thus, affecting the kind of personal and social adjustment they make.

Throughout the growth years, there are four cycles of growth, two of which are characterized by slow growth and development and two by rapid growth and development. Cycles of growth affect adjustment difficulties, energy level, maintains of homeostasis, and degree of awkwardness.

Baby size, which is controlled partly by heredity and partly by environmental condition before and after birth, is measured in terms of height and weight, both of which follow predictable patterns.

The psychological significance of body size comes from the way others both adults and peers-react to it.

Because not all parts of the body grow at the same rate, body proportions do not reach their mature level until the body completes its growth early in the adolescent years. Body disproportion leads to such consequences as awkwardness, unattractiveness, judgements of maturity status, concern about disproportions, and favourable and unfavourable attitude towards children.

In this way, the knowledge of the principles of growth and development helps much in the wellbeing of the youngsters.

Physical Development

It is important to know how children develop physically because physical development influences children's behaviour directly by determining what they can do and directly by influencing their attitudes toward self and others, thus affecting the kind of personal and social adjustment they make.

Throughout the growth years, there are four cycles of growth, two of which are characterized by slow growth and development and two by rapid growth and development. Cycles of growth affect adjustment difficulties, energy level, maintains of homeostasis, and degree of awkwardness.

Body size, which is controlled partly by heredity and partly by environmental conditions before and after birth, is measured in terms of height and weight, both of which follow predictable patterns.

The psychological significance of body size comes from the way others both adults and peers-react to it.

Because not all parts of the body grow at the same rate body proportions do not reach their mature level until the body completes its growth early in the adolescent years. Body disproportion leads to such consequences as awkwardness, unattractiveness, judgements of maturity status, concern about disproportions, and favourable and unfavourable attitudes towards children.

As body proportions change, children begin to take on the characteristics of endomorphic, ectomorphic, and mesomorphic body builds.

The development of bones psychologically significant because ossification effects the seriousness of accidents involving broken bones and the attractiveness of the shape of the children's head.

The fact-muscle ratio directly effects the quality of children's behaviour and, indirectly, children's reactions to their body builds.

There are five psychologically significant facts about teeth: they have an effects on emotionality, they can disturb body equilibrium, they serve as insignia of maturity, and they effect the child's appearance and speech.

Growth and development of the nervous system have their greatest effects on children's body proportions, their looks, the degree of helpless, they experience, and their intellectual capacity.

Puberty changes, which occurs as childhood draws to a close and require about 4 years to complete, include changes in size and proportions and the development of primary and secondary sex characteristics.

Puberty changes lead to changes in behaviour and concerns about normality and sex- appropriateness, some at which have only temporary effects while others have persistent effects.

Because hazards in physical development have psychological as well as physical effects, their importance to children's personal and social adjustments has leads to the extensive scientific research to determine what these effects are and how temporary and persistent they are.

Edmong the many hazards in physical development those that are now known to be most common are mortality, illness, physical defects, malnutrition, disturbances in homeostasis, accidents, deviant body builds, and homeliness.

The psychological significance of hazards in physical development comes from the fact that hazards not only effect children's behaviour but they also effect attitudes of significant people toward children and the way they treat children who are experiencing these hazards.

ppp

Q7. Write a short note on emotional development

Ans.

Emotion as feeling on effect that occurs when a person is in a state or an interaction that is important to him or her, especially to his or her well-being (compos, 2004). Emotion is characterized by behaviour that reflects the pleasantness or unpleasantness of a person's state or current transaction. Emotions also take more specific forms such as joy, fear, anger, and so on, depending on how a transaction effects the person. (For example, in the transaction a threat, a frustration, a relief, a surprise) and emotions can vary in their intensity. For example, an infant may show intense fear or only fear in a particular situation.

Development Of Emotions

Infancy: Early development changes in Emotion. In research only early emotional development, the classification of emotions into two broad types is useful (Leuis,2002).

Primarily emotions, which appears in humans and other animals. The primary emotions include surprise, interact, joy, anger, sadness, fear and disgust. They are present in the first six months of life.

Self-conscious emotions, which require cognition, especially consciousness. The self-conscious emotions include empathy, jealously, and embarrassment, which first appear at one and a half years (after the emergency of consciousness), and pride, shame and guilt, which first appear at two and a half years of age. In development this second set of self-conscious emotions), children require and are able to use societal standards and ruler to evaluate their behaviour

First Appearance

Emotions

Primary Emotions

3 months

Joy, sadness, disgust

2-6 months

Anger

First 6 months

Surprise

6-8 months

Fear (Peaks at 18 months)

Self-conscious Emotions

1.5 years to 2 years

Empathy, Jealousy, embarrassment.

2.5 years

Pride, shame, quilt.

When infants experience only the primary emotions their emotional expressions help create their first relationships. The ability of infants to communicate emotions permits. Coordinated interactions with their caregivers, and the beginning of an emotional bond-between them. Not only do parents change their emotional expressions in response to infants' emotional expressions in response to their parents' emotional expressions. These interactions are mutually regulated. Cries and smiles are two emotional expressions that infants' babies first forms of emotional communications.

Crying: Crying is the most important mechanism new-borns have for communicating with their world. The first carry verifies that the baby's lungs have filled with air. Caries also may provide information about the baby's central nervous system.

Babies have at least three types of cries:

Basic cry, 2) Anger cry, 3) Pain cry

Many years ago, the behaviourist John Watson (1928) argued that parent spend too much

time responding to infant crying. As a consequence, he said parents spend too much

time responding to infant crying. As a consequence, he said, parents reward crying and

increase its incident. More recently behaviourist Jacob Gewirtz (1977) found that a caregiver's quick, soothing response to crying increased crying. In contrast, infancy experts many Ars worth (1979) and john Bowly (1989) stress that you can't respond too much to in fact crying in the first year of life. They believe that a quiet, comforting response to the infant's cries is an important ingredient in the development of a strong bond between the infant and caregiver.

Smiling: Smiling is another important way that infants communicate emotion. Two kinds of smiling can be distinguished in infants.

Reflexive Smile: A smile that does not occur in response to external stimuli and appears during first month after birth, usually during sleep.

Social Smile: A smile that occurs in response to an external stimulus.

Social smile does not occur until 2 to 3 mentals of age.

Fear: one of the baby's earliest emotion is fear, which typically first appears at about 6 months of age and peaks at about 18 months.

The most frequent expression of an infant's fear involves stranger's anxiety, in which an infant shows a fear and wariness of strangers. Strangers' anxiety usually emerges gradually. It first appears at about 6 months of age in the form of wary reaction. By age 9 months the fear of strangers is often more intense and it continues to escalates through the infants first birthday. Infants experience fear of being separated from their caregivers.

The result is Separation Protest.

Social Referencing:

Infants not only express emotions like fear but 'read' the emotions of other people. Social referencing involves reading emotional cues in others to help determine how to act in a particular situation.

Infants become better at social referencing in the second year of life.

ppp

Q8. Explain the development of emotions at different stages.

Ans.

Emotional Regulation and Coping:

During the first year of life, the infants gradually develop an ability to inhibit, or minimize the intensity and duration of emotional reactions (Thomson, 2006).

Early Childhood:

Self-conscious Emotions: Self-conscious emotions, which require that children be able to refer to themselves and be aware of themselves as distinct from others. Self-conscious evaluative emotions-pride, shame, guilty-first appear at about two and half years of age. Expressions of these emotions indicates that children are beginning to acquire and are able to use social Standards and rules to evaluate their behaviour.

In one study, girls Showed more shame and pride than boys (Stipek et al, 1992). This gender difference is interesting because girls are more at risk for initializing disorders, such as, anxiety and depression.

Self-conscious emotions are specially influenced by parents' response to children's

behaviour.

Young children's emotion language and understanding of emotion.

Among the most important changes in emotional development in each an increased understanding of emotion.

Between 2 to 4 years to age, children considerably increase the number of terms they use to describe emotions.

4 to 5 years of age, children show an increase ability to reflect on emotions.

Parents, teacher, and other adults, can help children understand and control their emotions.

Emotions play a strong role in whether of child's peer relationships are successful on nat.

MIDDLE AND LATE CHILDHOOD:

These are some important development changes in emotions during the middle and late childhood years. An increase ability to understand such complex emotions as pride and shame. These emotions become more internalized and integrated with sense of personal responsibility. Increased understanding that more than one emotion can be experienced in a particular situation. Marked improvements in the ability to supress negative emotional reactions. The use of self-initiated strategies for redirecting feeling such as using distracting thoughts.

Adolescence:

Adolescence has long been described as a time of emotional turmoil Adolescence are not constantly in a state of 'storm and stress' but emotional highs and lows do increase during early adolescence- Reed Larson and Mayrse Richards (1994) found that adolescents reported more extreme emotions and more feting emotions that their parents did. For example, adolescence are five times more likely to report being "very happy" and three times more likely to report being "very sad" than their parents. These findings lend support to the perception of adolescents as moody and changeable. Some adolescence, such emotions can reflect serious problems. Girls are especially vulnerable to depression in adolescence.

Emotional fluxions in early adolescence may be related to the variability of hormones during this period. Pubertal changes are associated with an increase in negative emotions. (Brooks- Gunn, 2003). Environmental experience may contribute more to the emotions of adolescence than hormonal changes.

EMOTIONS AFFECT CHILDREN'S PERSONAL AND SOCIAL ADJUSTMENTS:

Emotions add pleasure to everyday experience: Even such emotions as anger and fear add pleasure to life by giving children some excitement. Mainly their enjoyment comes from their pleasant aftereffects.

Emotions Prepare the body for Action: The more intense the emotion, the more it upsets homeostasis to prepare the body for action. If this preparation is not needed, it will make children nervous and edgy.

Emotional Tension disturbs Motor Skills: Bodily preparation for action plays Havok with motor skills, causing children to become awkward and clumsy and leading to such speech disorders as sturring and stuttering.

Emotions Serve as form of Communication: Through the facial and bodily changes that accompany the emotions, children can communicate their feelings to others and determine what the feelings of others are.

Emotions interfere with mental activities: Because concentration, recall, reasoning, and other mental activities are severely affected by strong emotions, children perform below their intellectual potentials when emotionally disturbed.

Emotions act as sources of social and self- evaluation: People evaluate children in terms of both of how they express their emotions and of who their dominant emotions are. How they treat children based on their evaluations, serves as the basis of children's self-evaluations.

Emotions colour children's outlooks on life: How children view their roles in life and their roles in life and their position in the social group is markedly influenced by whether they are shy, frightened, aggressive, curious, or happy.

Emotions affect social interactions: All emotions pleasant or unpleasant, encourage social interaction. From them, children learn how to modify their behaviour to conform to social expectations and standards.

Emotion leaves their mark on Facial Expressions: Pleasant emotion improve children's looks while unpleasant emotion distorts the face and make children less attractive than they are. Because people are attracted or repelled by facial expressions, the emotions play an important role in social acceptance.

Emotions affect the psychological climate: In the home, the school, neighbourhood or the play group, Children's emotions effect the psychological climate and it, in turn, affect them. A childish temper tantrum annoys and embarrasses others, charging the emotional climate with anger and resentment. This makes children feel unloved and unwanted.

Emotional responses when repeated develop into habits: Any emotional expression the gives children satisfaction will be repeated and in time, develop into a habit. As children grow older, if they find social reactions to their emotional expressions unfavourable, unrooting the habit will be difficult.

Q9. Explain the concept of social development.

Ans.

SOCIAL DEVELOPMENT

There is little evidence that people are born social, unsocial, and much evidence that they are made that way by learning. However, learning to be social person does not come overnight. Children learn in cycles. With periods of rapid improvement followed by plateaus in which there is little improvement or even by phases or regression to lower levels of social behaviour. How soon children recover lost ground or rise from the plateaus depends largely on ground or rise from the plateaus depends largely on the strength of their motivation to become socialized.

PROCESSES IN SOCIALISATION:

Learning to behave in socially approved ways: Every social group has its standards of what is approved behaviour for its members. To become socialized, Children must not only know what this approved behaviour is, but they must also model their own behaviour along the approved lines.

Playing approved social roles: Every social group has its own patterns of astrometry behaviour that are carefully defined and are expected by members of the group. There are approved roles, for example, for parents and children and for teachers and pupils.

MEANING OF SOCIAL DEVELOPMENT:

Social development means acquisition of the ability to behave in accordance with social expectations. Becoming socialized three processes which, although they are separate and distinct, are so closely interrelated that failure in any one of them will lower the individual's level of socialization.

Relatively few people, either children or adults, totally succeed in all three of these processes. Most, however, wish to win social approval and, therefore, they conform to group expectations.

ÞÞÞ

Q10. Why social development is important?

Ans.

Essentials of Socialization: What children's attitudes towards people and social experiences will be and how well they will get along with other people will depends largely on their learning experiences during the early. Formative years of life. Whether they will learn to conform to social expectations and become socialized depends upon four factors, which are follows:

First: Simple opportunities for socializing are essential because children cannot learn to live socially with others if they spend most of their time alone.

Second: Children must not only be able to comminate with others when they are with them in words that others can understands, but they must also be able to talk about topics that are understandable and interesting to others.

Third: Children will learn to be social only if they are motivated to do so.

Fourth: An effective method of learning under guidance is essential. By trial and error, Children learn some of the behaviour patterns necessary for good social adjustment. They also learn by role practice by imitating the people they identify with. However, they will learn more quickly and the end results will be better if they are taught by a person who can guide and direct their learning and chose their associates so that they will have good models to imitate.

ÞÞÞ

Q11. Who are social and nonsocial people?

Ans.

Social people are those whose behaviour reflects success in the three processes of socialization. As a result, they fit into the group with which they are identified and are accepted as group members.

Gregarious people are social people who crave the presence of others and are lovely when by themselves. They are satisfied merely to be with others, regardless of the nature of the contact.

Non-social people are those whose behaviour does not reflect success in the three process that characterize a social person.

Un-social people are non-social people who are ignorant of what the social group expects and, as a result, behave in a manner that falls short at social expectations. Because of this, they are not accepted by the group and are forced to spend much of their time in solitude.

Antisocial people are non-social people who know what the group expects but, because of antagonistic attitudes toward people, they violate the group mores. As a result, they are neglected or rejected by the group.

ÞÞÞ

Q12. Explain social development at different stages of life?

Ans.

SOCIAL DEVELOPMENT IN INFANEY:

The behaviour of human infant is not social at birth. He is self-cantered with the satisfaction of his physical need. He does not even distinguish between people and inanimate objects.

Social behaviour is said to be taking its birth when the infant first communicates with the adults for the satisfaction of his needs. Therefore, normally the baby's first social contacts are with an adult. Hurlock in her book "child psychology" has beautifully explained the process of social development during the first two years of a child as a result of the contact with adults. Below we give summary of her findings.

Duration of Age

Patterns of Social behaviour

During the first month

Can't differentiate the human voices and other noises.

Second month

Recognises the sounds of human beings and gives smiles to the person.

Third month

Recognises its mother and feels unhappy on separation.

Fourth month

Shows selective attention to the human face and feels happy in company.

Fifth month

Reacts differently to smiling and scolding and disguises between friendly and angry voices.

FOLLOWING SOCIAL BEHAVIOUR LAID IN BABYHOOD: -

Imitation: Babies become a part of the social group by imitating others. They first imitate facial expressions, then gestures and movements, then speech, sounds and finally total patterns of behaviour.

Shyness: By the third or fourth months, babies can distinguish between familiar people and strangers until late in the first year, they react to strangers by whimpering, crying and clinging to the person who is holding them.

Dependency: The more babies are cared for by one person, the more dependent they become on that person, they show their dependency by clinging to the person, crying when left with someone else and expecting to be waited on when they are capable of doing things for themselves.

Acceptance of authority: Whether babies are learning to conform to be requests of those in authority will depend on how insistent those in authority are permissive attitudes encourage babies to reject authority.

Rivalry: Rivalry develops in associations with other babies or children. It is shown by attempts to snatch toys or other objects from them, not because the babies want them but it gives them pleasure to assert superiority.

Attention Seeking: During the second year, babies try to get the attention of adulty by vocalizations, especially crying, by grabbing at their clothes, by hitting them, and by doing bedridden things. If they are successful, they show their satisfaction by smiling as laughing.

Attachment Behaviour: When babies are able to establish warm, loving relationships with their mothers or mother substitutes, the pleasure they derive from this association motivates them to try to establish friendly relationships with other people.

Social Cooperation: Babies' cooperative play with adults is usually successful because adults are willing to do most of the shoring. With peers, social cooperation is usually unsuccessful because their peers are unwilling to share.

Resistant Behaviour: During the middle of the second year of life, resistant behaviour begins. It is expressed by tensing the body, crying and refusal to obey unless babies are given opportunities to be independent resistant behaviour usually leads to negativism.

SOCIAL DEVELOPMENT IN CHILDHOOD:

During the period 2 to 6 years, a child progresses from being relatively unsocial to becoming a distinctly socialized individual. They term to adopt themselves to others and how to cooperate in play activities. Follow up studies of group of children report that the social attitudes and behaviour established during these early years. Usually persists with little change.

Early childhood is often called the "preaging age". At this time the number of contacts children have with other children increases and this determines in parts, how their social development will progress children who attend pre-school nursery, schools, dog care centres or kinder-gardens usually have a decidedly large numbers of social contacts with peers and make better social adjustments, that children who have not had this pre-school for active group participation than children whose social activities have been limited mainly to family members or children in the immediate neighbourhood.

After children enter school, individual play gives way to group games. Since group games require a large number of playmates, the older child's circle of friends gradually widens with change in play interests comes and increasing desire to be with and to be accepted by, children outside the home.

With the entrance in childhood the area of their social contacts is now widened.

Following are the changes in the social behaviour of a child:

Social Awareness: The period is marked by greeted degree of social awareness. There is a great expansion of child's social world. Most of the important types of social behaviour, necessary to adjustment with others, begin to develop at this stage.

Independency: One tries to seek independence from his parents and other elders and spends less time with them. In actual since, one now drives no enjoyment from them. Thus, interest in playmates of his own age gets increased.

Segregation: We find of segregation among boys and girls at this age. They form their groups among members of their own sex because of a clear and definite differentiation between their habits, interests and attitudes etc.

Generosity: Generosity, as shown a willingness to share with others, increases as selfishness decreases and as children learn that generosity leads to social acceptance.

Peer Group: One becomes an active member of a "peer group" and this group gradually replaces the family group in its influence over his behaviour and attitudes. The members of such a group are almost of the same age. They believe in group loyalty and thus try to conform to the rules and values maintained by their group.

The interests and values of the peer group obtain clashes with the interests and values of the teacher and parents. The child at this age is caught between the two. On one hand, he aspires for the social values of his own group; on the other hand, he is equally anxious to win the loss and affection of his parents as well as teachers. Therefore, a proper balance between these two influencing forces peer group. Parents and teachers are essential. If neglected by other side he may develop a maladjusted and antisocial personality.

Till the end of the stage of childhood, i.e., 11th and 12th year, the child enters the peak of "gang age" with increasing loyalties towards his own gang and conflicts with other gangs, parents and teachers. The gang life develops many good and bad social qualities in a child.

Some of characteristics of children gangs are-

Gangs identify themselves by names, many of which are taken from the street or neighbourhood where the members live or from popular books, comics or movies.

Gang members we secret signals, passwords, communication codes, or a private language to maintain their secrecy.

Gangs socialize children in the following way-

The gang helps children to learn to get along with age mates and to behave in a way that is socially acceptable to them. The gang can help children's personal independence by giving them emotional satisfaction from friendship with peers.

ÞÞÞ

Q13. Explain moral development?

Ans

Early psychological interest in moral development was cantered in discipline the best type of use to ensure that children would learn to be law-abiding citizen and the effect of such discipline on their personal and to moral development the normal pattern for this rea of development and the ages at which children can be expected to behave in a socially approved way. With the serious increase in juvenile delinquency interest is studying the cause, cures and prevention of juvenile delinquency became a psychological as well as sociological concern. At first, this interest coast limited to studies of the adolescent years because, correctly speaking children are hot regarded as "juvenile delinquents". Regardless of how for their behaviour deviates from socially approved standards.

MEANING OF MORAL BEHAVIOUR:

Moral Behaviour: Moral behaviour means behaviour in conformity with the moral code of social group. "Moral" comes from the Latin word "mores", meaning manners, customs and folkways. Moral behaviour is controlled by moral concepts- the rules of behaviour to which the members of culture have become accustomed and which determine the expected behaviour patterns of all group members.

Immoral Behaviour: Immoral behaviour is the behaviour that fails to concern to social expectations. Such behaviour is not due to ignorance of social expectations, but to disapproval of social standards or to lack of feeling of obligation to conform.

Unmoral Behaviour: Unmoral or normal behaviour is due to ignorance of what the social group expects rather than intentional violation of group standards. Some of the misbehaviour of young children is unmoral rather than immoral.

ÞÞÞ

Q14. How morality is learned?/ explain Moral Development theory?

Ans.

At birth, no child has a conscience or a scale of values. Consequently, every new born infant may be regarded as unmoral or nonmoral. And no child can be expected to develop a moral code alone. Instead, every child must be taught the group's standards for right and wrong.

Kohlberg's stages in moral Development: Like piaget, Lowrance, Kohlberg stressed that moral reasoning unfolds in stages. They stage, Kohlberg theorized, are universal. Kohlberg arrived at his view after 20 years of using a unique interview with children.

The Kohlberg Stages: Kahlberg described three level of moral thinking each of which is characterised by two stages.

PRECONVENTIONAL REASONING:

Preconventional reasoning is the lowest level of moral reasoning said Kohlberg. At this level, good and bad are interpreted in terms of external rewords and punishments.

STAGE 1: HETERONOMOUS MORALITY:

Is the first stage in preconventional reasoning. At this stage, moral thinking is tied to punishment. For example, children think they must obey because they fear punishment for disobedience.

STAGE 2: INDIVIDUALISM, INSTRUMENTAL PURPOSE AND EXCHANGE:

Is the second stage of preconvention rearing. At this stage, individuals' reason that pursuing their own interests is the right thing to do but let other involves an equal exchange. They reason that if they are nice to others will be nice to them in return.

CONVENTIONAL REASONING:

Conventional conformity is the second, or intermediate level in Kohlberg's theory of moral development. At this level, individuals apply certain standards, but they are the standards set by others, such as parents or the government.

STAGE 3: Mutual interpersonal expectations, relationships, and interpersonal conformity is Kohlberg's third stage of moral development. At this stage individuals value trust, caring and loyalty to others as a basis of moral judgements. Children and adolescents often adopt their parent's moral standards at this stage seeking to be thought of by their parents as a "good girl" as a "good boy".

STAGE 4: Social system morality is the fourth stage in Kohberg theory of moral development. At this stage moral judgements are based on understanding the social order, law, justice and duty. For example, adolescents may reason than in order for a community to work are adhered to by its members.

POSTCONVENTIONAL REASONING:

This stage is the highest level in Kohlberg's theory of moral development. At this level the individual recognises alternative moral courses, explore the options, and then decides on a personal moral code.

STAGE 5: Social contact or validity and individual rights is the fifth Kohlberg's stage. At this stage individual reason that values, rights and principles order grid or transcend the law. A person evaluates the validity of actual laws and social systems can be examined in terms of the degree to which they preserve and protect fundamental human rights and values.

STAGE 6: Universal ethical principles is the sixth and highest stage in Kohlberg's theory of moral development. At this stage, the person has developed a moral standard based on universal human rights when based with a conflict between law and conscience, the person reasons that conscience should be followed, even though the decision might brink risk.

Kohlberg believed that these levels and stages occur in a sequence and are age related. Before age 9, most children use level 1, preconventional reasoning, when they consider moral choices.

By early adolescent, the reason in more conditional ways. Most adolescents reason at stage 3, some signs of stage 2 and 4. By early adulthood small number of individuals reason in postconventional ways.

KOHLBERG'S CRITICS:

Kohlberg is theory provokes debate, research and criticism 9walker, 2004). Key criticism involves the link between moral thought and moral behaviour, assessment of moral reasoning, the role of culture and the family in moral development, and the significance of concern by other.

⚐⚐⚐

Q15. Write a short note on period of storm and stress in adolescence?

Ans.

The period of Storm and Stress:

The term 'storm and stress' was coined by G. stanley hall in adolescence, written in 1904. Hall used this term because he viewed adolescent as a period of inevitable turmoil that takes place during the transition from childhood to adulthood. 'storm' refers to a decreased level of self-control, and 'stress' refers to an increased level of sensitivity. Hall's perception of adolescence continues to influence our view of this period of development.

Three main categories of storm and stress described by Hall are:

Conflict with parents: Adolescence tend or rebel against authority figures as they seek greater independence and authority.

Mood Disruption: Hormonal changes and the psychological stress of adolescence can cause uncontrollable shifted in emotions.

Risky Behaviour: The combination of a neurological need for stimulation and emotional immaturity lead to increased risk-taking behaviour during adolescence.

BIOLOGY AND ADOLESCENCE:

According to hall, some of the blame for this period of storm and stress is due to the biological changes of puberty. It takes time for developing bodies to get used to managing these biological changes. Hormone changes can account for many of the mood suing that occur. Physical growth at this time can make adolescents to seek stimulation.

Apart from the factors mention above earlier, conflicts with parents, mood disruption and behaviour, there are different factors responsible for why adolescence experience various storms and stress during this stage and this is due to rapid changes and transition going on in the body and in the environment around them. One factor responsible is the search of autonomy which according to (Erikson 1959) described it as a process of individualisation and (Freud, 1958) also analysed it as a developing sense of detachment from parent.

Most adolescent stress is also related to lack of identity which usually arise because they start to think about who they are what they want to become and this tend to put them under a pressure to discover their real identity and the pursuit of this leads to a sharpened sense of dignity which makes them want to gain their freedom and freedom of choice thus creating a gap between themselves and their parents because they see themselves as more of an individual and someone who can make decision on their own, and this whole process of transition causes a whole lot of confusion between them and the parents which is one big subject parents nowadays find difficult to cope with and tends to see adolescent as moody, self-cantered, detached or being too concealed.

CONCLUSION:

Adolescence period is a very important and exciting in life that are marred by many stages of development and challenge, it is a time whom adolescence experiment so many thing that can either make or break their life and future, a period of exposure, it is a very unstable, inconsistent and emotional period, there are different stress and storms attached with adolescent but Holmbeck (1996) suggested that less than 10% of family with adolescents experience conflicts while only 15-30% of most adolescent experience storm an stress.

Not all individual experience this process of storm and stress but it does happen and to only affect most adolescent but not all as it is widely perceived and portrayed by the media, society and parents.

FIFTEEN

PSYCHOLOGICAL TEST

Q1. Define test. Discuss different types of a test. What are the characteristics of a standardized psychological test?

Ans.

Meaning of Test in Psychology and Education:

According to the dictionary 'test' is defined as a series of questions on the basis of which some information is sought. In psychology and education, the meaning of test is something more than information this. A psychological (or an educational) test is a standardized procedure of measure quantitatively or qualitatively one or more than one aspect of trait by means of a sample of verbal or nonverbal behavior. The purpose of a psychological test is twofold. First, it attempts to compare the same individual on two or more than two aspects of trait; and second. two or more than two persons may be compared on the same trait. In the words of Bean (1053:11), a test is "an organized succession of stimuli designed to measure quantitatively or to evaluate qualitatively some mental process, trait or characteristic."

Classification OF TEST-

Psychologists and educators have taken pains over classifying the test from the point of view of different criteria. A brief introduction to this classification may be presented as under:

1. On the basis of the criterion of administrative conditions

Tests have been classified on the basis of administrative conditions into two types— individual tests and group tests, Individual tests are those tests that are administered to one person at a time. Koh's Block Design Test is an example of the individual test. Individual tests are often used by school psychologists and counselors to motivate children and to observe how they respond.

Group tests are tests which can be used among more than one person or in a group at a time. Bell Adjustment Inventory is an example of the group test. Besides assessing adjustment, group tests are adequate for measuring cognitive skills to survey the achievements, strengths and weaknesses of the students in the classroom.

2. On the basis of the criterion of scoring

Scoring is one of the vital parts of test. Based upon this criterion, tests are classified into two Types- objective test and subjective test. Objective tests are those whose items are scored by competent examiners or observers in such a way that no scope for subjective judgment or opinion exists and thus, the scoring remains unambiguous. Tests having multiple-choice, true-false and matching items are usually called objective tests. Such tests are also known as new-type tests or limited-answer tests.

Subjective tests are tests whose items are scored by the examiners or observers in a way in which there exists some scope for subjective judgment and opinion. As a consequence, some elements of vagueness and ambiguity remain in their scoring. These are also called essay tests. Such tests are intended to assess an examinee's ability to organize a comprehensive answer, recall and select important information, and present the same logically and effectively. Since in these tests the examinee is free to write and organize the answer, they are also known as free-answer tests.

3. On the basis of the criterion of time limit in producing the response

Another way of classifying tests is whether they emphasize time limit or not. On the basis of this criteria the tests are classified into power test and speed test. A power test is one which has a generous time limit so that most examinees are able to attempt every item. Usually, such tests have items which are generally arranged in increasing order of difficulties. Most of the intelligence tests and aptitude tests belong to the category of power test.

Speed tests are those that have severe time limits but the items are comparativeness and the difficulties involved therein are more or less of the same degree. Here, very few examinees are supposed to make errors. Speed tests, generally, reveal how rapidly, i.e., with what speed the examinees can respond within a given time limit. Most of the clerical aptitude tests belong to this very category.

4. On the basis of the criterion of the nature or contents of items

A test may be classified on the basis of the nature of the items or the contents used therein. Important type of the test on the is criterion are:

i) Verbal test

ii) Nonverbal test

ii) Performance test

iv) Non language test

i) A verbal test is one whose items emphasize reading, writing and oral expression as the primary mode of communication Herein instructions are printed or written. These are read by the examinees and, accordingly items are answered

ii) Nonverbal tests are those that emphasize but don't altogether eliminate the role of language y using symbolic materials like pictures, figures, etc. Such tests use the language in instruction but in items they don't use language. Test items present the problem with the help of figures and symbol.

iii) Performance tests are those that require the examinees to perform a task rather than answer some questions. Such tests prohibit the use of language in items. Occasionally, oral language is used to give instruction, or, the instruction may also be given through gesture and pantomime. Different kinds of performance tests are available. Some tests require examinees to assemble a puzzle, place pictures in a correct sequence, place pages in the boards as rapidly as possible, point to a missing part of the picture, etc.

iv) Non language tests are those which don't depend upon any form of written, spoken or reading communication. Such tests remain completely independent of the ability to use language in any way. Instructions are usually given through gestures or pantomime and the examinees respond by pointing at or manipulating objects such as pictures, blocks, puzzles, etc. Such tests are usually administered to those persons or children who can't communicate in any form of ordinary language.

5. On the basis of the criterion of purpose or objective

Tests are also classified in terms of their objectives or purposes. Based upon this criterion, tests are usually classified as intelligence tests, aptitude tests, personality tests and achievement tests. Intelligence tests intend to assess intelligence of the examinees. Aptitude tests assess potentials or aptitudes of the persons. Personality tests assess traits, adjustments, interests, values, etc., of the persons. Achievement tests assess what the persons have acquired in the given area as a function of some training or learning

6. On the basis of the criterion of standardization

Tests are also classified on the basis of standardization. Based upon this criterion, tests are classified into standardized test and teacher-made test.

Standardized tests are those which have been subjected to the procedure of standardization.

Teacher-made tests are those that are constructed by teachers for use largely within their class-room. The effectiveness of such tests depends upon the skill of the teacher and his knowledge of test construction. Items may come from any area of curriculum and they may be modified according to the will of the teacher. Rules for administration and scoring are determined by the teacher. Such tests are largely evaluated by the teachers themselves and no particular norms are provided; however, they may be developed by the teacher for his own class.

Five main characteristics of a good psychological test are as follows: 1 Objectivity 2. Reliability 3. Validity 4. Norms 5. Practicability.

1. Objectivity:

The test should be free from subjective-judgment regarding the ability, skill, knowledge, trait or potentiality to be measured and evaluated. It depends on the objectivity of the test and the objectivity of the scoring system.

2. Reliability:

This refers to the extent to which they obtained results are consistent or reliable. Reliability here refers to self-correlation of the test. When the test is administered on the same sample for more than once with a reasonable gap of time, a reliable test will yield same scores. It means the test is trustworthy. It thus includes the internal consistency and temporal consistency. There are many methods of testing reliability of a test.

3. Validity:

It refers to extent to which the test measures what it intends to measure. For example, when an intelligent test is developed to assess the level of intelligence, it should assess the intelligence of the person, not other factors. Validity explains us whether the test fulfills the objective of its development. There are many methods to assess validity of a test.

4. Norms:

Norms refer to the average performance of a representative sample on a given test. It gives a picture of average standard of a particular sample in a particular aspect. Norms are the standard scores, developed by the person who develops test. The future users of the test can compare their scores with norms to know the level of their sample.

5. Practicability:

The test must be practicable in-time required for completion, the length, number of items or questions, scoring, etc. The test should not be too lengthy and difficult to answer as well as scoring.

SIXTEEN
PERSONALITY

Q1. Explain the theory of personality given by Freud.

Ans: The personality is made up of three major systems – the id, the ego and the superego. According to this model of the psyche, the id is the set of uncoordinated instinctual trends, the super-ego plays critical and moralizing role, and the ego is the organized, realistic part that mediates between the desires of the id and the super-ego. The super-ego can stop one from doing certain things that one's id may what to do.

ID

At birth a baby's mind is all ID. It contains all the basic needs and feelings. It is the source for libido (Psychic energy). And it has only one rule, the pleasure principle. The id cannot tolerate increases of energy that are experienced as uncomfortable states of tension. When the tension level of the organism is raised, as a result of either external stimulation or internally produced excitations, the id functions in such a manner as to discharge the tension immediately and return the organism to a comfortably constant and low energy level.

Ego

Ego functions with the rational part of the mind. The ego develops out of growing awareness that you lant always get what you want. The ego relates to the real world and operates via the reality principle. The ego realizes the need for compromise and negotiates between the Id and the superego. The Ego's job is to get the Id's pleasures but to be reasonable and bear the long –term consequences in mind. The ego denies both instant gratification and pious delaying of gratification. The term ego-strength is the term used to refer to how well the ego copes with these conflicting forces. The ego controls the gateways to action, and helps in performing highly important executive functions.

Super Ego

It is the internal representative of the traditional values and ideals of society as interpreted to the child by its parents and enforced by means of a system of rewards and punishments imposed upon the child. The superego is the moral arm of personality. It represents the ideal rather than the real and strives for perfection rather than pleasure. Its main concern is to decide whether something is right or wrong so that it can act in accordance with the moral standards authorized by the agents of society.

Layers / components of personality – conscious, subconscious and Unconscious

Conscious (10%)

Subconscious

Unconscious (90%)

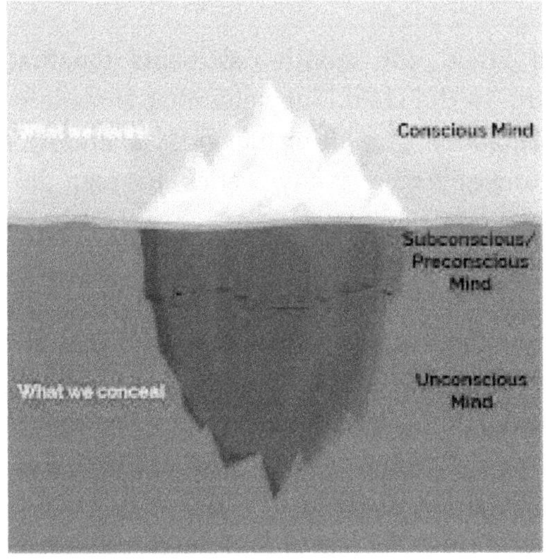

The conscious mind lies just above the surface of the water like the tip of an iceberg and occupies only one tenth of our local psyche or mental life. The ideas, thoughts and images that we are aware of at any moment of our mental life. The ideas, thoughts and images that we are aware of at any moment of our mental life are said to lie within this upper layer of our mind. Just beneath the conscious layer lies the subconscious mind. This middle portion of our mind stores all types of information just beneath the surface of awareness dormant or untapped which can be easily brought to the level of consciousness at a moment's notice whenever required. Thus, in the middle layer of the human mind there lie all experiences or knowledge which have been learned by an individual through various types of experiences or training.

Below the subconscious mind lies the unconscious, the most important part of our mind. It is related to the vast part of our mental life which is hidden and usually inaccessible to the conscious. It contains all the repressed wishes, desires, feelings, drives and motives, many of which relate to sex and aggression. All these repressed and forbidden desires and ideas are not destined to lie permanently in the unconscious. They usually strive and agitate to come up to the subconscious or the conscious layers of the mind, sometimes in distinguished forms, in dreams. This hidden treasure of mental life belongs to unconscious.

Stages of Psychosexual Development

1) The oral stage (0-2 years)

According to Freud, the mouth represents the first sex organ for providing pleasure to the child. The beginning is made with the pleasure received from the mother's nipple or the bottle. Therefore, the child derives pleasure by putting anything, candy, a stick, his own thumb, etc. into his mouth.

2) The Anal Stage (2 – 4 yrs)

At this stage, the interest of the child shifts from the mouth as the erogenous zone to the organism of elimination that is the anus or the urethra. He derives pleasure by holding back or letting go of the body's waste material through the anus or the urethra. The expulsion of the faeces removes the source of discomfort and produces a feeling of relief

3) The Phallic Stage (3 – 6 yrs)

This phase starts from the age of four years with shifting of the child's interest from the eliminating organs to the genitals. At this stage children come to note the biological differences between the sexes and derive pleasure by playing with and manipulating the genital organs. This stage may give rise to a number of complexes like deprivation and Electra complexes in girls and castration and Oedipus complexes in boys. The deprivation complex is the result of the feelings generated in the minds of the little girls that they have been deprived of the male organs by their mothers.

Castration complex is generated in boys through their fear of being deprived of the male organs certainly as a result of the threat received from elders that the organ would be cut off if they did not give up the habit of playing with it. About the Oedipus and Electra phases, Freud says that they are the result of the sexual attraction or pleasure that children experience in the company of the parent of the opposite sex.

4. The latency stage (6 - puberty)

This period starts from six years in the case of girls and seven to eight years in the case of boys and girls prefer to be in the company of their own sex and even neglect or hate members of the opposite sex.

5. The genital stage (Puberty to adult)

Puberty is the starting point of the genital stage. The adolescent boy and girl now feels a strange feeling of strong sensation in the genitals and attraction towards the members of the opposite sex. At this stage, they may feel pleasure by self-stimulation of the genitals, may full in love with their own self by taking interest in beautiful and adorning their bodies. In this stage, they are indulged in sexual inter course.

Defence Mechanism

Under the pressure of excessive anxiety, the ego is sometimes forced to take extreme measures to relieve the pressure. These measures are called defense mechanisms. All defense mechanism has two characteristics in common: they deny, falsity or distort reality and they operate unconsciously so that the person is not aware of what is taking place.

1) Repression: It means unknowingly placing an unpleasant memory or thought in the unconscious eg not remembering a traumatic incident in which you witnessed a crime. Repression can even interfere with the normal functioning of the body. Someone may become sexually impotent because he is afraid of sex impulse.

2) Regression: It implies reverting back to immature behavior from an earlier stage of development for example, throwing temper tantrums as an adult when you don't get your way.

3) Displacement: when a person redirects unacceptable feelings from the original source to a safer target. Taking your anger toward your boss out on your spouse or children by yelling at them and not your boss.

4) Sublimation: It means replacing socially unacceptable impulses with socially acceptable behaviors. For example, channeling aggressive drives into playing football or inappropriate sexual desires into out.

5) Reaction Formation: Acting in exactly the opposite way to one's unacceptable impulses. For example, being over protective and giving more attention on an unwanted child.

6) Projection: It involves attributing one's own unacceptable feelings and thoughts to others. And not yourself. For example, accusing your boyfriend of cheating on you because you have felt like cheating on him.

7) Rationalization: It means creating false excuses for one's unacceptable feelings, thoughts or behavior. For example, justifying cheating on an exam by saying that everyone else cheats.

8) Denial: When a person does not acknowledge that there is a problem it is known as denial. For example, a man has gotten a diagnosis from his doctor that he is HIV positive but is adamant that a mistake has been made and that his doctor is not good enough to diagnose.

9) Identification: taking on the characteristics of someone viewed as successful.

10) Fantasy: Gratifying frustrated desires by imaginary achievements.

ÞÞÞ

Q2. Explain Carl Roger theory of personality

Ans: Roger's theory is known as self-theory. He stressed the importance of an individual's self for determining the process of his growth, development, and appropriate adjustment to his environment. There are two basic systems – the organism and the self. The organism is an individual's entire frame of reference. It represents the totality of his experiences both conscious and unconscious. The second system, is the 'self' which the aware part of experience. The self as a system of one's phenomenal field which can be best understood in terms of I, me or myself.

The acquisition of the concept of self is a long and continuous process. Human beings have inherited the tendency to develop their self in the process of inter-personal and social experiences which they acquire in the environment. In other words, our inner world interacts with our total range of experiences to form the concept of our self. For example, if one is told that one is a handsome person, one tends to include in the concept of one's self, the idea that one is handsome. The concepts of self thus developed may differ from person to person as they are based purely on one's own personal experiences.

According to this theory, once a concept of self is formed, the individual strives to maintain it by regulating this behavior. Whatever is consistent with the concept of self is reading accepted and maintained at the conscious level while that which threatens that image may be totally ignored or buried deep in the unconscious.

The most unfortunate results in the development of personality occur in cases where an individual develops some false self-image. This false image is sometimes so strong that even indisputable reality is denied. Inconsistency between one's actual image and a false self-image, may then lead to abnormality in one's behaviors. Similarly, the development of ideal self from one's real self, may result in maladjustment and serious personality disorders. An individual's adjustment, happiness, growth and development all depend upon the union and harmony between the image of his self and the organism. That is the experience on situations he meets in his life. Stressing the psychological personality theory, Roger emphasizes that a person normally possesses considerable capacity for growth and the realization of his individual potential and thrusts to advance continuously towards the development of his self (i.e. self - actualization)

Roger believed that every person can achieve their goals, wishes and desires in life. The organism has one basic tendency and striving to actualize, maintain and enhance the experiencing organism.

Roger believed that people are inherently good and creative. They become destructive only when a poor self-concept or external constrains override the valuing process.

The self –concept incept includes:

Self – worth: what we think about ourselves, feelings of self-worth developed in early childhood and were formed from the interaction of the child with the mother and father.

Self-image: How we see ourselves, which is important to good psychological health. Self-image includes the influence of our body image on inner personality, A person thinks, feels and behaves in the worlds.

Ideal self: This is the person who we would like to be.

It consists of our goals and ambitions in life and is dynamic that is forever changing.

High self-worth means a person has confidence and positive feelings about him or herself, faces challenges in life, accepts failure and unhappiness at times, and is open with people.

A person with low self-esteem may avoid challenges in life, not accept that life can be painful and unhappy at times, and will be defensive and guarded with other people.

Roger believed feelings of self-worth developed in early childhood and were formed from the interaction of the child with the mother and father. As a child grows older, interactions with significant others will affect feelings of self-worth.

Rogers believed that we need to be regarded positively by others, we need to feel valued, respected, treated with affection and loved.

Unconditional Positive Regard means the person feels free to try things out and make mistakes, even though this may lead to getting it worse at times

Conditional Positive Regard is positive regard, praise and approval, and it depends upon the child. For example, behaving in ways that the parents think correct. Hence, the child is not loved for the person he or she is, but on condition that if he or she behaves in the way approved by the parents, then only he/she will get a reward.

According to Roger, we want to feel, experience and behave in ways which are consistent with our self-image and which reflect what we would like to be like, our ideal self.

The closer our self-image and ideal – self are to each other, the more consistent or congruent we are and the higher our sense of self-worth. A person is said to be in a state of incongruence if some of the totality of their experience is unacceptable to them and is denied or distorted in the self-image.

And thus, incongruence is "a discrepancy between the actual experience of the organism and self-picture of the individual in so for as it represents that experience."

Q3. Critically discuss Eysenck's theory of personality. Explain the theory based on the structure of mind.

Ans: Eysenck was a noted psychologist in the field of personality. He was born in Germany in 1916, but moved to England as the Nazis gained power early in the 1930s. Though Eysenck was known for many areas of study in psychology, including intelligence and mental illness, he is often cited today for his work in personality. Eysenck (1952, 1967, 1982) developed a very influential model of personality. Based on the results of factor analysis of responses on personality questionnaires he identified three dimensions of personality: extraversion, neuroticism and psychoticism.

During 1940s Eysenck was working at the Maudsley psychiatric hospital in London. His job was to make an initial assessment of each patient before their mental disorder was diagnosed by a psychiatrist. He found that the soldiers' answers seemed to link naturally with one another, suggesting that there were a number of different personality traits which were being revealed by the soldier's answers. He called these first order personality traits.

He used a technique called factor analysis. This technique reduces behavior to a number of factors which can be grouped together under separate headings, called dimensions. Eysenck (1947) found that their behavior could be represented by two dimensions: Introversion / Extroversion (I/E); Neuroticism/ Stability (N). Eysenck called these second-order personality traits. According to Eysenck the two dimensions of neuroticism (stable vs. unstable) and introversion-extroversion combine to form a variety of personality characteristics.

Traits:

Extraverts are sociable and crave excitement and change, and thus can become bored easily. They tend to be carefree, optimistic and impulsive. Introverts are reserved, plan their actions and control their emotions. They tend to be serious, reliable and pessimistic.

Neurotics / unstable tend to be anxious, worrying and moody. They are overly emotional and find it difficult to calm down once upset. Stables are emotionally calm, unreactive and unworried.

Psychoticism: Eysenck (1966) later added a third trait / dimension Psychoticism – e.g. lacking in empathy, cruel, a loner, aggressive and troublesome. Eysenck related the personality of an individual to the functioning of the autonomic nervous system (ANS). Personality is dependent on the balance between excitation and inhibition process of the nervous system. Neurotic individuals have an ANS that responds quickly to stress.

Limitations of Eysenck's type theory

Many would argue that the theory is too simplistic i.e. it boils something as complex as personality down to four categories. The assessment relies on the honesty of the participant when answering the questions. The answers they give may be influenced by mood. Eysenck believes that personality is genetic and fails to consider that it may change over time.

Q4. Critically discuss the theory of Erikson.

Ans. Erik Erikson proposed a lifespan model of development, taking in five stages up to the age of 18 years and three further stages beyond, well into adulthood. Erikson suggests that there is still plenty of room for continued growth and development throughout one's life. Erikson put a great deal of emphasis on the adolescent period, feeling" it was a crucial stage for developing a person's identity.

Erikson's (1959) theory of psychosocial development has eight distinct stages, psychosocial stages summary table Like Freud, Erikson assumes that a crisis occurs at each stage of development. For Erikson (1963), these crises are of a psychosocial nature because they involve psychological needs of the individual (i.e. psycho) conflicting with the needs of society (i.e, social).

According to the theory: successful completion of each stage results in a healthy personality and the acquisition of basic virtues. Basic virtues are characteristic strengths which the ego can use to resolve subsequent crises. Failure to successfully complete a stage can result in a reduced ability to complete further stages and therefore an unhealthier personality and sense of self. These stages, however, can be resolved successfully at a later time.

1. Trust vs. Mistrust Is the world a safe place or is it full of unpredictable events and accidents waiting to happen?

Erikson's first psychosocial crisis occurs during the first year or so of life (like Freud's oral stage of psychosexual development).

The crisis is one of trust vs. mistrust.

During this stage the infant is uncertain about the world in which they live. To resolve these feelings of uncertainty the infant looks towards their primary caregiver for stability and consistency of care. If the care the infant receives is consistent, predictable and reliable they will develop a sense of trust which will carry with them to other relationships, and they will be able to feel secure even when threatened. Success in this stage will lead to the virtue of hope. By developing a sense of trust, the infant can have hope that as new crises arise, there is a real possibility that other people will be there are a source of support. Failing to acquire the virtue of hope will lead to the development of fear. For example, if the care has been harsh or inconsistent, unpredictable and unreliable then the infant will develop a sense of mistrust and will not have confidence in the world around them or in their abilities to influence events.

2. Autonomy vs. Shame and Doubt

The child is developing physically and becoming more mobile. Between the ages of 18 months and three, children begin to assert their independence, by walking away from their mother, picking which toy to play with, and making choices about what they like to wear, to eat, etc. The child is discovering that he or she has many skills and abilities, such as putting on clothes and shoes, playing with toys etc. Such skills illustrate the child's growing sense of independence and autonomy. Erikson states it is critical that parents allow their children to explore the limits of their abilities within an encouraging environment which is tolerant of failure.

3. Initiative vs. Guilt

Around age three and continuing to age five, children assert themselves more frequently. These are particularly lively rapid developing years in a child's life. According to Bee (1992) it is a "time of vigor of action and of behaviors that the parents may see as aggressive". During this period the primary feature involves the child regularly interacting with other children at school. Central to this stage is play, as it provides children with the opportunity to explore their interpersonal skills through initiating activities Children begin to plan activities, make up games, and initiate activities with others. If given this opportunity, children develop a sense of initiative, and feel secure in their ability to lead others and make decisions. Conversely, if this tendency is squelched, either through criticism or control, children develop a sense of guilt. They may feel like a nuisance to others and will therefore remain followers, lacking in self-initiative. For example, rather than put on a child's clothes a supportive parent should have the patience to allow the child to try until they succeed or ask for assistance.

4. Industry (competence) vs. Inferiority

Children are at the stage (aged 5 to 12 years) where they will be learning to read and write, to do sums, to make things on their own. Teachers begin to take an important role in the child's life as they teach the child specific skills. It is at this stage that the child's peer group will gain greater significance and will become a major source of the child's self-esteem. The child now feels the need to win approval by demonstrating specific competencies that are valued by society and begin to develop a sense of pride in their accomplishments.

If children are encouraged and reinforced for their initiative, they begin to feel industrious (competent) and feel confident in their ability to achieve goals. If this initiative is not encouraged, if it is restricted by parents or teacher, then the child begins to feel inferior, doubting his own abilities and therefore may not reach his or her potential.

If the child cannot develop the specific skill, they feel society is demanding (e.g., being athletic) then they may develop a sense of Inferiority.

Some failure may be necessary so that the child can develop some modesty. Again, a balance between competence and modesty is necessary. Success in this stage will lead to the virtue of competence.

5. Identity vs. Role Confusion

During adolescence, the transition from childhood to adulthood is most important. Children are becoming more independent, and begin to look at the future in terms of career, relationships, families, housing, etc. The individual wants to belong to a society and fit in. This is a major stage of development where the child has to learn the roles he will occupy as an adult. It is during this stage that the adolescent will re-examine his identity and try to find out exactly who he or she is. Erikson suggests that two identities are involved: the sexual and the occupational. Erikson claims that the adolescent may feel uncomfortable about their body for a while until they can adapt and "grow into" the changes. Success in this stage will lead to the virtue of fidelity.

Fidelity involves being able to commit one's self to others on the basis of accepting others, even when there may be ideological differences.

During this period, they explore possibilities and begin to form their own identity based upon the outcome of their explorations. Failure to establish a sense of identity within society ("I don't know what I want to be when I grow up") can lead to role confusion. Role confusion involves the individual not being sure about themselves or their place in society.

6. Intimacy vs. Isolation

Intimacy versus isolation is the sixth stage of Erik Erikson's theory of psychosocial development. This stage takes place during young adulthood between the ages of approximately 18 to 40 yrs. During this stage, the major conflict centres on forming intimate, loving relationships with other people.

During this stage, we begin to share ourselves more intimately with others. We explore relationships leading toward longer-term commitments with someone other than a family member.

Successful completion of this stage can result in happy relationships and a sense of commitment, safety, and care within a relationship.

Avoiding intimacy, fearing commitment and relationships can lead to isolation, loneliness, and sometimes depression. Success in this stage will lead to the virtue of love.

7. Generativity Vs. Stagnation

Generativity versus stagnation is the seventh of eight stages of Erik Erikson's theory of psychosocial development. This stage takes place during middle adulthood (ages 40 to 65 yrs). By failing to find a way to contribute, we become stagnant and feel unproductive. These individuals may feel disconnected or uninvolved with their community and with society as a whole. Success in this stage will lead to the virtue of care.

8. Ego Integrity vs. Despair

Ego integrity versus despair is the eighth and final stage of Erik Erikson's stage theory of psychosocial development. This stage begins at approximately age 65 and ends at death. It is during this time that we contemplate our accomplishments and can develop integrity if we see ourselves as leading a successful life. As we grow older (65+ yrs) and become senior citizens, we tend to slow down our productivity and explore life as a retired person.

Erik Erikson believed if we see our lives as unproductive, feel guilty about our past, or feel that we did not accomplish our life goals, we become dissatisfied with life and develop despair, often leading to depression and hopelessness.

Success in this stage will lead to the virtue of wisdom. Wisdom enables a person to look back on their life with a sense of closure and completeness, and also accept death without fear.

Wise people are not characterized by a continuous state of ego integrity, but they experience both ego integrity and despair. Thus, late life is characterized by both integrity and despair as alternating states that need to be balanced.

Stage	Crisis	Basic Virtue	Age
1	Trust vs. Mistrust	Hope	0 - 1½
2	Autonomy vs. Shame	Will	1½ - 3
3	Initiative vs. Guilt	Purpose	3 – 5
4	Industry vs. Inferiority	Competency	5 – 12
5	Identity vs. Role Confusion	Fidelity	12 – 18
6	Intimacy vs. Isolation	Love	18 – 40
7	Generativity vs. Stagnation	Care	40 – 65
8	Ego Integrity vs. Despair	Wisdom	65+

SEVENTEEN
RESEARCH METHODOLOGY

Q1. Define variables. Discuss various types of variables. What are the techniques for controlling extraneous variables?

Ans. A variable, as the name implies, is something which varies. This is the simplest and the broadest way of defining a variable. However, a behavioral scientist attempts to define a variable more precisely and specially. Form his point of view, variables may be defined as those attributes of objects, events, things and beings, which can be measured. In other words, variables are the characteristics or conditions that are manipulated, controlled or observed by the experimenter, intelligence, anxiety, aptitude, income, education, authoritarianism, achievement, etc., are examples of variables commonly employed in psychology, sociology and education.

A. Dependent Variables and Independent Variables

The classification of variables into dependent and independent is frequently employed in experimental research.

The dependent variable (DV) is defined as one about which the experimenter makes a prediction. The independent variable (IV) is defined as one which is manipulated, measured and selected by the experimenter for the purpose of producing observable changes in the behavioral measure (or DV). In other words, the independent variable is the variable on the basis of which the prediction about the DV is made. The occasional synonym of IV is controlled variable, which is rarely used because of its confusing nature with control variable. An example may illustrate the distinction between the IV and the DV.

If the experimenter wants to study the effect of a religious group upon attitude towards family planning, he may take the Hindu, the Muslim, the Sikh and the Parsi as the four religious and study their attitude towards family planning. Subsequently, he may be able to predict which religious groups have a favorable attitude or unfavorable attitude towards family planning. In this example, the religious groups constitute the example of the IV and the attitude towards family planning constitutes the example of the DV.

As it has been said above, the IV is manipulated by the experimenter and its effect is examined upon the DV. Some experts, depending upon the DV. An example may illustrate the distinction between the Type-E and Type-S independent variable. Suppose the experimenter wants to study the effect of temperature upon the rate of production in an industry. Here the IV is the temperature and the DV is the rate of production. He may manipulate the temperature by dividing it into three categories— high, medium and low- and examine its effect upon the rate of production. Here the temperature is being directly manipulated by the experimenter and hence, it constitutes the example of Type- E independent variable.

a) Test Variables: The task variables refer to those characteristics which are associated with a behavioral task presented to the subject. It includes the physical characteristics of the apparatus as well as many features of the task procedures.

b) Environment Variables: Environmental variables refer to those characteristics of the environment, which are not the physical parts of the task as such, but tend to produce changes in the behavioral variables.

c) Subject-Variables: Subject variables refer to those characteristics of the subjects which are likely to produce change in the behavioral measures. Sex, age, weight, anxiety, intelligence, etc... are the characteristics of the subjects (animals or human), which may be conveniently termed as subject variables. Subject variable can be divided into two types: the natural subject variable and the induced subject variable.

Techniques of Controlling Extraneous Variables

AS we know, the extraneous variables are those that operate in the experimental situation in addition to the independent variables and affect the dependent variables. It is therefore, essential threat extraneous variables must be controlled. If the researcher falls to control the extraneous variables it results in confounded experiment. The following arc the five important ways to control the extraneous variables

|. Technique of elimination
2. Constancy of conditions
3. Balancing
4. Counterbalancing
5. Randomization

These methods can be discussed as follows

Technique of Elimination

The simplest way to control the extraneous variable is to eliminate it completely from the experimental situation. For example, if noise in any experiment is an extraneous variable, the simple way to control it is to make the experimental situation sound-proof. But this technique is too simple to control many extraneous variables. For example, controlling extraneous variables like age, sex intelligence through the technique of elimination is very difficult.

Constancy of Conditions

Where the extraneous variables can't be controlled through the technique of elimination, they can be controlled by holding their values constant for all participants in all conditions. This is known as constancy of conditions. By holding constant the instructions to be given to every participant by holding the time of the day constant for all participants, and by holding lighting conditions constant, extraneous variables related to instruction, time of the day and lighting conditions can be controlled. The apparatus for administering the experimental treatment and for recording the results should also be kept constant in all conditions for all participants. Sometimes the organismic variables like sex, age, intelligence also become important extraneous variables. To control these extraneous variables the researcher chooses only those participants or subjects who are homogeneous with respect to either sex or age or intelligence.

3. Balancing

When due to some reasons, it is not possible for the researcher to hold the various conditions constant, he may try to control the extraneous variables by balancing a technique used in the following two situations:

i) Where the researcher remains unable to identify the extraneous variables.

ii) Where they are readily identified and the researcher takes special steps to control them

The first situation where the researcher has no idea about the likely extraneous variables that might be influencing the dependent variable. In such a situation the researcher gives equal treatment to all subjects, but the experimental group is treated in a different way from the control group. Consequently, wherever the extraneous variables operate the influence both the experimental group and the control group in equal manner and their effect is, thus, balance. The changes occurring in the dependent variables are clearly attributed to the changes done in the independent variable. Suppose a set of four extraneous variables is influencing the experimental group in addition to the independent variable. The effects of these extraneous variable can be balanced out by allowing them to operate also on the control group. As a consequence, the independent variable will be the only one that can differentially influence the two groups.

4. Counterbalancing

The technique of counterbalancing is used for controlling the extraneous variables of amount of practice and fatigue. There are such experiments in which each subject is required to serve under two or more different experimental conditions and there is the probability that the participants performance might improve due to practice or their performance might decrease due to fatigue. The technique of counterbalancing is used to distributed these practice and fatigue effects together called order effects, equally over all conditions.

5. Randomization

Randomization is a very popular technique of controlling extraneous variable. Randomization refers to a technique in which each member of the population or universe has an equal and independent chance of being selected. Randomization is used where the experimenter assumes that some extraneous variables operate, but he can't specify them and therefore can't apply the other techniques of controlling extraneous variables. The technique is also applied where the extraneous variables are known but their effects can't be controlled by known techniques. In this way it is obvious that the extraneous variables can be controlled in several ways. Of these various ways, randomization, balancing and counterbalancing are relatively more popular.

ÞÞÞ

Q2. Define hypothesis. Discuss the characteristics of a good hypothesis.

Ans. In conducting research the next step after the selection of the problem is to formulate a hypothesis. When the problem has been stated, a tentative solution in the form of a testable proposition is offered by the investigator. This testable proposition is called a hypothesis. Therefore, a hypothesis is nothing but a suggested testable answer to a problem. Enlarging on this meaning of a hypothesis, we may say: A hypothesis is a testable relationship between two or more than two variables.

McGuigan (1990: 370) has defined hypothesis as, "a testable statement of a potential relationship between two (or more) variables.

Kerlinger (1973: 18) has defined hypothesis as, "a conjectural statement of the relationship between two or more variables. First, a hypothesis is a testable statement. Second, a hypothesis exhibits either a general or specific relationship between variables.

When a hypothesis has been formulated, the investigator must determine whether or not the formulated hypothesis is good. There are several criteria or characteristics of a good research hypothesis. A good hypothesis is one which meets such criteria or incorporates such characteristic to a large extent. Some of these characteristics are enumerated below.

1. The hypothesis should be conceptually clear. A good research hypothesis is one which is based upon operationally defined concepts.

2. The hypothesis must be testable. It should be formulated in a way that can be tested directly and found to be probably true or probably false.

3. The hypothesis should be economical and parsimonious. If several hypotheses are offered to test a research problem the more economical and parsimonious ones should be preferred to hypotheses involving higher monetary expenses and less time currency.

4. The hypothesis should be related to the existing body of theory and fact. If the investigator advances a hypothesis, which seems to him of interest but which is not related to the existing body of theory of facts, cannot be a good research hypothesis.

5. The hypothesis should have logical unity and comprehensiveness. If several hypotheses can be formulated regarding the same research problem, the most logical comprehensive one should be preferred.

6. The hypothesis should be general in scope. A general hypothesis permits several deductions and thus, explains several facts at a time. Therefore, a general hypothesis should be preferred.

7. The hypothesis should be related to available scientific tools and techniques. A hypothesis about which data cannot be collected because no scientific tools or techniques are available, cannot be a good research hypothesis.

8. The hypothesis should be in accord with other hypotheses of the same field. While this is not an essential condition, if any hypothesis satisfies this criterion, it can be claimed to be a good research hypothesis. A hypothesis that contradicts other hypotheses of the same field can also be regarded as a good hypothesis provided it is followed by scientific rationale, which in tum, has experiment support.

Formulating a Hypothesis

It is difficult to tell precisely how a scientist formulates a hypothesis because the process of formulation itself is vague and idiosyncratic. Good & Hatt (1952) have pointed out three major possible difficulties in formulation of a good research hypothesis. The absence of knowledge of a theoretical framework is a major difficult in formulating a good research hypothesis.

ÞÞÞ

Q3. What is sample? Discuss various sampling techniques.

Ans. A sample is any number of persons selected to represent the population according to some rule or plan. A sample is smaller representation of the population. A measure based upon a sample is known as a statistic

The general meaning of probability is less than certain and for which there exists some evidence. In sampling theory, the term 'probability is used as equivalent to the relative frequency

If one says that the probability of having of a male child is 0.8. it is meant that on previous occasions the relative frequency of birth of a male child has been 0.8. Probability may be expressed in terms of a fraction or in decimal numbers.

Following Block (1960) most sampling methods can be categorized into two

(A) Probability Sampling Methods

(B) Nonprobability Sampling Method

· Sampling Techniques:

Probability Sampling Methods

Probability sampling methods are those that clearly specify the probability or likelihood, of inclusion of each element or individual the sample. Technically, the probability sampling methods must satisfy the conditions given below.

The size of the parent population or universe from which the sample is to be taken, must be known to the investigator.

Each element or individual in the population must have an equal chance of being included in subsequent sample.

The desired sample size must be clearly specified

The positive point of probability sampling method is that the obtained samples arc considered representative and hence, the conclusions reached from su 0u samples are worth generalization and comparable to similar populations to which they belong.

Major Probability sampling methods are the following:

1. Simple random sampling
2. Stratified random sampling

a) Proportionate stratified random sampling

b) Disproportionate stratified random sampling

3. Area or cluster sampling

B. Nonprobability Sampling Methods:

Nonprobability sampling is one in which there is no way of assessing the probability of the element or group of elements of population being included in the sample. In other words, non-probability sample approximate the parameters of population from which the sample don't use the technique of random sampling. Important techniques of nonprobability sampling methods are:

1. Quota sampling
2. Accidental sampling
3. Judgmental or purposive sampling
4. Systematic sampling
5. Snowball sampling
6. Saturation sampling
7. Dense sampling

SIMPLE RANDOM SAMPLE:

A simple random sample (also known as an unrestricted random sample) may be defined as one in which each and every individual of the population has an equal chance of being included in the sample and also the selection of one individual is in no way dependent upon the selection of another person. For example, if we are to select a sample of 10 students from the seventh grade consisting of 40 students. We can write the name (or roll number) of each of the 40 students on separate slips of paper-all equal in size and color-and fold them in a similar way.

Subsequently, they may be placed in a box and reshuffled thoroughly. A blindfolded person, they may be asked to pick up one slip. Here, the probability of each slip being selected is 1/40. Thus, random sample nig may be defined as one in which all possible combinations of samples of fixed size have an equal probability of being selected.

1. A sample prepared on the basis of simple random sampling plan is regarded as the representative of the population

from which it was drawn. This is because in such a sampling plan all the elements in the population have an equal and independent chance of being included in the sample. A sample drawn in such a way that does not ensure equal chance for all elements to be included in the population rather increases or decreases the likelihood of an element being included, the resultant sample is called a biased sample

2. In sample random sampling the investigator need not know the true composition of the population beforehand Such a sample theoretically reflects all important characteristics and segments of the population.

3. With a view to understanding and application, simple random sampling is the easiest and simplest technique of all probability sampling plans.

4. Simple random sampling serves as a foundation upon which all other types of random sampling are based because this method of sampling can be readily applied in conjunction with all other probability sampling plans.

5. In simple random sampling the sampling error associated with any given sample drawn can easily be assessed.

6. In simple random sampling the investigator does not commit classification errors because he need not know thoroughly the population characteristics prior to selection of the sample, By classification error is meant the error which results from the improper classification of population characteristics or segments

However, simple random sampling has also some disadvantages given below:

1. One of the major disadvantages is that simple random sampling docs not ensure that those elements which exist in small numbers in the population will be included in the given sample.

2. Another disadvantage of simple random sampling is that it does not fully exploit the knowledge the instigator has concerning the segments of the population.

3. In the case of simple random sampling the error of a sample of size n is greater as compared with the-sampling error incurred in the case of a stratified random sample of the same size.

Despite these limitations simple random sampling has been preferentially used for assignment of elements randomly to different experimental conditions in psychological experiments as well as in raising a random sample for generalizing the obtained findings

2. STRATIFIED RANDOM SAMPLE

In stratified random sampling the population is, first, divided into two or more strata, which may based upon a single criterion such as sex, yielding two strata-male and female, or upon a combination of two or more criteria such as sex and graduation, yielding four strata, namely male undergraduates, male graduates, female undergraduates and female graduates. These divided population are called subpopulations, which are non-overlapping and together constitute the whole population. Having divided the population into two or more strata, which are considered to be homogeneous internally, a simple random simple for the desired number is taken from each population stratum. Thus, in stratified random sampling the stratified random sampling the stratification of population.

Two of them are mentioned below.

1. Stratified tends to increase the precision in estimating the attributes of the whole population. If the whole population is divided into several internally homogeneous units, the chances of variations in the measurements from one unit to another are almost nil. In such a situation a precise estimate can be made for each unit and by combining all these estimates, we can make a still more precise estimate regarding the population.

2. Stratification gives some convenience in sampling. When the population is divided into several units, a person or group of persons may be deputed to supervise the sampling survey in each unit. Or, the possibility is that the institution conducting the sampling survey may have field branches to supervise the survey in each part or unit of the population.

Stratified random sampling is of two types.

A. Proportionate stratified random sampling

B. Disproportionate stratified random sampling

A. Proportionate stratified random sampling

As its name implies, in this sampling plan the researcher stratifies the population according to the know characteristics of the population and subsequently, randomly draws the individuals in a similar proportion from each stratum of the population.

B. Disproportionate stratified random sampling

Disproportionate stratified random sampling bears similarity with the proportionate stratified random sampling. The only difference is that the substrata of the drawn sample are not necessarily distributed according to their proportionate weight in the population from which they were randomly selected. In fact, some of the strata of the population may be overrepresented or some underrepresented.

Suppose the investigator divides a given population of 10,000 individuals into 6.000 males and 4,00) females. If he has decided to draw a simple of 1,000 individuals from the set of 10,000 and if he draws randomly both the males and the females in equal number, say, 500 each, it will constitute the example of a disproportionate stratified random sampling, But, if he randomly draws 600 males and 400 females in his sample in his sample, it will constitute the example of proportionate stratified random sampling. From this example it becomes obvious that in the disproportionate stratified random sampling.

From this example it becomes obvious that in the disproportionate stratified random sample the investigator tries to give equal weight to each stratum, that is he tries to draw equal number of individuals from each stratum. In doing so he over represents on stratum while under presents the other strata. In this example, when he randomly draws 500 males and 500 females, he is over representing a female stratum and underrepresenting a male stratum.

Disproportionate stratified random sampling has both advantages and disadvantages, its major advantages are indicated below:

1. Disproportionate stratified random sampling is comparatively less time-consuming than proportionate stratified random sampling because here the investigator is not worried about making proportionate representation of each stratum of the population.

2. In disproportionate stratified random sampling the investigator is able to give weight to the particular groups of elements that are not represented as frequently in the population as compared with other elements.

The major disadvantages of disproportionate stratified random sampling are given below:

1. In this method of sampling certain stratum of the population is overrepresented and some other strata are underrepresented in the samples drawn.

2. Disproportionate stratified random sampling assumes that the investigator knows the composition of original population.

3. In this method of sampling the investigator is required to classify the population into different substrata and from each substratum he takes more or less equal number of cases.

3. AREA OR CLUSTER SAMPLING

Area or cluster sampling is another important method of probability sampling. Such sampling method has its origin in the field of agriculture. Farming experiments that were conducted to determine the effect of various kinds of fertilizers, soil treatments and a variety of planting methods on crop yield, mostly used this method of sampling. In social sciences application of area sampling has been extensive in survey research and field research.

In area of cluster sampling generally geographical divisions to territory, community, neighborhood, cities, states, etc., are made on a map a certain number of them is drawn at random and called sample. The investigator or interviewer proceeds to interview all elements of the randomly drawn areas of clusters. That is the reason why this method of sampling is also known as Cluster sampling.

Suppose the investigator wants to assess the attitude of the people of Tamil Nadu towards family planning, for this, it will be convenient for the investigator to have the map of Tamil Nadu before him and then divide them into various sections according to a number of vertical and horizontal grid lines drawn across the total area. He will then number each section from 1 to N. N being equal to the total number of sections. With the help of the table of random numbers. he will draw a specified number of sections to constitute the sample that he will finally study. The investigator will, then. interview all persons or members of families living in those sections. If any drawn section contains extremely different types of families, again, random selection from among subdivision and selection of sampling can be done to different stages. This is called multistage sampling.

Area sampling has some advantages and disadvantages. The important advantages are given below:

1. When larger geographical areas are to be covered, it is easier to use area sampling than any other method of probability sampling.

2. In area sampling respondents can readily be substituted for other respondents within the same random section.

3. Area sampling saves both time and money. The investigator can concentrate his efforts in one specific region and. thus, can save time.

4. Area of cluster sampling possesses the trait of flexibility. In a multistage are sampling design the investigator can successfully employ different forms of sampling in several successive stages.

5. Still another advantage of area sampling is that the respondents can readily be substituted for other respondents within the same random section. This further increases the degree of flexibility in the area sampling.

Area sampling has some disadvantages too. The important disadvantage are given below.

1. In area sampling the degree of sampling error is usually high.

2. In area sampling there is no correct way to ensure that each sampling unit included in an are simple will be of equal size.

3. In area sampling it is also difficult to ensure that the individuals included in one cluster are independent of other randomly drawn clusters.

NON-PROBABILITY SAMPLING:

QUOTA SAMPLING:

Quota sampling is one of the important types of non-probability sampling methods which is apparently similar to stratified random sampling. In quota sampling the investigator recognizes the different strata of population and from each stratum he selects the number of individuals arbitrarily.

Quota sampling has both advantages and disadvantages. The major advantages of quota sample are stated below:

1. Quota samples are the most satisfactory means when quick and crude results are desired.

2. This method of sampling is convenient and less costly than many other methods of sampling, whether probability or non-probability.

3. Quota sampling, to a greater extent, can guarantee the inclusion of individuals from different strata of population. However, quota sampling has some disadvantages also as given below:

1. In quota sampling there is no means of establishing randomness. As such, the selected samples remain no longer representative of the population. The conclusion, therefore, lacks external validity or generalizability.

2. In quota sampling the investigators or interviewers get ample opportunity to select the most accessible individuals influencing their friends and relatives. Such readily accessible individuals may not be typical of the population they are going to study.

3. Quota sampling is amenable to classification error. Here the interviewer or the investigator bases his classification of respondents on the way they apparently look to him. In fact, he possesses no knowledge concerning the way respondents should be classified. The investigator remains ignorant of many important variables that might otherwise be used in classifying them. All these tend to make quota sampling less dependable and reliable.

4. In Quota sampling the researcher, to a greater extent, controls one variable such as sex or caste etc. but he can 't control other variables that may have both theoretical or practical significant. This mars the dependability of quota sampling.

Despite these limitations, quota sampling is a popular method among non-probability methods of sampling. because it enables the researcher to introduce a fee controls into his research plan.

2. PURPOSIVE SAMPLING

Purposive sample, a kind of non-probability sample is one which is based on the typicality of the of the cases to be included in the sample. The investigator has some belief that the sample being handpicked is typical of the population or =is a very good representative of the population. A purposive sample is also known as a judgmental sample because the investigator on the basis of his impression makes a judgment regarding the concerned cases, which are thought to be typical of the population. For studying attitudes towards any national issue, a sample of journalists, teacher and legislators may be taken as an example of purposive samples because they can more reasonably be expected to represent the correct attitude than other classes of persons residing in the country. Before the start of general elections, purposive samples are often taken in an attempt for forecast the national elections. The investigator selects the persons from those states whose election results on previous polls have approximated the actual results and thus, have been typical of the whole population.

Purposive sampling has some advantages and disadvantages. The important advantages are given below:

1. Since purposive sampling does not involve any random selection process, it is somewhat less costly and more readily accessible to the investigator.

2. Purposive sampling is a very convenient method of sampling as compared to other methods of non-probability sampling.

3. Purposive sampling guarantees that those individuals will be included in the sample that are relevant to the research-design. The investigator does not get such guarantee in any other methods of non-probability sampling.

Purposive sampling has some disadvantages also as given below:

1. In purposive sampling there is no way to ensure that the sample is truly random or representative of the population despite the belief in typicality of the sample by the investigator. This inhibits his ability to generalize the findings.

2. In purposive sampling too much emphasis is placed on the ability of the investigator to assess which elements or individuals are typical of population and which are not. This leaves ample scope for introducing subjectivity in the sampling. Once has selected the sample he assumes that errors arising from his selection method will be minimal, but actually there is no legitimate stand for arguing his position.

3. In the case of purposive sampling the inferential statistics can't be used legitimately, because, under all inferential statistical techniques, there is an assumption of randomness. This criticism also applies to other forms of non-probability sampling method.

3. ACCIDENTAL SAMPLING

Accidental sampling, also known as incidental sampling, is another popular method of non-probability sampling plan. It refers to a sampling procedure in which the investigator selects the persons according to his convenience. Here he does not care about including the people with some specific or designated trait, rather he is mainly guided by convenience and economy. This is a crude method of sampling, and the investigator knows that little can be generalized from the sample thus drawn.

Accidental sampling has some advantages and disadvantages. The important advantages are given below:

1. Accidental sampling is the most convenient method of sampling.

2. This method of sampling possesses the trait of economy. This method saves time, money and labor of the investigator.

However, accidental sampling has the undernoted disadvantages as well:

1. From, accidental samples nothing can be generalized with confidence because the samples remain no longer representative of the population.

2. In accidental sampling the investigator gets ample opportunity to show his bias and prejudice in selecting the individuals. As such, this method of sampling is not much dependable.

3. In accidental sampling the probability of sampling error is high. Therefore, the validity and reliability of this method are badly affected.

Despite these disadvantages, it will not be an exaggeration to say that in many psychological and sociological researches this method of sampling is frequently used.

4. SYSTEMATIC SAMPLING

Systematic sampling is another method of non-probability sampling plan, though the label systematic' is somewhat misleading in the sense that all probability sampling methods are also systematic sampling methods. Due to this, it often sounds that systematic sampling should be included under one category of probability sampling, but in reality, this is not the case.

Systematic sampling may be defined as drawing or selecting every nth person from a predetermined list of elements or individuals. Selecting every 5th roll number in a class of 60 students will constitute systematic sampling. Likewise, drawing every 8th name from a telephone directory is an example of systematic sampling.

Systematic sampling has some advantages and disadvantages. The important advantages are mentioned below:

1. Systematic sampling is relatively a quick method of obtaining a simple of elements. If the investigator has short time schedule, this method of sampling eliminates several steps otherwise taken in different methods of sampling.

2. Systematic sampling makes it very easy to check whether every nth number of name has been selected. In case, there occurs and error in counting, that is, if the investigator selects 6th number instead of 5th number, his sample will not be seriously affected.

3. System sampling is very easy to use. In fact, it is much simpler than having to employ a table of random numbers for drawing the sample or fixed quota from each stratum of the population in order to have proportional representation.

Despite these advantages, there are some limitations of systematic sampling as indicated overleaf:

1. Systematic sampling ignores all persons every nth element chosen. Obviously, then, it is not a probability sampling plan.

2. In systematic sampling, the sampling error increases if the list is arranged in a particular order, say, the list increases or decreases with respect to some trait such as age, education, income, caste, etc.

5. SNOWBALL SAMPLING

Snowball sampling which is a non-probability sampling method, is basically sociometric. It is defined as having all the persons in a group or organization identified their friend who in turn identify their friends and associates until the researcher observes that a constellation of friendships converges into some type of a definite social pattern. Some selected behavior is usually used as the basis of contact and / or association. Obviously, then, snowball sampling is used for obtaining an impression of informal social relations among individuals.

Snowball sampling has important research application in relatively small business and industrial organizations where N is expected not to exceed 100.

Snowball sampling has some advantages and disadvantages, The important advantages are given below:

1. Snowball sampling which is primarily a sociometric sampling technique, has proved very important and is helpful in studying small informal social group and its impact upon formal organizational structure.

2. Snowball sampling reveals communication pattern in community organization concepts like community power; and decision-making can also be studied with the help of such sampling technique.

3. The method of snowball sampling is amenable to various scientific sampling procedures at various stages such as use of random numbers or computer determination.

Despite these advantages, snowball sampling has some limitations also as described below:

1. Snowball sampling becomes cumbersome and difficult when N is large or say it exceeds 100.

2. This method of sampling does not allow the researcher to use probability statistical methods.

6. SATURATION SAMPLING AND DENSE SAMPLING

Coleman (1959) has emphasized these two types of sampling techniques which are used less frequently as compared to other techniques of sampling. Saturation sampling is defined as drawing all elements or individuals having characteristics of interest to the investigator. Drawing all physicians having at least the age of 45 (from a small community), would be called saturation sampling. Dense sampling is a method of sampling which lies somewhere between simple random sampling and saturation sampling. When the researcher selects 50% or more from the population and takes a majority of individuals having specified traits or characteristics which are of interest to him, it is called dense sampling. For example, if the researcher selects 500 to 600 students from a population of 1,000 students, it will constitute dense sampling.

7. DOUBLE SAMPLING

Double sampling, as its name implies is defined as drawing a sample of individuals from another sample of them, Suppose the investigator randomly draws a sample of 1,000 from a population have N = 10,000. From these 1,000 individuals, he again randomly a sample of 300 for further study. This is called double sampling.

Q4. What are the requisites of Good Sampling method?

Ans. Any sampling method to be good and scientifically sound must possess at least the two following properties:

1. It must ensure the representativeness of the sample
2. It must ensure the adequacy of the sample.

ÞÞÞ

Q4. Write a short note on normal probability curve.

Ans. The major characteristics of a normal curve are enlisted below:

A normal curve is always symmetrical, that is, the right half of the curve is equivalent to the left half of the curve.

A normal curve is unimodal, and the mode is always at the center of the distribution. In fact, in a normal curve the mean, the median and the mode are numerically identical and fall at the center of the distribution.

A normal curve is asymptotic to the x-axis. Hence, a normal curve never touches the baseline no matter how far the curve is stretched.

In a normal curve the highest ordinate is at the center. All ordinates on both sides of the distribution are smaller than the highest ordinate.

A normal curve is continuous.

Area Under the Normal Curve

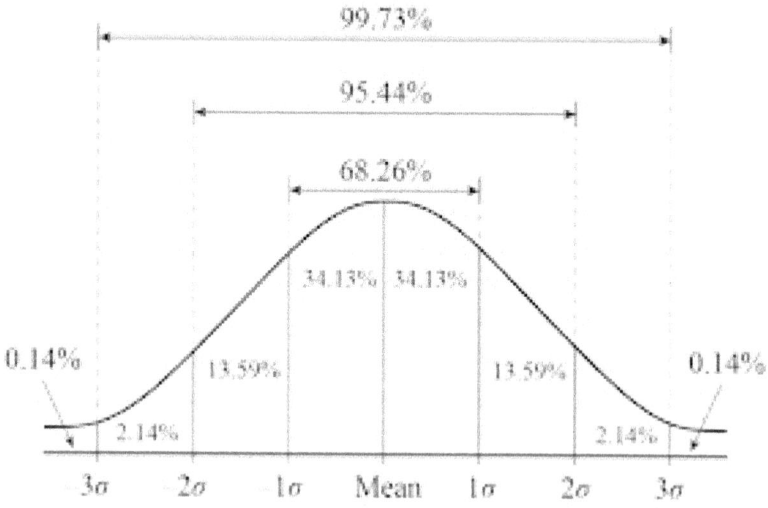

As we know, there is a definite relationship between standard deviation units and the normal curve. The figure below shows the different percentages of areas falling under a normal curve at different standard-deviation units. One standard-deviation unit taken on each side of the mean includes a total area of 34.13%+34.13%= 68.26% of the curve. This is approximately two-third of the cases. In terms of probability, it can be said that in any normally distributed sample chances are that two out of three scores will fall within the area of one standard-deviation unit on each side of the mean. A second standard-deviation unit taken beyond the first standard deviation cuts off 13.59% of the area on each side of the mean. Thus, up to two standard-deviation units on each side of the mean we have 68.26% of 27.18%= 95.44% of the total area. If we take another, or a third standard deviation, we have 2.15% of area on each side of the mean. The total areas included by all the six standard-deviation units (three standard-deviation units on each side), have accounted for 99.74% area of the normal curve. This means that only 0.26% of the cases are left which lie beyond three standard- deviation units from the mean. For convenience in statistical computation, we generally take and analyses cases up to three standard-deviation units on each side of the mean in normal distribution.

In psychological and educational researches, the normal curve has the main practical applications given below:

A normal curve helps in transforming the raw scores into standard scores.

A normal curve helps in calculating the percentile rank of the given scores.

If we want to normalize the obtained distribution, a normal curve is of immense importance.

A normal curve helps in testing the significance of the obtained measures against a chance hypothesis and thus enables the researcher to make a generalization about the population from which the sample was drawn.

Applications of the Normal Probability Curve

Normal curve has guide significance and applications in the field of measurement concerning education, Psychology and Sociology. Some of its main applications are as follows:

Use as a model: Normal curve represents a model distribution. It can be used as a model to

(a) Compare various distributions with it i.e. to say, whether the distribution is normal or not, in what way it diverges from the normal;

(b) Evaluate student's performance from their scores.

(2) Computing percentiles and percentile ranks: Normal probability curve may be conveniently used for computing percentiles and percentile ranks in a given normal distribution.

(3) Understanding and applying the concept of standard errors of measurement: The normal curve is also known as the normal curve of errors or simply the curve of error on the grounds that it helps in understanding the concept of standard errors of measurement

(4) Ability Grouping: A group of individuals may be conveniently grouped into certain categories as A, B, C, D, E (very good, good, average, poor, very poor) in terms of some trait, with the help of a normal curve.

(5) Transforming and combining Qualitative data: Under the assumption of normality of the distributed variable, the sets of qualitative such as ratings, latter grades and categorical ranks on a scale may be conveniently transformed and combined to provide an average rating for each individual.

(6) Converting raw scores into Comparable Standard Normalized Scores: Sometimes, we have records of an individual's performance on two or more different kinds of assessment tests and we wish to compare his score on one test with the score on the other. Unless the scales of these two tests are the same, we cannot make a direct comparison. With the help of a normal curve, we can convert the raw scores belonging to different tests into standard

normalized scores like sigma (or Z scores) and T – Scores.

(7) Determining the relative difficulty of test items: Normal curve provides the simplest rational method of scaling test items for difficulty and therefore, may be conveniently employed for determining the relative difficulty of test questions, problems and other test times.

EIGHTEEN

STRESS

Q1. Define stress

Ans: Stress is defined as the response to events that threaten or challenge a person. Whether it be a paper or exam deadline, a family problem, or even a cumulative series of small events such as those faced by people on the job, life is full of circumstances, known as stressors, that produce threats to our well-being. Even pleasant events such as planning a party or beginning a sought-after job can produce stress, although negative events result in greater consequences which can be detrimental

Q2. Explain GAS Model

Ans: It was given by Hans Selye. This model, the general adaptation syndrome (GAS), suggests that same set of physiological reactions to stress occurs regardless of the particular cause of stress. The model has three phases.

1. The first stage, the alarm and mobilization stage, occurs when people become aware of the presence of a stressors. For example, your learned at the end at the first term of college that you were on academic probation because of your low grades. You likely would respond first with alarm, feeling concerned and upset. Subsequently you would probably begin to mobilize your efforts, making plan and promises to yourself to study harder for the rest of the school year.

2. In the next stage, the resistance stage, you would prepare yourself to fight the stressor. During resistance, a person uses various means to cope with the stressor – sometimes successfully but at a cost of some degree physical or psychology general well-being. For instance, your resistance might take the form of devoting long hours to studying. You may ultimately be successful in raising your grades, but it may be at the expense of a loss of

sleep and hours of worry.

3. If resistance is not adequate, the lost stage of the model, exhaustion, is reached. During exhaustion stage, a person's ability to adapt to the stressor, declines to the point where negative consequences of stress appear, physical illness, psychological symptoms in the form of an inability to concentrate, heightened irritability, or in several cases, loss of touch with reality. In a sense, people wear out. Of course, not everyone reaches the exhaustion stage. Its people can resist a stressor in the second stage, their physical resources are not drained and they can bounce back, thereby avoiding exhaustion

Q3. What are the causes of stress?

Ans.

Environmental stress

Stresses like earthquake, flood, fire etc that are sudden and have a powerful impact and is universal in terms of impact these are not the factors which are affecting one person at a time, it will have a mass effect. For example, a place which is hitted by an earthquake, the people who are living at the particular place would experience stress because of the loss that has happened to them.

Social stress

The issues related to society can cause stress among people. For example, death or illness in the family, or divorce, strained relationships, are one of the causes of stress sometimes, hostile neighbours can also cause stress.

Psychological Stress

These are personal and unique to the person Experiencing them and are consider as internal sources of stress. They can be divided into: frustration, conflict, tension etc.

Frustration: - It results from the blocking of needs and motives by something that prevents or hinders vs from achieving a desired goal e.g. An adolescent who wants to attend a college party, over - restrictive parents would be source of frustration.

Pressure: - When someone is forcefully required to do any work, or is trying to meet some expectations but is not able to do it. Example. If one student is expecting to clear the competitive exam in first round, but is unable to do so, He will face pressure, when he will be sitting for the second time of that particular exam.

Conflict: - Stress from conflict between interest and motives.

It is divided into four types.

Approach-approach conflict:

In this type of conflict individual will have two desires with positive valence which are equally powerful. For example, a person has two attractive job offers and he has to choose any one of them- tension arises.

Such conflicts are not so harmful, because after selecting one, the other one automatically subsides or loses its importance to him. But in some situation choice will be very difficult. For example, a girl has to choose either loving parents or a boyfriend for inter-caste marriage. Such cases are like 'you cannot have the cake and eat it too'.

2. Avoidance-avoidance conflict:

This conflict involves two goals with negative valence. At times the individual is forced to choose one among two negative goals. In such conflicts, both are unwanted goals, but he cannot keep quiet without opting also. For example, a woman must work at a job which she dislikes very much or else she has to remain unemployed.

Here the individual is caught between two repelling threats, fears or situations. When she cannot choose either of them, she may try to escape from the field itself. But the consequences of the escape may also be harmful. For example, a person who cannot convince the mother or the wife may resort to Alcohol consumption which is otherwise dangerous or some people may even commit suicide.

3. Approach-avoidance conflict:

This is also a most complex conflict and very difficult to resolve. Because in this type of conflict a person is both attracted and repelled by the same goal object. Here the goal object will have both positive and negative valences.

The positive valence attracts the person, but as he approaches, the negative valence repels him back. Attraction of the goal and inability to approach it leads to frustration and tension.

For example, a person is approaching to accept a job offer, because the salary is attractive- but at the same time he is repelled back as the job is very risky. A man wants to marry to lead a family life, but does not want the responsibilities of family life.

4. Double approach-avoidance conflict:

Some of the situations in life we come across will involve both positive and negative valences of multiple nature. Suppose a woman is engaged to be married. The marriage to her has positive valences like-providing security to life and marrying a person whom she loves very much.

Suppose, on the other hand, if the marriage is repellent to her because she has to quit her attractive job and salary, recognition which makes her dependent, the situation builds up tension in her.

The resolution of this conflict depends upon the sum total of both valences. If the sum total of attractive valence takes upper hand, she will quit the job and go for marriage; otherwise, she may reject marriage and continue the job if the sum total of negative valence is powerful.

NINETEEN
MENTAL HEALTH

Q1. Discuss various causes of abnormal behavior.

Ans. The causes of abnormal behaviour are complex, and it is not always possible to isolate and evaluate the multiple factors involved. Some of the difficulties are listed below.

1.There are many varieties of mental deficiencies, psychoneuroses, psychoses, and antisocial personalities, and each variety tends to have an independent etiology.

2. Psychological disorders are usually due to the interaction to two or more agents. It is frequently difficult to ascertain the relative importance of each contributory factor.

3.The same symptom pattern may arise from a variety of different causes. Even when it is known that certain factors are responsible for a specific type of psychological disorder, it does not follow that these factors are always present in the same degree in all patients exhibiting similar symptoms.

Causes :

1.Heredity :

Heredity is the enigma of psychopathology. Its importance is usually either exaggerated or underestimated. Almost every form of psychological deviation has been attributed by some writers to hereditary and by others to nonhereditary ones. Experimental data with respect to individual diseases are reported in subsequent chapters. A summary of these findings indicates that approximately three-fourths of mental defectively and one-third of psychotic individuals owe their condition mainly to unfavorable heredity. Heredity is a contributory factor in an additional 15 per cent of psychoses, in many psychoneuroses, and in some cases of chronic antisocial or criminal behavior. It is relatively unimportant in juvenile delinquency and in most instances of mild or occasional criminality.

What is Inherited : One never inherits nervousness, anxiety, delusions, excitability, hallucinations, antisocial tendencies, convulsions, depressive, states, urge ton drink or defective intelligence. All that one inherits are genes, which are submicroscopic chemical units that in some unknown way control the development of the nervous system and other parts of the body. The quality of the organs and tissues inherited in turn influences behaviour potentialities, since in the final analysis all psychological reactions have a physiological foundation.

Genetic Principles : The billions of cells that make up the human organism at birth are derived from the repeated division and re-division of the initial fertilized cell. Located in linear order in the chromosomes, like beads on a string, are the genes, which are directly responsible for the transmission of inherited characteristics. An important quality of genes is that each maintains its integrity, particular constitution and properties in unaltered form from one generation to the next. They are in no way affected by the life experiences of their temporary host. Traits, skills, and diseases that are acquired by the parent do not modify the genes he passes on to his children.

2.Constitutional Factors :

As generally used in psychiatry, the term constitution refers to the total biological assets and liabilities of an individual, whether innate or acquired, that determine his reactive potentialities and his resistance or susceptibility to disease. Included under this more stable component of the individual's makeup, for example his bodily build, sex, and temperament, as contrasted with his social attitudes, habits, and other more changeable components. Constitution is mainly determined by heredity and endocrine function, but it is by no means fixed and unalterable. It is subject to modification by age and environmental factors, especially those that affect the physiology of the individual, such as diet and physical disease.

Physique and Personality: The intriguing game of classifying people into physical types and predicting personality on the basis of bodily traits antedates Hippocrates. About every half century it is "discovered" that individuals fall into certain physical categories and that there exists a close affinity between physique and personality. For a time, each new theory is enthusiastically received. Gradually it is discredited, but above the death knell of the rejected theory rises the birth cry of the succeeding theory, which is hailed as "original and penetrating."

3.The Endocrines

Hormones are internal secretions that are discharged into the blood stream, which carries them to various tissues. Though minute in quantity, they are unbelievably potent in their effect upon body structure and function.

Individuals with profound endocrine imbalance are rarely happy or well adjusted. In a small percentage of cases, the psychological symptoms are probably a direct result of hormonal dysfunction. The apathy of the hypothyroid, the anxiety and restlessness of the hyperthyroid, and the fatigue and irritability associated with certain deficiency might be included under this heading. More commonly, however, the only direct effect of glandular dysfunction is to produce physical anomalies that in turn provide fertile soil for the growth of distorted personalities. It is not easy for midgets, bearded ladies, giants, and obese persons to remain good-natured and mentally serene when they are continuously exposed to ridicule, jest, and social isolation. This harsh and unfair treatment makes many of them indorse, hypersensitive, seclusive, depressed and misanthropic.

4.The Nervous System

In describing the human nervous system, a distinction, is usually made between the cerebrospinal and autonomic system. The former consists of the brain and the spinal cord. The autonomic system is a semi-independent collection of nerve cells located mainly outside and along either side of the spinal cord. The two systems are closely interrelated structurally and functionally. Many of the nerve cells and fibers of the autonomic system lie within the cerebrospinal system. This structural relationship makes for functional interaction. In general, however, the cerebrospinal division is primarily concerned with receiving and organizing sensory impulses, delivering motor impulses to the skeletal musculature, and engaging in higher mental processes. The autonomic system is more concerned with the control of the internal environment through stimulation of the endocrine glands, the heart, and the smooth muscles of the gastrointestinal, respiratory, and circulatory systems.

Spinal Cord: Apart from mediating simple reflex actions, the main function of the spinal cord is to conduct afferent, or sensory, impulses from various parts of the body to the brain and to conduct efferent, or motor, impulses from the brain to the muscles and limbs.

The Brain: As the "seat" of intelligence, judgement, memory, and integrative behaviour, and as the neural center for controlling excitation-inhibition and the experiencing of emotions, the brain undoubtedly plays an important role in almost all forms of psychological disorders. However, attempts to establish causal relationships between abnormalities in brain stricture and abnormalities in psychological functioning have met with meager success. In anatomical detail, the brains of delinquents, criminals, and psychoneurotic individuals are indistinguishable from those of normal people.

Autonomic Nervous System : The autonomic nervous system consists of three parts, the cranial, the thoracic lumber, and the sacral. The cranial division originates from the base of the brain, the thoracic lumber from the middle portion of the spinal cord at about the level of the chest; and the sacral originates from the tail end of the spinal cord.

5.Environmental And Cultural Factors:

a)Cultural Level: The psychological ills of man are not a product of modern civilization. References pertaining to the symptoms, legal aspects, and treatment of mental defective, criminals, psychoneurotics and psychotics are contained in the earliest records of the ancient Egyptians, Greeks, and Romans. From descriptions in the Bible it even appears that the nature of mental symptoms was the same then as now. Nor are psychological deviants found only among civilized peoples. Anthropological studies have shown that even the most primitive people are affected with mental deficiency, psychoses, psychoneuroses, and criminality.

b)Stress and Strain : In investigating the life histories of psychological deviants, it is often noted that these individuals have been exposed to various emotional traumata such as unhappy or broken homes in childhood, poverty or financial reverses, terrifying situations, disappointing love affairs loss of position, death of loved ones, and other disturbing experiences.

c) War and Depression : The most satisfactory test of the etiological importance of distressing emotional experiences is provided by national catastrophes that acutely disturb the lives of millions. There are three recent periods in American history when the general stress and strain of existence bore heavily and fairly consistently on the entire population, namely, the periods of the First and Second World Wars, and the economic depression that began in 1929.

d) Race : Every race has its quota of psychological deviants. The same clinical varieties of psychological disorders noted among whites are also present a abnormalities among whites, Indians, and Orientals. As yet no studies have been made with respect to the relative incidence of mental abnormalities among Whites, Indians, and Orientals.

e) Nationality : The many national groups that constitute the white race all exhibit the same forms of mental abnormalities There are no groups for assuming that any national group is innately more susceptible or more immune to psychological diseases than another. Cultural influences within a nation may, however, modify the types of disorders encountered. Crimes of violence, for example, will be more common in countries tolerating feuds and lawlessness, and the incidence of alcoholic psychoses will depend on the alcoholic habits of a given population. Nations that provide adequate facilities for the institutional care of mental defectives will have a greater number of recorded cases than nations that ignore this problem.

ꝒꝒꝒ

Q2. Write a short note on mental health and hygiene.

Ans. Mental health and hygiene- After having fair ideas on educational physiology, physiology of growth and development, various stages of development, memory and forgetting, learning and personality in the previous units, now we are going to discuss one of the important aspects of physiology that is mental health and hygiene. Mental health and hygiene is the two sides of a coin. Hygiene is the pre-requisite condition for maintaining good and sound health l. Besides these, this unit also deals with the various mechanisms of adjustment. Infact, adjustments mechanisms are the instrument for maintaining the balanced personality as well as the instrument to rescue from the various mal-adjusted behaviours and problems.

Most of us probably were not intentionally taught good mental health hygiene habits. These habits also bring consistency to our lives, promote wellness and resilience, and protect us from becoming overwhelmed by mental illness. While mental health hygiene habits may vary from person to person, it is important to identify those that work best for us and to integrate them into our day-every day-through reminders and practice until they become a routine that we anticipate with pleasure.

Freudians lay emphasize on an awareness of one's unconsciousness motivations and subsequent self control, based on the awareness.

Jahoda (1963), proposes six criteria of the mentally healthy individual. These ate-

The ability to love adequacy in interpersonal relationship, efficiency in meeting situation requirements; efficiency in problem solving.

Undistorted perception of reality including empathy and social sensitivity.

Possessing a balance of psychic forces in the individual and a unifying outlook on life and resistance to stress.

Can make decisions his or her own.

Growth, self development and self actualization including conception of self etc.

Attitude towards self concept and sense of identity.

From the above discussion we can easily distinguish between the mentally healthy and unhealthy person in the following ways-

Mentally Healthy

1.Aware about their self and have some respect for others

2.Understand one's own limitation and also tolerate other limitations.

3.They can understand that all behavior is causal.

4.They can understand the basic needs that motivate behaviour.

Mentally Unhealthy

1.Not aware about their own self and have no respect for others

2.Cant understand one's own limitation and can't other limitation.

3.They can't understand the cause of behaviour.

4.They can't understand the basic needs which motivate behaviour.

Mental health is, this, a condition of physiological maturity. It is a condition of personal and social functioning with a maximum of effectiveness and satisfaction. A mentally healthy person is responsible, self reliant and has a true sense of individuality. He has a realistic life goal as well as philosophy of life and values. Differentiate between the right and the wrong.

Mental hygiene is a Science which deals with the process of attaining mental health and preserving mental health in the society. The term mental health is closely related with the term mental hygiene as the main objective of mental hygiene is to attain mental health. In other words, mental hygiene is a means of mental health. That is why we can say that mental hygiene is the means and mental health is the end.

Objectives of mental hygiene :

Mental Hygiene is a science. The main objective of mental hygiene is to build up one's ego rather than tearing down another's ego. It tries to develop the power of tolerance and praise and discourages the habit of blaming others. Hence, we can say that the approach of mental hygiene is positive rather than negative.

The main objectives of the mental hygiene can be summarized as shown below-

To help to realizes one's potentiality:

Every individual possess certain potentialities. Mental hygiene tries to help each individual to develop his/her potentialities.

To develop self-respect and respect for others:

Loss of self-respect is one of the factors for the great majorities of emotional disorders. A person who likes himself can like others and one who dislikes himself cannot like anybody. Hence, the main aim of mental hygiene is to help one to respect oneself.

To understand one's limitations and tolerate the limitations of others:

Mental hygiene helps one to understand his own limitations as well as to tolerate others" limitations.

To cause harmonious development :

Mental hygiene aims at the harmonious development of the physical mental and spiritual capacities of the individual so that he can adjust himself in the environment.

To create happiness:

Another objective of mental hygiene is to develop a positive attitude towards life so as to create a sense of happiness in a person who can live happily in this world.

To enable one to make effective adjustment:

Mental hygiene also prepares an individual for effective adjustment in all sphere of life and all situations such as in school, home, society work and also with self.

To enable one to know his or her self :

Many of us do not know our own self. We are not at all aware about our potentialities, weaknesses, limitations etc. for which many individuals suffer from different types of confusion. Mental Hygiene helps an individual to know himself.

TWENTY

Psychological Disorders

Q1. Elucidate the etiology and symptoms of generalized anxiety disorder.

Ans. People who experience generalized anxiety disorder (GAD) exhibit excessive concern about multiple events or activities most days of the week. While it is not unusual for people to experience some stress as they go about their daily lives, GAD sufferers rarely get a break from worrying. Although some of the symptoms and reactions may be similar to those of a phobia (an extreme, irrational fear), GAD is not a direct response to a specific situation or experience. Sufferers experience unease that casts a shadow over all of their activities. While not merely as intense as a panic attack, the unease lasts much longer and almost doesn't let up. GAD sufferers describe it as a feeling of being "wired" all of the time, according to the National Institute of Mental Health (NIHM).

Signs and symptoms

Not everyone with generalized anxiety disorder has the same symptoms, but most people experience a combination of emotional, behavioral, and physical symptoms that often fluctuate, becoming worse at times of stress.

DSM-5 criteria

The diagnostic criteria for GAD as defined by the diagnostic and statistical manual of mental disorders DSM-5 (2013) published by the American Psychiatric Association, are as follows:

Excessive anxiety and worry(apprehensive expectation), occurring more days than not for at least 6 months about a number of events or activities (such as work or school performance).

The individual finds it difficult to control the worry.

The anxiety and worry are associated with three(or more) of the following six symptoms (with at least some symptoms having been present for more days than not for the past six months):

Note: only one item is required in children.

Restlessness or feeling keyed up or on edge.

Being easily fatigued.

Difficulty concentrating or mind going blank.

Irritability.

Muscle tension.

Sleep disturbance (difficulty falling or staying asleep, or restless, unsatisfying sleep)

The anxiety, worry, or physical symptoms cause clinically significant distress or impairment in social, occupational, or other important areas of functioning.

The disturbance is not attributable to the physiological effects of a substance (e.g. , a drug of abuse, a medication) or another medical condition (e.g. , hyperthyroidism).

The disturbance is not better explained by another mental disorder (e.g. , anxiety or worry about having panic attacks in panic disorder, negative evolution in social anxiety disorder social phobia, contamination or other obsessions in obsessive-compulsive disorder, separation from attachment figures in separation anxiety disorder, remainders of traumatic events in post-traumatic stress disorder, gaining weight in anorexia nervosa, physical complaints in somatic symptom disorder, perceived appearance flaws in body dysmorphic disorder, having a serious illness in illness anxiety disorder, or the content of delusional beliefs in schizophrenia or delusional disorder)

Symptoms of GAD

Emotional symptoms:

Constant worries running through the head

Filling like anxiety is uncontrollable; there is nothing one can do to stop the worrying

Intrusive thoughts about things that make you anxious; one try to avoid thinking about them, but you can't

An inability to tolerate uncertainty; one needs to know what's going to happen in the future

A pervasive feeling of apprehension or dread

Behavioural symptoms:

In ability to relax,

Difficulty concentrating or focusing on things

Putting things off because one feels overwhelmed

Avoiding situations that make anxious

Physical symptoms:

Feeling tensed; having muscle tightness or body aches

Having trouble falling asleep or staying asleep because mind won't quit

Feeling edgy, restless, or jumpy

Stomach problems, nausea, diarrhea

Causes

Genetics

About a third of the variance for generalize anxiety disorder has been attributed to genes. Individuals with a genetic predisposition for GAD are more likely to develop GAD, especially in response to a life stressor.

Substance-induced

Long-term use of benzodiazepines can worsen underline anxiety, with evidence that reduction of benzodiazepines can lead to a lessening of anxiety symptoms. Similarly, long-term alcohol using associated with anxiety disorders, with evidence that prolonged abstinence can result in a disappearance of anxiety symptoms. However, it can take up to two years for anxiety symptoms to return to baseline in about a quarter of people recovering for alcoholism.

Sometimes anxiety pre/existed alcohol or benzodiazepines dependence, but the dependence was acting to keep the anxious disorders going and often progressively making them worse. Recovering from benzodiazepines tends to take a lot longer than recovery from alcohol, but people can regain their previous good health.

Tobacco smoking has been established as a risk factor for developing anxiety disorders.

Excessive caffeine usage has been linked to anxiety.

Mental disorders are difficult to prevent, but many techniques are available to health relief and manage anxiety. Many sufferers have found ease by relaxation exercises, deep breathing practice and meditation. Additionally, avoidance of caffeine may prevent GAD. Avoiding nicotine also can decrease the risk for the development of anxiety disorders including generalized anxiety disorder. Meta-analysis indicates that both cognitive behavioral therapy (CBT) and medication have been shown to be effective in reducing anxiety.

ꝒꝒꝒ

Q2. Write a short note on OCD.

Ans. A) OCD: obsessive-compulsive disorder (OCD) is a common, chronic and long-lusting disorder in which a person has uncontrollable, reoccurring thoughts (obsessions) and behaviors (compulsions) that he or she feels the urge to repeat over and over. Signs and symptoms

People with OCD may have symptoms of obsessions, compulsions, or both. These symptoms can interfere with all aspects of life, such as work, school, and personal relationships.

Obsessions are repeated thoughts, urges, or mental images that cause anxiety. Common symptoms include:

Fear of germs or contamination

Unwanted forbidden or tobacco thoughts involving sex, religion, or harm

Aggressive thoughts towards others or self

Having things symmetrical or in a perfect order

Compulsions are repetitive behaviors that a person with OCD feels the urge to do in response to an obsessive thought. Common compulsions include:

Excessive cleaning and/or hand washing

Ordering and arranging things in a particular, precise way

Repeatedly checking on things, such a repeatedly checking to see if the door is locked or that the oven is off compulsive counting

Not all rituals or habits are compulsions. Everyone double checks things sometimes. But a person with OCD generally:

Can't control his or her thoughts or behaviours, even when those thoughts or behaviours are recognized as excessive

Spends at least one hour a day on those thoughts or behaviours

Does not get pleasure when performing the behaviours or rituals, but may feel brief relief from the anxiety the thoughts cause

Experiences significant problems in their daily life due to these thoughts or behaviours

Some individuals with OCD also have a tic disorder. Motor tics are sudden, brief, repetitive movements, such as blinking and other eye movements, facial grimacing, shoulder shrugging, and head or shoulder jerking. Common vocal tics include repetitive throat-clearing, sniffing, or grunting sounds.

Symptoms may come and go, ease over time, or worsen. People with OCD may try to help themselves by avoiding situations that trigger their obsessions, or they may use alcohol or drugs to calm themselves. Although most adults with OCD recognize that what they are doing does not make sense, some adults and most children may not realise that their behavior is out of the ordinary. Parents or teachers typically recognise OCD symptoms in children.

PPP

Q3. What are symptoms of schizophrenia?

Ans. Symptoms of schizophrenia: Schizophrenia is a challenging disorder that often makes it difficult to distinguish between what is real and unreal, to think clearly, manage emotions, relate to others, and function normally.

There are five types of symptoms characteristic of schizophrenia: delusions, hallucinations, disorganised speech, disorganised behaviour, and the so-called "negative" symptoms. However, the symptoms of schizophrenia very dramatically from person to person, both in pattern and severity. Not every person with schizophrenia will have all symptoms, and the symptoms of schizophrenia may also change over time.

Positive Symptoms :

Delusions :

A delusion is a firmly – held idea that a person has despite clear and obvious evidence that it isn't true. Delusions are extremely common in schizophrenia, occuring in more than 90% of those who have the disorder. Often, these delusions involve illogical or bizarre ideas or fantasies, such as :

Delusions of persecution- belief that others, often a vague "they, "are out to get you. These persecutory delusions often involve bizarre ideas and plots (e.g. "Martians are trying to poison me with radioactive particles delivered through my tap water").

Delusions of reference- a neutral environmental event is believed to have a special and personal meaning. For example, you might believe a billboard or a person on TV is sending a message meant specially for you.

Delusions of grandeur- believe that you are a famous or important figure such as Jesus Christ or Napoleon. Alternately, delusions of grandeur may involve the believe that you have unusual powers, such as the ability to fly.

Delusions of control- believe that your thoughts or actions are being controlled by outside, alien forces. Common delusions of control include thought broadcasting ("my private thoughts are being transmitted to others"), thought insertion ("someone is planting a thought in my head"),and thought withdrawal ("the CIA is robbing me of my thoughts").

Hallucinations:

Hallucinations are sounds or other sensations experienced as real when they exist on in your mind. While hallucinations can involve any of the five senses, auditory hallucinations (e.g. hearing voices or some other sound) are most common in schizophrenia, often occurring when you misinterpret your own inner self-talk as coming from an outside source.

Schizophrenic hallucinations are usually meaningful to you as the person experiencing them. Many times, the voices are those of someone you know, and usually they are critical, vulgar, or abusive. Visual hallucinations are also relatively common, while all hallucinations tend to be worse when you are alone.

Disorganised speech :

Schizophrenia can cause you to have trouble concentrating a train of thought, externally manifesting itself in the way that you speak. You may respond to queries with an unrelated answer, start sentences with one topic and end somewhere completely different, speak incoherently, or say illogical things.

Common signs of disorganised speech include :

Loose associations- rapidly shifting from topic to topic with no connection between one thought and the next.

Neologisms- made-up words or faces that only have meaning to you.

Perseveration- repetition of words and statements; saying the same things over and over.

Clang- meaningless use of rhyming words ("I said the bread and read the shed and fed ned at the head")

Disorganised behaviour

Schizophrenia disrupts goal-directed activity impairing your ability to take care of yourself, your work, and interact with others. Disorganised behaviours appears as:

A decline is overall daily functioning

Unpredictable or inappropriate emotional responses

Behaviors that appear bizarre and have no purpose

Lack of inhibition and impulse control

Negative symptoms(absence of normal behaviours)

The so-called "negative" symptoms of schizophrenia refer to the absence of normal behaviours found in healthy individuals, such as:

Lack of emotional expression- inexpressive face, including a flat voice, lack of eye contact and blank or restricted facial expressions.

Lack of interest or enthusiasm- problems with motivation; lack of self-care.

Seeming lack of interest in the world- Apparent unawareness of the environment; social withdrawal.

Speech difficulties and abnormalities- inability to carry a conversation; short and sometimes disconnected replies to questions; speaking in monotone.

The most effective treatment strategy for Schizophrenia involves a combination of medication, therapy, lifestyle changes and social support.

Q4. What are the causes of schizophrenia?

Ans. The causes of schizophrenia are not fully known. However, it appears that schizophrenia usually results from a complex interaction between genetic and environmental factors.

1.Genetic causes of schizophrenia:

Schizophrenia has a strong hereditary component. Individuals with a first-degree relative (parent or sibling) who has schizophrenia have a 10 percent chance of developing the disorder, as opposed to the 1 percent chance of the general population.

But schizophrenia is only influenced by genetics, not determined by it. While schizophrenia nuns in families, about 60% of schizophrenics have no family members with the disorder. Furthermore, individuals who are genetically predisposed to schizophrenia don't always develop the disease, which shows that biology is not destiny.

2.Environmental causes of schizophrenia:

Twin and adoption studies suggest that inherited genes make a person vulnerable to schizophrenia and then environmental factors act on this vulnerability to trigger the disorder.

As for the environmental factors involved, more and more research is pointing to stress, either during pregnancy or at a later stage of development. High levels of stress are believed to trigger schizophrenia by increasing the body's production of the hormone cortisol.

Research points to several stress-inducing environmental factors that may be involved in schizophrenia, including: Prenatal exposure to a viral infection, Low Oxygen levels during birth (from prolonged labor or premature birth), Exposure to a virus during infancy, Early parental loss or separation, Physical or sexual abuse in childhood.

3.Abnormal brain structure or anatomical factors:

In addition to abnormal brain chemistry, abnormalities in brain structure may also play a role in schizophrenia. Enlarged brain ventricles are seen in some schizophrenics, indicating a deficit in the volume of brain tissue. There is also evidence of abnormally low activity in the frontal lobe, the area of the brain responsible for planning, reasoning, and decision-making.

Some studies also suggest that abnormalities in the temporal lobes, hippocampus, and amygdala are connected to schizophrenia's positive symptoms. But despite the evidence of brain abnormalities, it is highly unlikely that schizophrenia is the result of any one problem in any one region of the brain.

When the signs and symptoms of schizophrenia are ignored or improperly treated, the effects can be devastating both to the individual with the disorder and those around him or her. Treatment options for schizophrenia are good, and the outlook for the disorder continues to improve. With medication, therapy, and a strong support network, many people with schizophrenia are able to control their symptoms, gain greater independence, and lead fulfilling lives.

PPP

Q5. State the etiology of substance abused disorder (substance related and addictive according to DSM-V).

Ans. In the fifth edition of the Diagnostic and Statistical Manual of Mental Disorders (DSM-5), the revised chapter of "Substance-Related and Addictive Disorders" includes substantive changes to the disorders grouped there plus changes to the criteria of certain conditions. Substance Use Disorder Substance use disorder in DSM-5 combines the DSM-IV categories of substance abuse and substance dependence into a single disorder measured on a continuum from mild to severe. Each specific substance (other than caffeine, which cannot be diagnosed as a substance use disorder) is addressed as a separate use disorder (e.g., alcohol use disorder, stimulant use disorder, etc.), but nearly all substances are diagnosed based on the same overarching criteria. In this overarching disorder, the criteria have not only been combined, but strengthened. Whereas a diagnosis of substance abuse previously required only one symptom, mild substance use disorder in DSM-5 requires two to three symptoms from a list of 11. Drug craving will be added to the list, and problems with law enforcement will be eliminated because of cultural considerations that make the criteria difficult to apply internationally. In DSM-IV, the distinction between abuse and dependence was based on the concept of abuse as a mild or early phase and dependence as the more severe manifestation. In practice, the abuse criteria were sometimes quite severe. The revised substance use disorder, a single diagnosis, will better match the symptoms that patients experience. Additionally, the diagnosis of dependence caused much confusion. Most people link dependence with "addiction" when in fact dependence can be a normal body response to a substance.

The definitions for the different levels of drinking include the following:

• Moderate Drinking-According to the Dietary Guidelines for Americans, moderate drinking is up to 1 drink per day for women and up to 2 drinks pet day for men.

• Binge Drinking-SAMHSA defines, binge drinking as drinking 5 or more alcoholic drinks on the same occasion on at least 1 day in the past 30 days. The National Institute on Alcohol Abuse and Alcoholism (NIAAA) defines binge drinking as a pattern of drinking that produces blood alcohol concentrations (BAC) of greater than 0.08 g/dl. This usually occurs after 4 drinks for women and 5 drinks for men over a 2 hour period.

• Heavy Drinking-SAMHSA defines heavy drinking as drinking 5 or more drinks on the same occasion on each of 5 or more days in the past 30 days.The Eleven Symptoms of Alcohol Use Disorder

1. Alcohol is often taken in larger amounts or over a longer period than was intended.

2.There is a persistent desire or unsuccessful efforts to cut down or control alcohol use.

3. A great deal of time is spent in activities necessary to obtain alcohol, use alcohol, or recover from its effects.

4. Craving, or a strong desire or urge to use alcohol.

5. Recurrent alcohol use resulting in a failure to fulfill major role obligations at work, school, or home.

6. Continued alcohol use despite having persistent or recurrent social or interpersonal problems caused or exacerbated by the effects of alcohol.

7. Important social, occupational, or recreational activities are given up or reduced because of alcohol use.

8. Recurrent alcohol use in situations in which it is physically hazardous.

9. Alcohol use is continued despite knowledge of having a persistent or recurrent physical or psychological problem that is likely to have been caused or exacerbated by alcohol.

10. Tolerance, as defined by either of the following : a) A need for markedly increased amounts of alcohol to achieve intoxication or desired effect b) A markedly diminished effect with continued use of the same amount of alcohol.

11. Withdrawal, as manifested by either of the following : a) The characteristic withdrawal syndrome for alcohol (refer to criteria A and B of the criteria set for alcohol withdrawal) b) Alcohol (or a closely related substance, such as a benzodiazepine) is taken to relieve or avoid withdrawal symptoms.

The presence of at least 2 of these symptoms indicates an alcohol use disorder (AUD). The severity of an AUD is graded mild, moderate, or severe :

Alcohol abuse has the potential to destroy people's lives. Hopefully, raising awareness of the eleven symptoms for diagnosing alcohol use disorders will lead more individuals to seek help if they have two or more of the eleven symptoms listed above.

ÞÞÞ

Q6. What do you know about mood disorders?

Ans. A mood disorder is a prolonged and disturbed emotional state that effect all of a person's thought feeling and behaviours. Most of the individuals have experienced continuous of moods, with depression on one end and elation and the other. The D. S. M. IV TR lists ten different mood disorder. But for the present purpose the symptoms of three of the more common forms are going to be discussed.

Major depressive disorder; Bipolar disorder, Bipolar I disorder, Bipolar Il disorder, Dysthymic disorder. Before describing the clinical features of different forms of mood disorders. Some common mood episode should be mentioned so that the diagnosis of the different forms can be possible.

Mood episode:

Major depressive episode : Find of the following symptoms have been present during the same to week period and represent a change from previous functioning; at least one of the symptoms is either (i) depressed mood or (ii) loss of interest or pleasure

(I)Depressed mood most of the day.

(II)Markedly diminished interest or pleasure in almost all activities most of the details.

(III)Significant weight lost or weight gain.

(IV)Insomnia or Hypersomnia nearly everyday.

(V)Psychomotor agitation or retardation everyday.

(VI) Fatigue or loss of energy every day.

(vii)Feelings of worthlessness or excessive inappropriate guilt

(VIII) Diminished ability to think or concentrate or indecisiveness.

(IX) Recurrent thoughts of death or suicidal ideation or attempt.

Manic Episode :

(a) A distinct period of abnormally and persistent elevated, expansive or irritable mood, lasting at least one week.

(b) During the period of mood disturbance some symptoms like –

(I)Inflated – self esteem

(II)Decreased need for sleep

(III)Talkativeness

[iv] Flight of ideas

(v] Excessive involvement in pleasurable actively etc. are found.

3. Mixed Episode:

(a) The criteria are met both for a manic episode and for a major depressive episode nearly every day during at least one week period

(b) The mood disturbance is sufficiently severe to cause marked empowerment in occupational functioning or in usual social activities or relationships with others.

Hypomanic Episode:

(a) A distinct period of persistently elevated, expansive or irritable mood, lasting through out, at least four days i.e., clearly different from the usual non depressed mood.

(b) Some of the symptoms like grandiosity, decreased need for sleep destructibility, talkativeness etc. are found.

(c) The disturbance in mood and the change in functioning are observable by others.

(d) The episode is not severe enough to cause marked impairment in social or occupational functioning and there are no psychotic features.

Major Depression : Major depressive disorder is marked by at least a two weeks of continuously being in a bad mood having no interest in anything, and getting no pleasure for activities. In addition a person must have at least four of following symptoms.

(I)Problems with eating
(II) Sleeping
(III)Thinking
(Iv)Concentrating or making decision.
(V)Lacking energy.
(vi) thinking about suicide.
(Vii) feeling worthless or guilty.

BIPOLAR I DISORDER : Bipolar I Disorder is marked by fluctuation between episode of depression and mania. A manic episode goes on for at least a week, during which a person is unusually euphoric, cheerful and high and has at least there of following symptoms; has great self esteem little need for sleep. Speaks rapidly & frequently has racing thought, is easily destructed, and persons pleasurable activities (American Psychiatric association 200). About 13 of the population suffer from bipolar I disorder, and 1.6 suffer from only monic episode. (Rush 2003).

BIPOLAR II DISORDER :

Bipolar II disorder is characterized by recurrent major depressive episode with hypomanic episode – presence of one or more major depressive episode presence of at least 1 hypomanic episode has never been a monic episode, has never been a monic episode or mixed episode and mood symptoms in the mention criteria are not better accounted for by schizo affective disorder and are not super imposed on schizophrenia, delusional disorder etc.

The symptom causes clinically significant distress or impairment in social occupational or other important areas of functioning.

4.Dysthymic disorder : Another mood disorder that is less serious than major depression is called dysthymia disorder is characterized by being chronically but not continuously depressed for a period of two years while depressed, a person experiences at least two of the following symptoms : poor apatite, insomnia, fatigue, low self-esteem, poor concentration and feelings of hopelessness (American psychiatric association 2000)

There has never been a manic episode, a mixed episode or a hypomanic episode. The symptoms are not due to the direct physiological effect of a substance or a general medical condition. Its early onset takes place before age 21 years and late onset takes place at age 21 years or older.

Criteria for Cyclothymic disorder :

A .For at least 2 years, the presence of numerous periods with hypomanic symptoms and numerous periods with depressive symptoms that do not meet criteria for a major depressive episode.

B .During the 2nd year, the person has not been without symptoms or criterion for more than 2 months a time.

C. No major Depressive Episode, manic episode, or mike episode has been present during the first two years of the disturbance.

D.The symptoms in criterion are not better accounted for by another disorder.

E The symptoms cause clinically significant distress or impairment in functioning.

Q7. What are the causes of depression? / etiology of manic depressive psychosis?

Ans.

In considering the development of major mood disorder are find it useful to examine the roles of biological, psychosocial and sociocultural factors.

Biological Factors:

(I)Hereditory predisposition : The incidence of mood disorder is considerably higher among the blood relatives of individuals with clinically diagnosed mood disorder than in the population at large. In an early Steedy Staler (1994) found that approximately 15 percent of the brothers, sisters, parents and children of "manic depressive" (bipolar) patients had developed the same disorder, as compared with an expectancy of about 0.5 percent for the general population. Kallmann (1958) found the concordance for those disorders to be much higher for identical than fraternal twins. Other studies have supported these earlier findings.

(II)Biochemical Factors : According to Kraepelin, depression and mania both may arise from disruptions in the delicate balance of biochemical substances that regulate and mediate the activity of the brain's nerve cells or neurons, curtain of these substances called neurotransmitters, mediate the transfer of nervous impulses across the synaptic cleft from one neuron to next one in a particular neuronal path way. Mood disorders one due, according to this general view, to faulty communication between neuron caused by disruption of the transmission process.

Based on the known-level of complexity of brain biochemical functioning it is clear that there is no such straight forward mechanism, that is likely to provide the answer we need. (Thare, Frank and Kupfer 1985, Zis and Goodwin, 1982).

(III) Neurophysiologic and Neuroendocrine Factors : A good deal of research has focused on the role of neurophysiological disturbances in manic depressive psychosis. The success of this line of investigation has so far not been especially impressive and to an extent has been over showed by developments in other areas of biological research, notably the neurophysiologic and neuroendocrine (hormonal) correlates of some distinguishable forms of mood disorder (Thare, Fronk and Kuplar 1985) For example, it is now clear that some depressed persons shows disturbances in their electroencephalographic (brain wave) sleep rhythms.

2.PSYCHOSOCIAL FACTORS: Growing awareness of biological factors in the etiology of affective disorders does not of course imply that psychosocial factors are irrelevant. There some psychosocial factors which may found to be the causes of Mood Disorder.

(I)Stress as a precipitating factor : Psychosocial stressors may lead to altered body functioning and may also affect biochemical balances and other conditions in the brain, at least in predisposed persons. Branches and his colleagues(1978) in a summary of research in this area, suggest that psychosocial stressors may cause long term changes in the manner in which the brain functions and that these changes may play a role in the development of mood disorder. Essentially, the same paint has been made by other leading researches in the field, notably Akislaol(1979) and Kupfer (1985).

(II)Predisposing Personally Characteristics: Beek (1967) argues convincingly that psychosocial stress or provoke severe depressive reactions only in persons who already have a negative cognitive set, consisting of negative of the future. According to this hypothesis, the stressor merely serves to activate negative views cognitions that have heretofore been dormant. The result in an abnormally negative affect. Obviously, Beck's negative affect. Obviously Beck's "negative cognitive set" is in the nature of a psychological predisposing variables.

(III)Feeling of helplessness and loss of hope : Feelings of helpless and hopelessness have been emphasized as basic to depressive reactions by investigators. A sense of hopelessness may be central in the aged (Fry, 1984). Other investigators have referred to learned helplessness in severe depression, presumably, the individual, perceiving no likelihood that coping efforts will remove the sowzees of stress, eventually, stop fighting and gives up. (Hiroto and seligman 1975), (Weiss 2974).

(IV)Extreme Defense Against Stress : Manic and depressive disorder may be viewed as two different but related defense oriented strategies for doubling with server stress.

In the case of mania, individual try to escape their difficulties by a flight into testily- that is, they try to avoid pain of their inner lives through outer world distractions.

In case of depression, the person apparently gains some relief from the intolerable stress situation by admitting defeat and withdrawing psychologically from the fight.

(V)Interpersonal Effects of Mood Disorder : The manic individual apparently feels that wishing to rely on others or to be taken care of is threating and unacceptable. Instead such on individual maintains self-esteem and feelings of adequacy and strength by establishing a social role in which control of other people is possible. (Janowoshky, et. al 1974).

On the other hand, the depressed individual tends to adopt a role that attempts to place others in the position of providing supports and care and thus reinforcement. (Ferster 1973, Jonowsky 1970), positive reinforcement does not necessarily follow however. Depressive behaviour can and frequently does, illicit negative feelings and rejection in other persons. Infact, merely being around a depressed person may include depressed feelings in others.

GENERAL SOCIOCULTURAL FACTORS

The incidence of mood disorders seem to vary considerable among different societies : in some , manic episodes are more frequent, while in others depressive episodes are more common.

In the present society, the role of socio cultural factors in mood disorders, is gradually becoming clarified. It would appear that conditions that increase life stress lead to a higher incidence of these as well as other disorder. server stress.

PPP

Q8. Write a short note on panic disorders.

Ans. Panic Disorders:

Panic disorder is characterized by recurrent & unexpected panic attacks. The person becomes so worried about having another panic attack that this intense worrying interferes with normal psychological functioning.(APA, 2000).

About 4% of adults in the United States suffer from panic disorder & women are 2 to 3 times more likely to report it than men (Hal Breich, 2003). People who suffer from panic disorder, have an increased risk of alcohol & other drug abuse, an increased incidence of suicide, decreased social functioning & less marital happiness. About a third suffer from depression (Durand & Barlow 2003).

Symptoms :

Keren's symptoms in the beauty shop indicate that she was having a panic attack, which may occur in several different anxiety disorders but is the essential feature of panic disorder.

A panic attack is a period of intense fear or discomfort in which four or more of the following symptoms are present pounding heart, sweating, trembling, shortness of breath feelings of choking, chest pain, nausea feeling, dizzy and fear of losing control of dying (American Psychiatric Association, 2000).

Treatment :

Panic disorders are usually treated with drugs-benzodiazepines, antidepressant(prozac-like drugs which are selective serotonin reputed inhibitors or SSRIS) and / or psychotherapy successful treatment may require 3-8 months or drug therapy & psychotherapy (Sheehan 2002). However, some clients relapse after drug treatment has stopped. Researchers found that, one year after treatment with a combination of psychotherapy & drugs, about 30% to 50% of clients were symptom free (Page, 2002).

Another kinds of anxiety disorder, i.e., relatively common involves different kinds of phobias.

Phobias : Phobia is an anxiety disorder characterized by an intense & irrational fear that is out of all proportion to the possible danger of the object or situation. Because of this intense fear, which is accompanied by increased psychological arousal a person goes to great length to avoid the feared event. If the feared event can't be avoided, the person feels intense anxiety.

Researchers report that because 75% of individuals with phobias traced their onset to specific dramatic events, many phobias are learned through conditioning or observing a person showing a fear of something. However, since 25% of those with phobias could not recall their onset, there may also be other causes of phobias (Ranchman 2002).

Social Phobias : Social phobias are characterized by irrational, marked & continuous fear of performing in social situations. The individuals fear that they will humiliate or embarrass themselves (American Psychiatric Association 2000).

As a fearful social situation approaches, anxiety builds up & may result in considerable bodily distress, such as nausea, sweating & other signs of heightened physiological arrival. Although a person with a social phobia realizes that the fear is excessive or irrational he or she may not know to deal with it, other than by avoiding the situation.

Specific phobias : Specific phobias, formerly called simple phobias, are characterized by marked & persistent fear that are unreasonable & triggered by anticipation of or exposure to a specific object or situation (flying, heights, spiders seeing blood) (APA, 2000).

Among the more common specific phobias seen in clinical practice are fear of animals (zoophobia). Fear of heights (acrophobia), fear of confinement (claustrobia), fear of injury or blood & fear of flying (dwand & Barlow 2003).

The content & occurrence of specific phobias vary with culture, e.g. fear of spirits or ghosts are present in many cultures but become specific phobias only if the fear turns excessive & irrational (APA, 2000).

Agoraphobia: Agoraphobia is characterized by anxiety about being in places or situations from which escape might be difficult or embarrassing, if a panic attack or panic like symptoms (sudden dizziness or onset of diarrhea) were to occur (APA, 2000).

Agoraphobia arises out of an underlying fear of cither having a fault blown panic attack or having a sudden and unexpected onset of panic like symptoms.

After any of these phobias are established, they are extremely persistent & may continue for years if not treated(Heaby & Holland, 2000).

TWENTY-ONE
SOCIAL PROBLEMS

Q1. Discuss various psychosocial problems related to old age.

Ans. The elderly people not only face physical problems as they are aged, but they also experience emotional challenges as well, elderly people are faced with stresses that may include living on a reduced retirement income or being unable to care for themselves independently. They may be facing the loss of a spouse, siblings or close friends.

Most older adults enjoy good mental health. However, it is anticipated that the number of older adults with mental and behavioral health problems will almost quadruple, from 4 million in 1970 to 15 million in 2030. Mental health disorders including anxiety and depression, adversely affect physical health and ability to function, especially in older adults. Some late-life problems that can result in depression and anxiety include coping with physical health problems, caring for a spouse with dementia or a physical disability, grieving the death of loved ones, and managing conflict with family members.

The Growing Need for Psychological Services for Older Adults : The demand for mental health practitioners with expertise in older adult care will expand as the older population grows. Demand for mental health services is expected to rise as large cohorts of middle-aged individuals-who are more accepting of mental health services than the current generation of older people-move in to old age.

Researchers estimate that almost two-thirds of older adults with a mental disorder do not receive needed services. This problem is particularly acute in rural and underserved groups, such as those living in poverty and some ethnic and racial groups. CE Research suggests that a majority of older adults would want to be treated should they become depressed. When given a choice for the treatment of depression, older adults often prefer psychological services to antidepressant medication. Older adults report feeling comfortable receiving mental health services from qualified mental health professionals. The Interface Between Physical and Mental Health Care CE Studies indicate that 50-70% of all primary care medical visits are related to psychological factors such as anxiety, depression, and stress. In rural and underserved areas, it may be that primary care medical services are the only health care available. CE Physical and mental health affect each other. For example, older adults with medical problems such as heart disease have higher rates of depression than those who are medically well. Conversely, untreated depression in an older person with heart disease negatively affects the outcome of the disease. Even mild depression lowers immunity and may compromise a 2 person's ability to fight infections and cancers.

Psychologists conduct research on and provide treatment for a wide range of mental health disorders and life problems that affect older adults including the following.

1.Adjustment to the stressors of late life. Psychologists work with older patients to deal with the many life stressors that accompany aging, such as decline in health, loss of loved ones, and relocation to a new living situation.

2. Anxiety disorders, Psychologists use psychotherapy and supportive counseling to treat anxiety disorders in older adults, the frequency of which is comparable to that of depression in older people. Anxiety-related disorders include generalized anxiety disorder, panic disorder, post-traumatic stress disorder, and obsessive-compulsive disorder.

3. Capacity assessment. Families, health care providers, attorneys, and judges concerned about an older person's capacity to make medical or legal decisions call upon psychologists. Psychologists have been leaders in the development of the instruments that assess specific capacities in older adults.

4. Caregiving. Family caregivers provide care to most of the 10 million older adults in the United States who have a disabling condition. Although the role of caregiving can be rewarding, it can also be quite stressful and taxing. Caregivers may suffer from depression, anxiety, substance abuse, anger, and stress-related health problems, including cardiovascular disease. Psychologists help family members to better deal with the practical and emotional demands of caring for a physically or cognitively impaired older relative.

5. Dementia. Psychologists help individuals who are in early stages of dementia build coping strategies and reduce distress through psychotherapy and psychoeducational support groups. Memory training strategies help to optimize remaining cognitive abilities. Psychologists also teach behavioral and environmental strategies to caregivers of those with dementia to deal with common behaviors such as aggression and wandering. Unlike sedating medications, these strategies do not lead to additional confusion or impairment of mental functioning. In addition, as individuals with dementia often also suffer from depression, paranoia, and anxiety, the psychologists' skills in differential diagnosis and treatment are helpful in these complex cases. CE

6. Depression. Depression in older adults is a very treatable disorder. However, symptoms of depression in older adults are often overlooked because they are inaccurately assumed to be a normal part of aging or may coincide with medical illnesses or life events that commonly occur as people age. Psychologists successfully identify and treat both major depressive disorder and subclinical forms of depression with psychotherapy.

7. End-of-life care. Psychologists assist older adults and their families with advanced care planning. They counsel terminally ill patients and their families on how to manage feelings, decrease distress, and manage pain, and after the death grief. As depression and anxiety are often associated with a terminal diagnosis and the progression of a disease, psychologists assess and treat these mental health conditions to minimize suffering and distress. Psychologists also train physicians to recognize and ameliorate patient and caregiver psychological distress.

8. Health promotion. As experts in human behavior, psychologists have been at the forefront in developing effective health promotion programs and strategies to enhance healthy behaviours. Two examples of health promotion effort that have proven beneficial for older adults include memory-training programs that enhance memory performance and physical activity programs that elevate mood, relieve symptoms of depression, and contribute to the effective management of hypertension and diabetes.

9. Incontinence. Psychologists use behavioral training methods, such as biofeedback, bladder training, goal setting, and self-monitoring, to reduce incontinence. These treatments have proven to be more effective than drug therapy. Incontinence has significant implications for the independence of older adults. It is the second most common reason why families admit an

elder relative to a nursing home, which in itself is associated with depression in older adults.

10. Insomnia. Insomnia is prevalent among older adults, especially medically ill elders. Older adults are especially vulnerable to the adverse effects of sleep medications, including memory impairment and impaired daytime performance. Psychologists have developed effective nonpharmacologic treatments for insomnia, including cognitive-behavioral techniques, sleep restriction and stimulus control, and sleep hygiene instruction.

11. Long-term care. There is a very high prevalence of mental health disorders in long-term care institutions, such as nursing homes. Psychologists' presence in these settings has greatly increased in the past decade. Psychologists work with facility staff to more effectively manage resident behavioral problems, such as aggression and wandering, and to improve quality of life for both staff and residents. Psychologists work with individuals and with groups of residents to help them better adjust to life in long-term care, medical problems, depression, anxiety, and the loss of cognitive abilities.

12. Management of chronic diseases. Psychologists help older adults manage multiple chronic medical conditions that often accompany aging, such as heart disease, stroke, and arthritis. A major goal of such management is to prevent excess disability and hospitalization through treatment adherence and behavioral interventions, including physical activity, biofeedback, nutrition, and stress reduction techniques.

13. Substance abuse. Alcohol abuse is a significant problem for some older adults and is one the eight leading causes of death among older Americans. Psychologists can help older adults boost their motivation to stop drinking, identify circumstances that trigger drinking, and learn new methods to cope with high-risk drinking situations. Some older adults have problems with addiction to prescription medication for anxiety and need help in reducing or stopping medication. In addition, as the baby boomer cohort enters old age, the prevalence of both alcohol and illicit drug use will likely increase.

14. Suicide. Older adults, particularly White men, have the highest rates of suicide in the United States. Depression is suicide's foremost risk factor. Psychologists are skilled at identifying depression and assessing for suicide risk. Those at risk for suicide are often not identified by primary health care providers. It has been reported that two-fifths of older adults who commit

suicide visited a physician within the past week and three-quarters within the past month. Primary care providers often overlook the potential link between physical symptoms and mental health problems.

Psychologists provide services to older adults in a variety of settings, including health care facilities, community-based private or group practices, and places where older adults reside-in their homes, long-term-care and assisted-living facilities, and hospices. Psychologists work both independently and as members of interdisciplinary teams. As team members, psychologists collaborate with a variety of professionals, including medical and other mental health care services providers, to ensure comprehensive care.

PPP

Q2. Write a short note on social integration.

Ans. SOCIAL INTEGRATION

Social integration in sociology and other social sciences, is the movement of minority groups such as ethnic minorities, refugees and underprivileged sections of a society into the mainstream of societies. Social integration requires proficiency in an accepted common language of the society, acceptance of the laws of the society and adaptation of a common set of values of the society. It does not required assimilation and it does not require persons to give up all of their culture, but it may require to forgo some aspects of their culture which are inconsistent with the laws and the values of the society. In tolerant and open societies, members of minority groups can often use social integration to gain full access to the opportunities, rights and services available to the members of the mainstream of society.

Caste : Cast is an elaborate and complex social system that combines some or all elements of endogamy, hereditary transmission of occupation, social class, social identity, hierarchy, exclusion and power, have land defines caste as a closed form of social stratification in which membership is determined by birth and remains fixed for life, castes are also endogamous and off springs are automatically members of their parent's caste.

Social class : Social class is a set of concepts in the social science and political theory centered on models of social stratification in which people are grouped into a set of hierarchical social categories. Social class is usually synonymous with 'socio-economic class', it can be defined as 'people having the same social, economic and educational status', for e.g., 'the working class', 'an emerging professional class'.

Religion : Religion is a collection of cultural systems, belief systems and world views that relate humanity to spirituality, and some times moral values. Many religions have narratives, symbols, traditions and sacred histories that are intended to give meaning to life or to explain the origin of life or the universe. They tend to derive morality, ethics, religious laws or a preferred lifestyle from their ideas about the cosmos and human nature. The word religion is sometimes used interchangeably with faith or belief system, but religious differs from private belief in that it has a social aspect. Many religious have organised behaviors, clergy, a definition of what constitutes adherence or membership, regular meetings or services for the purposes of veneration of a deity or for prayer, holy places or scriptures. The practice of a religion may also include sermons, commemoration of the activities of a God or Gods, sacrifies, festivals, feasts, trance, initiations, funerary, services, matrimonial services, meditation music, art, dance, public, service or other aspects of human culture.

ppp

Q3. Who are criminals and sociopaths?

Ans. CRIMINAL BEHAVIOUR-DELINQUENCY AND CRIME

The terms sociopath or sociopathy in contrast with the legal base of the terms criminal or crime have psychological and psychiatric grounds. whereas all sociopaths generally exhibit criminal behavior, it is not essential that all criminals (adults or minor) should be sociophobes. The following points make a distinction between criminals and sociopaths:

Criminals

Criminals usually show normal or extra-ordinary concentration.

Criminal offences are planned and well organised.

Criminals oparate under a conscience peculiar to themselves and are loyal to each other, but not to society, by whom they frequently feel rejected. They may be hostile to one particular group of people or section of the society, but may be generous to others.

It is not essential for the criminals to be inadequate in all forms of behaviour.

Criminals exhibit skill and proficiency and develop a sophistication in committing a crime. They are ruthless in their approach which is their work. They act with judgement and keen insight.

Criminals have an affect; this means that they commit an offence with a motive and frequently care for their family and children. They get upset and punish children if they commit crimes.

Sociopaths

Sociopath exhibit complete lack of concentration.

They offences are usually impulsive, often poorly carried out.

There is no evidence of a conscience in sociopathy behavior. Sociopaths even do not hesitate to steal from fellow patients. They may be observed to wonder from woman to woman, having many children and supporting no one, not even themselves.

Sociopaths are usually inadequate in all forms of behaviour.

Sociopaths are not very serious about their criminal behaviour. They repeat the same offences and never learn from their past experiences. They suffer from poor judgement and lack insight.

Sociopaths have only the shallowest affect. They show no serious concern for their life partners, family or children. For themselves is always great.

Q4. What do understand by the term delinquency and crime?

Ans.

Delinquency and crime

The terms 'crime and 'delinquency' are legal ones and their meaning varies from country to country and in the same country from one state to another. In India, any person of 21 years and above convicted by the court for violating the provision of Indian Penal Code (IPC) and the Criminal Procedure Code (CPC) is a criminal. Of course, there are state laws which vary from state to state. For example, in some states or part of a state liquor consumption, except for medical reasons, may be considered a crime, whereas in others it may not be so.

Similarly, for legally levelling an individual in the age group seven to eighteen as delinquent, he must be convicted by the court for violating the provisions of the Children's Acts, the IPC and the CPC.

The individuals between 18 and 21 who violate the provisions of IPC and CPC are midway between criminals and delinquents and are leveled young or youthful' offenders. After the trial by the court, they are sent either to the institution or to prisons depending on the seriousness or nature of their crimes and circumstances.

The individuals below the age of seven even although committing such offences are covered legally in the term delinquency- it is felt that they are not mature enough to distinguish between the legal and the illegal or between right and wrong.

Delinquency

Criminal behaviour or tendency to commit crime in any society nation, is not only found among the adults, but minor children and adolescents also. These individuals are known as juvenile or young delinquents. (Juvenile delinquents, therefore, are criminal minor in age legally from seven to eighteen in our country) and usually referred to as minors with major problems. They violate the law of the land and commit offences like thefts, gambling, cheating, peak-pocketing, murder, robbery, dacoity, destruction of property, violence and assault, intoxication vagrancy, begging, kidnapping, abduction and sexual offences. The term 'juvenile delinquent or young delinquent' means a child or youth (minor in age) who deviates seriously from the norms of his culture or society and commits offences such as murder and robbery or those that are strictly age related such drinking liquor and sexual activities. Juvenile delinquency should, therefore, be considered a serious challenge to the well-being of the society. The young delinquents, if not handled properly, become a source of concern for the society.

Q5. What are the causes of delinquency?

Ans.

Causes of delinquency

1. Hereditary factor: The early researches held heredity responsible for delinquency. The claim of hereditarians like Henry, Maudsley, Tredgold, and Dugdale that delinquency is inherited was tested by William Healey, Cyril Burt, Conrad and Jones, Wingfield and Sandiford. They concluded that delinquency is not inherited and therefore it is unjustified to blame heredity for delinquent behaviour.

2. Constitutional or physiological factors: Defective constitution or glandular systems were also thought to be the cause of delinquent behavior. It was observed that "poor health, short or too big stature or some deformity which give rise to feeling of inferiority, dispose one to more aggression, as a compensatory reaction for his inadequacies". Consequently, this leads to delinquent behaviour. Apparently, this alienation seems to be well founded but it is not so, for not much scientific evidence has been reported in its support so far. However, in some cases, it may be taken as one of the causes of delinquent behaviour.

3. Intelligence factor : While earlier writers like Lombroso and Goddard emphasize that the most important cause of delinquency and crime is low grade mentality, Burt, Healey, Bronner, Merrill and others deny that

delinquents are mentally retarded. In fact, a direct causal relationship between intelligence and delinquency is doubtful. High intelligence is no guarantee for good behaviour. Often persons with superior intelligence have been found to be the leaders of notorious gangs and antisocial organisations. Sometimes it is argued on the basis of the statistics that since the majority among the delinquents possess low intelligence, defective intelligence therefore causes delinquency. But this conclusion is not well founded. The collected statistics, in such cases, may represent an unreal picture. An intelligent individual may not be caught red handed, whereas someone with low intelligence may always be taken in custody. Moreover, defective intelligence may lead to delinquency is one situation and may be a barrier to it in another situation. Hence, low intelligence along cannot be held responsible for delinquent behaviour.

4. Environmental and social factors : It has been proved that delinquent behaviour is a learned reaction. Delinquents do not inherit delinquent characters from their parents or ancestors but are made so by the uncongenial environment and social conditions. It was observed that "delinquency is not inherited : it is the product of social and economic conditions and is essentially a coefficient of the friction between the individual and the community. The most important causes of antisocial behaviour are environmental and sociological in character." It is therefore the uncongenial environment of the family, school, neighbourhood and society which should be blamed for the delinquent behaviour of the child since he picks up delinquent traits in such situations. We shall now see how environment is responsible for the delinquent character formation among minors.

(a)Home environment and delinquency

A defective and deficient family environment is a fertile ground for the germination of delinquency. As a matter of fact, family life and delinquency are closely related. Findings of various studies indicate that the family environment, where the following relationships or conditions prevail, is most susceptible to delinquency.

Broken home-where the family is incomplete due to death, desertion, separation or divorce.

Improper parental control.

Unusual jealousy and rivalry among the siblings or children within the family and reactions like, "My parents gave him more love than they gave me".

The delinquent and criminal behaviour of the parents or other family members.

Domestic conflicts.

Economic difficulties and poverty of the family.

Dull, monotonous and uninteresting home environment.

Denial of reasonable freedom and independence to the youngsters.

Maltreatment and injustice done to the youngsters.

Lack of proper physical and emotional security.

In these situations, and environment, the child does not get the opportunity for the satisfaction of his basic needs. He becomes victim of the emotional problems like inferiority, insecurity, jealousy or being thwarted which make him a maladjusted individual and consequently turn him into a hostile, rebellious and antisocial personality. Thus, uncongenial home conditions deserve to be blamed for juvenile delinquency and in all circumstances the root cause of delinquent behavior must be investigated in family background and home environment.

(b)Uncongenial environment outside the home

Whereas home provides the roots for the delinquent behaviour, the social environment outside the home nourishes it by supplying some substitute for the satisfaction of unsatisfied basic needs and urges. For example, the peer-group or gang presents itself as a substitute for family love and belongingness. It also satisfies the need for recognition and gives an individual the opportunity for self-dependence and adventurism. Delinquent acts of peer-group Iead him to delinquent behaviour and engage in delinquent acts. Neighbourhood and the places of social contracts and situations where the elder members of the society engage in antisocial activities, or the mass media like newspapers, books, magazines and cinema that acquaint children with immoral and anti-social acts, provide temptation for the youngsters to become delinquents.

(c)Maladjustment in school

In many cases of delinquency, uncongenial school environment can be a significant stimulating factor. It brings about serious maladjustment and consequently increases the probability of delinquent character formation. Such environment may involve the following elements:

* Defective curriculum.

* Improper teaching element.

*Lack of cocurricular activities.

*Lack of proper discipline and control.

* Slackness in administration and organisation.
* Antisocial or undesirable behaviour of the teachers.
* Maltreatment and injustice done to the child.
* Failure or backwardness.

To conclude, delinquency is an environmental and social disease. Delinquent nor is delinquent behaviour the product of genes. Thus delinquents are not a specific type of human beings born with innate, physical, mental or emotional characteristics. They are normal individuals with normal needs and desires. Like other normal children they also want to love, to be loved, and to satisfy the need for security and recognition. The denial of these basic needs leads to maladjustment and makes them hostile and rebellious. Thus delinquent behaviour is a reaction or resentment against the prevailing social and environmental conditions. It is a revolt against parents, teachers or social organisations which do not provide them the essential environment for the satisfaction of their basic needs and urges.

Q6. How can we prevent criminal behaviour among youths?

Ans. CURATIVE MEASURES

The problem of juvenile delinquency should not be regarded as panel problem. It is an educational and welfare problem. Juvenile delinquents should not be put behind bars and treated through the panel system. Delinquents require rehabilitation and re-education for which special legal provisions should be made. The legal dealings with the juvenile delinquents have been changed in the progressive communities of the world. The "Children's and Young Person's Act" of U.K. can be adopted with some modifications in our country. Its essential features are as follows:

Establishment of special juvenile courts with trained magistrate to deal with the juvenile delinquents.

Appointment of trained social workers or probation officers for taking change of delinquent cases.

Taking help from clinical psychologists and psychiatrists for understanding the delinquent behaviour of children.

Establishment of special schools where the education, correction and rehabilitation is possible.

Provision of keeping the children in the custody of responsible persons or social agencies.

Establishment of remand homes where juvenile delinquents are placed while they wait for their trial or for approved school placement or for being given to the custody of responsible persons or as asked by probation officer before employment on being discharged from the approved schools.

Prevention and treatment

The remedy for criminal behavior demands preventive and curative measures.

Prevention : The preventive measures involve improvement of social factors and environmental conditions that are responsible for the germination and perpetuation of criminal behaviour. The problem is a gigantic one and needs the cooperation of parents, members of the family, neighborhood, community, school or college authorities, religious heads, police and government officials responsible for the social and psychological environment of the inhabitants of a society. The following measures may be fruitful in the prevention task :

1. Since today's delinquents are tomorrow's criminals, maximum efforts should therefore be made for the prevention, control and treatment of all the identified delinquents.

2. There is a great need for social reforms and breaking social and caste barriers.

3. The task of narrowing the gulf between the rich and the poor, linguistic groups and religious sects should be given priority.

4. The importance of moral values should be inculcated. There should be an end to the crisis of character threatening the existence of the moral base and legal codes of our society.

5. The system of education and national planning need rethinking and re-modification for minimizing economic difficulties of our youth and adults.

6. The problem of unemployment has to be checked and the professional dissatisfaction as well as frustration affecting the vast population of the younger generation should be curbed.

7. Attempts should be made to minimize undesirable influence of literature, films and other mass media.

8. The parents, elder, government authorities, social, religious, educational and political leaders should be such that they become ideals of socially desirable behaviour.

9. The society should feel the necessity of providing social and legal justice to its citizens. In case of environmental deprivations and hazards of life, the affected individual should be helped, protected and rehabilitated.

Thus there is a need for modifying the environmental conditions so that one does not fall victim to social and emotional maladjustment or lured by the criminals and drifted by instinctive behaviour to commit crimes.

Treatment and rehabilitation : The old notion that a criminal is born and nothing can be done for reforming and rehabilitating him still holds its ground. The law enforcement is still largely punitive and revengeful. Even in many civilized societies and developed countries the treatment meted out to criminals is still in terms of tooth for tooth and eye for eye. The criminals are isolated from society, kept in prisons and punishments such as lashing, severing of hands and legs, hanging are given in public not to deter the criminal from further offences but also to prevent others from indulging in such acts. However, as a result of an increase in the knowledge of human behaviour and criminal psychology, there have been changes in the attitude of the general public, police officials and government authorities towards criminals and crime. It is now felt that for most criminals, their behaviour is a part of the larger pattern of personality maladjustment. Criminal behaviour is nothing but a social disease and criminals are ill primarily in terms of their inability to conform to the social milieu. With serious psychological and psychiatric problems, they need hospitalization, medical and psychological treatment as curative measures for their illness.

Q7. What can be the preventive measures taken to reduces crime in society?

Ans.

Prevention and treatment

Delinquency, besides being a legal problem, is basically a psycho-social problem. All delinquents are essentially maladjusted personalities and the result of faulty up-bringing and maltreatment. The solution of the problem requires preventive and curative measures.

PREVENTIVE MEASURES

Initially these involve improvement of the social or environmental conditions which thwart the satisfaction of the basic needs of the individual. Some of the following suggestions may work well in this direction.

Parental education : Parents should be aware of the psychology of delinquency so that they can treat and handle their children with understanding and provide them an environment for the satisfaction of their basic needs and urges. It requires parental education which may be provided through guidance services, clinics and voluntary social services.

The child's company : Parents, family members and school authorities should keep a close watch on the activities and social environment of the children and take care so that they do not fall in bad company. Antisocial elements and criminals often sock out youngsters for their own purpose. Attempts should be made to save the children from them and they should be educated in keeping away from such Clements.

Substitute environment: It is difficult to bring a change in the defective family environment or the influences of the neighbourhood and peer group. In such circumstances children should be removed from their original environment and placed either in foster homes or well-managed reformatories and special schools so that they may be provided with healthy environment for their emotional and social adjustment.

Rectifying school education and environment : School environment should be healthy and congenial. The curriculum, methods of teaching, discipline, class-room behaviour of the teacher and the social atmosphere of the school should be rectified so that children do not involve themselves in emotional and social maladjustment problems. The attitude of teachers who impose their authority on children and do not understand their basic needs should be changed. The headmaster as well as the teachers should be familiar with the psychology of individual difference and delinquency.

TWENTY-TWO

REHABILITATION PSYCHOLOGY

Q1. What are Primary, Secondary and Tertiary prevention?

Ans. Primary, Secondary and Tertiary prevention :

Scientists are always looking for new and better ways of preventing diseases and injury both to avert human suffering and to control the tremendous economic costs of ill health. Thus, today researchers are talking of prevention which means fixing a problem at the source. In general, prevention includes a wide range of activities known as "interventions" which are mainly aimed at reducing risks / threats to health. They are basically grouped into 3 categories-

1.Primary prevention-Here the goal is to protect healthy persons from developing a disease or Primary experiencing an injury in the first place for example –

·Education about good nutrition, the importance of regular exercises, and the dangers of tobacco, alcohol and other drugs.

·Regular examination & screening tests to monitor risk factors for illness.

·Immunization against infectious diseases.

·Controlling potential hazards at home & in the work place.

·Example of primary prevention of mental health problems include measures to strengthen family & community support system, teaching conflict management etc.

2.Secondary Prevention- These interventions happen after an illness or serious risk factors have already been diagnosed. The goal is to halt or slow the progress of disease (if possible) in its earliest stages, in the case of injury, goals include limiting long-term disability and preventing re-injury.

For example-

·Telling people to take daily, low-dose aspirin to prevent a first or second heart-attack or stroke.

·Recommending regular exams and screening tests in people with known risk factors for illness.

·Providing suitably modified work for injured workers.

Thus, with early detection & diagnosis, it may be possible to cure a disease, slow its progression or minimize complications.

3.Tertiary Prevention- This focuses on helping people manage complicated, long-term health problems such as diabetes, heart disease, cancer, and chronic musculoskeletal pain. The goals include preventing further physical deterioration & maximizing quality of life. For example-

·Cardiac or stroke rehabilitation programme.

·Chronic pain management programmes.

·Patient support groups.

Thus, tertiary prevention programs aim to improve the quality of life for people with various diseases by limiting complications and disabilities, reducing the severity & progression of diseases and providing rehabilitation. Unlike primary and secondary prevention tertiary prevention involves actual treatment for the disease and is conducted primarily by the health care practitioners.

Psychological principles underlying teaching learning process :

Teaching and Learning both are behavioral acts that are governed by specific psychological principles. The goal of teaching may be learning but not all teaching facilitates learning. Because not all teaching facilitates learning, a teacher must employ a teaching strategy. Teaching strategy refers to the techniques employed by teachers to facilitate learning.

Teaching and learning relationship considers 4 processes of education- 1.Teacher, 2. Student, 3. Learning process, 4.Learning situation.

Q2. Write a short note on application of psychology in education.

Ans: 1) Child-Centred Education

In early times, the teachers were mainly engaged in imparting various kinds of information to the children. Today, it is the child who is the center of attention in education. Every child is individually considered and treated.

2) Emphasis on extracurricular activities

Previously, education was believed to be a comprehensive process that trained the individual, provided him with a moral character and made him more cultured. At present variety is believed to be essential in education and it is hold to be true that the education of one individual subject includes many different activities and functions, of which the teacher should be aware of

3) Reform in the curriculum

Psychology has also managed to bring about important variations and reforms in educational curriculum. Now, it is the mental age and not the chronological age of the child that helps to determine the course of study to which he is to be subjected. Intelligence tests reveal the mental age of the child. Different courses are devised for brilliant and deficient children. With the use of audio-visual aids such as television, film projection etc. education has become more interesting and appealing. Many schools are equipped with radio sets that provide both entertainment and information to the child.

4) New Methods of Discipline: Previously, physical punishment was one of the chief methods of teaching and imparting discipline among the children. The main motive behind discipline was fear of physical violence and injury. Psychologists attracted the attention of the enlighten people to the injurious effect of physical punishment and also suggested alternative means of making children disciplined. Now a days it has become customary in schools to allow the children to adopt discipline rather than foist it upon them.

5) Education of the total personality

Modern methods of education place great emphasis upon the education of personality. Education is now understood to mean something more than mere reading or writing. It is also understood to in value the development of personality.

Many schools have resident psychologists who solve problems related to the personality of the students and give advice to teachers and parents in this regard. At places there are also child guidance clinics that make special efforts towards the correction and normal rehabilitation of problem children of juvenile delinquents.

6) Psychological testing Methods: In this manner, psychology has changed teaching methods. All new research aims at evolving teaching methods that induce the child to learn for himself and thus himself achieve his development. The means of the new teaching methods are radio, picnics, tours of historical places, games, election contests, students' unions etc.

7) Emphasis on Individual Differences

In previous days, the same curriculum was prescribed for all students in the class. The development of psychology led to the fact that different individuals differ from each other in respect of their interests, intelligence, ability, capabilities etc. Now a- days the essential pre-requisite to guidance of an educational nature is knowledge of the subject's ability and interests.

8) Reform of the problem children:

One of the most notable contributions of psychology to education is the improvement and reform of juvenile delinquents, and problem children and advise their parents regarding them

9) Mental Testing and Guidance:

Teachers need the help of psychologists in either of these two matters. Psychologists solve the problems of students through personal guidance and inform them of the job, they are best suited to, through vocational guidance. In this way the cooperation and coordination between the teacher and the psychologists in the field of education is on the increase.

TWENTY-THREE
THERAPIES

Q1. Discuss psychoanalytic therapy in details.

Ans. Psychoanalytic therapy is a type of treatment based upon the theories of Sigmund Freud, who is considered one of the forefathers of psychology, and the founder of psychoanalysis. This therapy explores how the unconscious mind influences thoughts and behaviours, with the aim of offering insight and resolution to the person seeking therapy. Psychoanalytic therapy tends to look experiences from early childhood see if these events have affected the individual's life, or potentially contributed to current concerns. This form of therapy is considered a long-term choice and can continue for weeks, months or even years depending on the depth of the concern being explored.

Assumptions of psychoanalytic therapy : It can be helpful to know what assumptions psychoanalysts work from when considering a therapy type. While each therapist will work in different ways according to the needs of the individual seeking therapy, many work on the following assumptions:

- Psychological problems are rooted in the unconscious.
- Manifest symptoms are caused by hidden or 'latent' disturbances.
- Typical causes for psychological upset include unresolved issues during development or repressed trauma.
- Treatment looks to bring repressed conflicts to the surface where individuals can deal with it.

By working through and understanding conflicts, this type of therapy aims to change the participant on a deeper level.

Psychoanalytic therapy contains many different therapeutic techniques. These techniques are intended to increase awareness and foster insight into the client's behavior. Four techniques will be discussed in this lesson:

Free association

Dream analysis

Analysis of transference

Analysis of resistance

Free Association : Free association involves exploring a person's unconscious through spontaneous word association. Clients are encouraged to say whatever comes to mind when the therapist presents them with a word, no matter how trivial, illogical, or irrelevant the response may seem. It is the therapist's job to interpret the responses as patterns in the associations are identified. This is a central technique in psychoanalytic therapy. It is used to uncover unconscious desires or intense emotions that have been blocked by the client.

Dream Analysis : Dream analysis is the investigation of repressed feelings that can be expressed in our dreams. Psychoanalytic theory believes repressed feelings often manifest themselves in our dreams. This happens because our defenses are lowered when we sleep. Dream analysis helps uncover this unconscious material.

Dreams have two levels of content:

Latent content, or hidden motives, wishes, or fears

Manifest content: this refers to the dream as it actually appears

Dream analysis takes place as the therapist uncovers the disguised, latent content within the actual, manifest content of the dream. Usually this involves identifying symbolic meaning in the dream. Sometimes, free association with different dream elements is used in the process.

Analysis of Transference : Transference relates to the way you may be transferring thoughts or feelings connected to influential figures in your life (for example your parents or siblings) onto your therapist. While this may not happen in every case, if it does your therapist should discuss transference with you to help you gain further insight into the way you deal with people in your daily life.

Interpretation : A key element of psychoanalytic therapy is interpreting and 'reading between the lines'. While your therapist is likely to stay relatively quiet and allow you to talk freely, they will occasionally interject with thoughts or interpretations of the topics the clients discuss. The psychoanalyst may also about the dreams: Freud wrote a lot on the subject of dream analysis and believed that dreams were important resources for understanding the unconscious.

Q3. What is behavior therapy? Describe the process for conducting this therapy.

Ans. Behavior therapy refers to psychological treatments, which are bused on experimental psychology and intended to change symptoms and behavior. It assumes the role of learning in the etiology, maintenance and treatment of some psychiatry disorders. Some of these disorders are due to a learning, some to overlearning; and others to loss of previous learning, e.g. institutionalization. Behavioral therapy has beneficial change in behavior as the goal. The methods used may be based on Pavlovian classical conditioning (1927), Skinnerian operant conditioning (1938), learning principles, experimental psychology, or behavioral sciences in general.

Behavioral Analysis

This requires a detailed behavioral analysis: 1. Problem behaviours: Major complaints are categorized into behavioral excesses and deficits, including the frequency, intensity and duration. 2. Antecedents: Events, which precede and elicit problem behaviors. 3. Consequences: These refer to the circumstances or responses of people following the occurrence of the problem behaviors. They often reinforce or else maintain the problem behaviors.

Behavioral approaches may be categorized into:

a)Relaxation therapy, b) autogenic training, c) guided imagery, d) systematic desensitization, e)exposure therapy, f) response prevention, g) modelling, h) thought stopping, I) biofeedback, j)aversion therapy, k)habit reversal l) mass practice, m) response cost, n) modelling, o) shaping, p) token economy.

Autogenic Training

Developed by Schultz (1905) from the work of Oskar Vogt, this involves a series of standard relaxation exercises followed by meditative ones to induce feelings of heaviness, warmth or cooling in parts of the body and to slow respiration. Autogenic training can be used to treat generalized anxiety disorders and stress related disorders.

Relaxation Therapy

The simplest form of relaxation therapy involves regular deep breathing exercises. Another form of relaxation exercise is muscle relaxation. First described by Jacobson (1938), it was an elaborate procedure intended to bring about reduction of individual groups of skeletal muscle tone. It involves alternate contraction followed by relaxation of different muscle groups e.g. the arms, shoulders, neck, jaw, face, etc.

Guided Imagery

Here the patient is presented with a series of mental images depicting peace and rest. Sceneries such as the tranquility of a clear blue lake, the morning break by the golden beach, or the cool and refreshing dew in the woods, are used to induce relaxation. Often soothing music or sounds of chirping birds or waves in the background help enhance the relaxed state further. The purpose is to involve as many sensory modalities as possible in the imagery in order to achieve optimal relaxation.

Systematic Desensitization

Developed by Wolpe (1958), it begins with the construction of a list of anxiety-evoking situations in an ascending order (hierarchy). Relaxation is taught, and the patient is presented with the hierarchy of feared situations (either live or by imagination), beginning with the least feared one. Mild anxiety is experienced initially, and this is paired with relaxation exercise. Once the anxiety diminishes, the next level of feared stimulus is presented. In this way, while never experiencing intolerable anxiety, the patient proceeds from mildly anxious situations to progressively more terrifying ones. Gradually he will be able to cope with the most anxiety evoking situations. Systematic desensitization is commonly used for the treatment of phobic disorders.

Exposure Therapy

This is similar to systematic desensitization except that no attempt is made to relieve the anxiety during the period of exposure. Instead, with time, the anxiety will subside or disappear through a psychological process of habituation. This deliberate exposure aims at confronting the fear instead of avoiding, and can be graduated (graded-exposure) or else “flooding” the patient with the most feared situations all at once. Exposure therapy is now the mainstay of behavioral treatment for obsessive-compulsive disorder and phobias.

Modelling

Modelling refers to the acquisition of new behaviors by the process of imitation. The patient observes someone else carry out an action, which he has problem with. It is often used in conjunction with other techniques like exposure therapy and role- playing for the treatment of obsessive-compulsive disorder and phobias, as well as in social skills training. In the phobic child modelling is especially useful e.g. the phobic child watches other children play with dogs and is then encouraged to join in subsequently.

Biofeedback

Biofeedback involves the use of electronic instruments to monitor small and otherwise undetectable changes in the biological state of the patient. These are then fed back to him (visually e.g. colours or by auditory means e.g. Low or high pitched sounds), so that he can in turn gradually learn to alter and control them. Biofeedback has been used to train individuals to gain control over heart rate, blood pressure, skin temperature, EEG activity and muscle tension. It has been used in the treatment of cardiac arrhythmias, hypertension, tension headache, migraine, tics, generalized anxiety and stress related.

Aversion Therapy

In aversion therapy, the undesirable behavior is paired with an unpleasant consequence. It may take the form of imaginable aversion (also called covert sensitization) or physical aversion e.g. electric shock. A pedophile when imagining touching a naked child shocks himself or imagines himself being arrested and publicly humiliated. Besides deviant sexual behavior, aversion therapy has also been used in the treatment of alcohol dependence and pathological gambling. The ethanol-alcohol reaction following alcohol ingestion with disulfiram is an example of chemical aversion.

Mass Practice

In mass practice, the patient is asked to deliberately practice the undesirable behavior e.g. motor ties. This will lead to boredom and eventually extinction of the behavior.

Response Cost

This is a form of aversion in which the patient agrees to pay a forfeit, not necessarily monetary, for every exhibition of an undesirable behavior. Widely practiced as the form of fines for offending the law for instance, the person could prearrange to make a donation to his least liked charitable organization for every stick of cigarette he smokes.

Social Skills Training

Social skills consist of verbal and non-verbal behaviours, which a person needs in order to form and/or maintain social relationships with ether people. It can be taught to those who are deficient in such skills. The training involves a step-by-step programme including the breaking down of a social interaction into different stages like initiating, maintaining and terminating social contact, personal grooming, modelling, rehearsal and role-plays, and finally video feedback. Attention is drawn to details like eye contact, voice volume, body language, posture and social distance. It has been employed successfully to institutionalized chronic schizophrenics, depressives, Psychopaths and the mentally retarded. Although it may not play a direct therapeutic role like drugs in terms of cure for the illness, it has an important role in the overall management of the patient in enhancing a better quality of life during rehabilitation.

Shaping

It is a form of operant conditioning in which rewards are given for successive approximations towards the desired new behaviour e.g. a mentally retarded child dressing himself. The desired behaviour is broken into many steps, and often the therapist also acts as a model for the child to follow. It is a laborious process, and used only if a new behaviour is totally absent from the patient's repertoire.

Token Economy

Also based on operant conditioning as in shaping, desired behaviours necessary for day-to-day functioning are specified. A unit of exchange (the token) is presented to the patient contingent upon the occurrence of the desired behaviours. The tokens accumulated can then be exchanged for other objects or privileges. Token economy is often used to avoid institutionalization of long stay psychotic patients and the mentally retarded.

It has been estimated that as many as ten percent of adult psychiatric patients are suitable for behavioural therapy. As the lay person becomes more aware of the adverse effects of pharmacological treatment, he would like to help himself and seek alternative methods of treatment. The behaviour therapist role is more that of an instructor and the patient a potential student. It is the latter's responsibility to choose whether he wants to try to learn the new and desired behaviour, or to discontinue the old and undesirable one. Ultimately he has to understand that this is under his own control.

PPP

Q3. Explain in detail Cognitive Behavioural Therapy.

Ans. Cognitive Behavioral therapy (CBT) is a form of psychological treatment that has been demonstrated to be effective for a range of problems including depression, anxiety disorders, alcohol and drug use problems, marital problems, eating disorders, and severe mental illness.

Numerous research studies suggest that CBT leads to significant improvement in functioning and quality of life. In many studies, CBT has been demonstrated to be as effective as, or more effective than, other forms of psychological therapy or psychiatric medications.

Cognitive behavioral therapy (CBT) is a form of talking therapy which can be used to treat people with a wide range of mental health problems.

CBT is based on the idea that how we think (cognition), how we feel (emotion) and how we act (behavior) all interact together. Specifically, our thoughts determine our feelings and our behavior.

Therefore, negative and unrealistic thoughts can cause us distress and result in problems. When a person suffers with psychological distress, the way in which they interpret situations becomes skewed, which in turn has a negative impact on the actions they take.

CBT aims to help people become aware of when they make negative interpretations, and of behavioral patterns which reinforce the distorted thinking. Cognitive therapy helps people to develop alternative ways of thinking and behaving which aims to reduce their psychological distress.

It is important to emphasize that advances in CBT have been made on the basis of both research and clinical practice. Indeed, CBT is an approach for which there is ample scientific evidence that the methods that have been developed actually produce change. In this manner, CBT differs from many other forms of psychological treatment.

CBT is based on several core principles, including:

Psychological problems are based, in part, on faulty or unhelpful ways of thinking.

Psychological problems are based, in part, on learned patterns of unhelpful behavior.

People suffering from psychological problems can learn better ways of coping with them, thereby relieving their symptoms and becoming more effective in their lives.

CBT treatment usually involves efforts to change thinking patterns. These strategies might include:

Learning to recognize one's distortions in thinking that are creating problems, and then to reevaluate them in light of reality.

Gaining a better understanding of the behavior and motivation of others.

Using problem-solving skills to cope with difficult situations.

Learning to develop a greater sense of confidence in one's own abilities.

CBT treatment also usually involves efforts to change behavioral patterns. These strategies might include:

Facing one's fears instead of avoiding them.

Using role playing to prepare for potentially problematic interactions with others.

Learning to calm one's mind and relax one's body.

Not all CBT will use all of these strategies. Rather, the psychologist and patient/client work together, in a collaborative fashion, to develop an understanding of the problem and to develop a treatment strategy.

CBT places an emphasis on helping individuals learn to be their own therapists. Through exercises in the session as well as "homework" exercises outside of sessions, patients/clients are helped to develop coping skills, whereby they can learn to change their own thinking, problematic emotions, and behavior.

CBT therapists emphasize what is going on in the person's current life, rather than what has led up to their difficulties. A certain amount of information about one's history is needed, but the focus is primarily on moving forward in time to develop more effective ways of coping with life.

TWENTY-FOUR

INDUSTRIAL PSYCHOLOGY

THEORIES OF MOTIVATION

Q1. Explain Herzberg's theory of motivation.

Ans. Frederick Herzberg has developed a theory on the premise that worker mental health is associated with performing meaningful work. His theory grew out of a research study conducted with 200 accountants and engineers. The research consisted of personal interviews being conducted with each subject. The essence of the interview was to ask "Can you describe, in detail, when you felt exceptionally good about your job?".

The responses showed that the accountants and engineers generally stated that some content aspects of the job were associated with feeling good about the job. Herzberg called these job content factors. Concerning experience in which people felt bad about their job, Herzberg noted that these tended to be associated with surrounding or peripheral aspects of the job. Herzberg called these context factors. With this general categorization, Herzberg concluded that job content factors were satisfies and that job context factors were dissatisfies.

According to Herzberg, two kinds of factors affect motivation, and they do it in different ways.

i) Hygiene factors: These are factors whose absence motivates, but whose presence has no perceived effect. They are things that when you take them away, people become dissatisfied and act to get them back. A very good example is heroin to a heroin addict. Long term addicts do not shoot up to get 'high; they shoot up to stop being stick-to get normal

Other examples include decent working conditions, security, pay, benefits (like health insurance), company policies, interpersonal relationships. In general, these are extrinsic items low in the Maslow / Alderfer hierarchy.

ii) Motivators. These are factors whose presence motivates. Their absence docs not cause any particular dissatisfaction, it just fails to motivate. Examples are all the things at the top of the Maslow hierarchy, and the intrinsic motivators,

So hygiene factors determine dissatisfaction, and motivators determine satisfaction. The two scales are independent, and you can be high on both

It is noteworthy that rarely were content factors mentioned as dissatisfies or that context factors were rarely mentioned as satisfiers. From this Herzberg concluded that the opposite of satisfaction is not dissatisfaction, but rather that the absence of satisfaction is simply no satisfaction. Similarly, the opposite of dissatisfaction is no dissatisfaction, rather than satisfaction. Satisfaction and dissatisfaction are discrete feelings and they do not occur on a continuum, i.e., they are not polar opposites on the same scale. In other words, one set of factors can lead to satisfaction while another set of factors can lead to dissatisfaction Thus, this is called the two-factors theory.

The job content factors or satisfiers were generally classified as relating to some of the following:

Achievement Recognition

Work Itself Responsibility

Advancement Growth

These factors are motivators that can be realized when completing a job, solving problems, seeing the results of one's efforts, being recognized for a job well done, performing interesting work, successful completing a (difficult, demanding or challenging) task. having control over one's own job, being given responsibility for the work of others, upward movement in the organization, increased opportunities, and learning new skills.

The job context or environment factors associated with dissatisfaction were classified as relating to the following

Company Policy Company Administration

Supervision Working Conditions

Salary Interpersonal Relations (with superiors, peers, etc.)

Status Job Security

Personal Life

There are "hygiene" factors which include feelings about the inadequacy of company management, poor lines of communication, poor direction as to the tasks to be performed, unclear lines of authority, lack of authority to complete a task, incompetent supervisors, excessive amount of work, poor environmental conditions (light, temperature, space, ventilation), poor wages, lower than expected salary increases, restrictions because of status (work conditions, worker liberties, etc.), company stability transfers to undesirable locations,

Herzberg's theory bears considerable similarity to Maslow's hierarchy of needs. Herzberg noted that the higher level of needs, the growth needs, are the only true motivators. The content factors tend to motivate by their presence while context or hygiene factors dissatisfy individuals when they are deficient, i.e., dissatisfiers are deficit needs. For example, poor working condition are commonly named as the source of dissatisfaction, but good physical working conditions are rarely named as being the source of worker satisfaction

If a firm is to motivate its workers, it must be cognizant of the fact that the lack of dissatisfiers does not create satisfaction.

Another way of considering satisfaction and dissatisfaction is to consider the difference between job enrichment and job enlargement. A worker that is asked to do a more challenging task (job enrichment or vertical loading) will probably be more satisfied than will a worker who is simply expected to do an increased amount of the same work (job enlargement or horizontal loading) that has been performed in the past Management must simply realize that hygiene factors and motivators are different and that both must be addressed,

Job enrichment or vertical job loading is associated with the content factors given above. To maximize satisfaction and thus to motive workers, the following actions might be considered:

Remove some job controls

Increase worker accountability for their own work

Give workers complete units of work to produce

Give greater job freedom or additional authority to workers

Make periodic reports directly to the workers (not through the supervisor) Introduce new and more difficult tasks.

Assign specialized tasks to workers so they can become experts

Subsequent research or the two-factor theory on construction workers has shown that there might be a subtle difference in the motivation of construction workers. In essence, Herzberg stated that workers will be motivated when they are satisfied. For construction workers, there may be a slight twist to this causal relationship. What is so special about construction work is that each structure is unique. As a result, workers derive a strong sense of pride and satisfaction from having completed a project Thus, the driver or motivation for construction workers may be to complete their projects as a means of realizing the satisfaction that accompanies this effort. While this may explain a different relationship between satisfaction and production, management can utilize the two-factor theory to good advantage even on construction projects. They must simply make it possible for workers to efficiently complete their construction tasks. While the above may appear to be a contraction, it might also be argued that this is further validation of the two-factor theory. Note that even though a construction project may take months to complete. daily satisfaction surely accompanies the work as it is done.

Q2. Explain Maslow's Theory of work motivation.

Ans. One of the most popular needs theories is Abraham Maslow's hierarchy of needs theory. Maslow proposed that motivation is the result of a person's attempt at fulfilling five basic needs: physiological, safety, social, esteem and self- actualization. According to Maslow, these needs can create internal pressures that can influence a person's behavior.

Physiological needs are those needs required for human survival such as air, food, Water, shelter, clothing and sleep. As a manager, you can account for physiological needs of your

employees by providing comfortable working conditions reasonable work hours and the necessary breaks to use the bathroom and cat and/or drink.

Safety needs include those needs that provide a person with a sense of security and well-being. Personal security, financial security, good health and protection from accidents, harm and their adverse effects are all included in safety needs. As a manager, you can account for the safety needs of your employees by providing safe working conditions, secure compensation (such as a salary) and job security, which is especially important in a bad economy.

Social needs, also called love and belonging, refer to the need to feel a sense of belonging and acceptance.

Social needs are important to humans so that they do not feel alone, isolated and depressed. Friendships family and intimacy all work to fulfill social needs. As a manager, you can account for the social needs of your employees by making sure each of your employees know one another, encouraging cooperative teamwork, being an accessible and kind supervisor an good work-life balance.

Abraham Maslow's hierarchy of needs theory:

Safety: The five basic human needs

Esteem needs refer to the need for self-esteem and respect, with self-respect being slightly more important than gaining respect and admiration from others. As a manager, one can account for the esteem needs of the employees by offering praise and recognition when the employee does well, and offering promotions and additional responsibility to reflect your belief that they are valued employees.

Self – actualization needs describe a person's need to reach his or her full potential. The need to become what one is capable of is something that is highly personal. While someone might have the need to be a good parent, another person might have the need to hold an executive-level position within your organization. Because this need is individualized, as a manager, you can account for this need by providing challenging work, inviting employees and giving them flexibility and autonomy in their jobs.

As the name of the theory indicates, Maslow believed that these needs exist in a hierarchical order. This progression principle suggests that lower-level needs must be met before higher-level needs. The deficit principle claims that a once a need is satisfied, it is no longer a motivator because an individual will take action only to satisfied unmet needs. If you look at this pyramid you can see how Maslow's needs are organized with basic physiological need such as air, food, water and sleep, at the bottom and the idea of self-actualization, or, when a person reaches the full potential in life, at the top. Again, according to Maslow, before a person can take action to satisfy a need at any level on this pyramid the needs below it must already be satisfied.

Criticism : The order in which the hierarchy is arranged (with self-actualization described as the highest need) has been criticized as being ethnocentric by Geert Hofstede, Maslow's hierarchy of needs fails to illustrate and expand upon the difference between the social and intellectual needs of those raised in individualistic societies and those raised in collectivist societies. The needs and drives of those in individualistic societies tend to be more self-centered than those in collectivist societies, focusing on improvement of the sell, with self-actualization being the apex of self-improvement. In collectivist societies, the needs of acceptance and community will outweigh the needs for freedom and individuality

The term "Self-actualization" may not universally convey Maslow's observations, this motivation refers to focusing on becoming the best person that one can possibly strive for in the service of both the self and others Maslow's term of self-actualization might not properly portray the full extent of this level; quite often, when a person is at the level of self-actualization, much of what they accomplish in general may benefit others or, "the greater good."

Q3. Explain ERG Theory?

Ans. Related to Maslow 's needs hierarchy theory is the ERG theory of work motivation developed by Clayton Alderfer. He proposed three basic needs. Existence needs, Relatedness needs, and Growth needs. These needs encompass the needs proposed by Maslow and they can be satisfied within the work environment (Alderfer, 1972) (ERG theory The theory of motivation based on three types of needs, existence needs, relatedness needs, and growth needs.)

Existence needs, at the lowest level, are concerned with physical survival and include the needs for food, water, shelter, and physical safety. Organizations can satisfy these needs through pay, fringe benefits, a safe working environment, and job security. Relatedness needs involve interaction with other people and the satisfaction these social relationships bring in terms of emotional support, respect, recognition, and belonging. The relatedness needs can be satisfied on the job by interactions with co-workers and mentors and off the job by family and friends. Growth needs focus on the self, such as our need for personal growth and development. These needs can be satisfied by using our skills and abilities to the fullest. Growth needs include Maslow's self-esteem and self-actualization needs. A job can satisfy growth needs if it involves challenge, autonomy, and creativity.

The ERG needs are not arranged in a hierarchy, all the needs can influence us at the same time. Therefore, satisfaction of one set of needs does not automatically lead to the emergence of higher needs. However, frustration of the relatedness or growth needs can lead us to revert to the existence needs. Whereas Maslow believed that a person will persevere to satisfy a need, Alderfer suggested that a person will give up on that need and refocus attention on a more basic need. For example, if employees cannot find emotional support or recognition on the job (relatedness needs), they may demand higher pay or better health care coverage (existence needs) as compensation for failing to satisfy the other needs.

Maslow suggested that once a need is satisfied, it no longer motivates us. By contrast, Alderfer said that satisfying a need may increase its strength. For example, if a job provides a great deal of challenge and creativity, our growth needs might become stronger, leading us to seek greater challenges at work.

The ERG theory has considerable empirical research support as well as an intuitive appeal. It is more directly applicable to employee motivation than is Maslow's needs hierarchy theory .

⩦⩦⩦

GROUPS

Q4. What are the functions of the group?

Ans. FUNCTIONS OF GROUPS

The study of human society is essentially the study of human groups. Society consists of groups of innumerable kinds and variety. No man exists without a society and no society exists without groups. Groups have become a part and parcel of our life. Out of necessity and inevitability human beings are made to live in groups. Knowingly or unknowingly or unwillingly, with pleasure or contempt, people live in groups and societies. Man's life is to an enormous extent lived and controlled by groups of deterrent kinds.

Groups Help Social Survival Also: Not only from the point of view of survival but also from the viewpoint of leading a successful life man depends on groups. By engaging himself in constant relations with others he learns things and mends his ways. He keeps eyes wide open, lends his ears to what others say, tries to keep his memory ever fresh to remember the good things of the past and to refrain from repeating the blunders of the past. In brief, from birth to death, man is engaged in the process of socialization. Socialization or the process of humanization helps man to develop a personality of his own.

Groups Contribute to the Development of Personality: Personality is the product of the group life. The 'self' that every individual develops, though unique, is itself a product of the group. No 'self' arises in isolation. Groups provide scope for the individuals to express their real nature their talents and abilities. Hidden potentialities can find their expression only in the context of social groups. What is latent in man becomes manifest only in groups. The groups shape man's attributes, him beliefs, his morals and his ideals. Emotional development, intellectual maturity, satisfaction of physical and social needs is unthinkable without groups. Group is a part of our mental equipment and we are a part of group.

Q5. Explain the effect of group on individual behavior?

Ans. INFLUENCE OF GROUP ON INDIVIDUAL BEHAVIOUR

Social Facilitation

Think of the situations when you are running alone trying to compete with your own standard, or when you are running a race competing with others. In which situation will you run faster? Probably you will run faster when you are competing with others. We all are affected in different ways by other people. Do you know that even the mere presence of the other person effects our behavior? It is a common observation that we tend to eat more when in a group than when we are alone.

Individual behavior is 'facilitated' in several ways while performing in the presence of others. Floyd H. Allport conducted a series of studies in which the performance of individuals was compared on a variety of tasks when they performed alone, and when they were doing the same in the presence of others. Floyd H. Allport conducted a series of studies in which the performance of individuals was compared on a variety of tasks when they performed alone, and when they were doing the same in the presence of others. In one study, the participants were asked to write down on paper as many associations for the given words as they could think of the participants were allowed to work alone and in the presence of two other persons. The results showed that participants produced more associations when working in the presence of other people than when working alone. This positive effect on performance due to the presence of others is known as Social-Facilitation. In general, it is observed that performance is facilitated in the presence of others. However, this is not true in all cases neither for all individuals.

Sometimes, people's performance is adversely affected by others presence. People sometimes tend to make greater number of errors in the presence of others. Such adverse effects on performance due to others presence are called "Social Inhibition". Stutterers, for example, stutter more when reading a passage aloud in front of an audience than when they do the same alone. Facilitation affect is found in case of simple, automatic, over learned behaviors, such as running copying text, etc. and is not observed for complex tasks.

Why does the presence of others sometimes enhance and sometimes impairs performance? There are different reasons for this type of behavior. I) The presence of others seems to energies people or generate feelings of increased arousal, which enhances performance. II) The second reason for social facilitation is apprehension of evaluation of concern of being judged by others which is often arousing the fear of negative evaluation can arouse people to do well, especially on simple tasks. On complex tasks, when a performer makes mistakes and assumes a negative reaction, she/ he gets flustered, and then makes more mistakes. III) Another reason contributing to social facilitation is the concern over self-presentation-looking or performing well in front of others. Try to recall how you had felt when you were on stage in front of the school assembly or audience. Were you more tense or excited? In general, the social facilitation stems from evaluation apprehension concerns over being judged by others (which is often arousing), or from concerns over self-presentation-looking good in front of other, and not only due to the mere presence of others.

Social Loafing: Suppose you and your class-fellows were asked to shift a heavy table to the next room, all of you try to push the table. Do you think all the people will be putting equal effort? May be or may not be. A few persons will be putting in their efforts, while some others would only appear to be helping, or pretending to do more than they really are. This pattern is commonly observed when a group is required to make efforts together for completing a task on such tasks, some persons work hard while the others pretend to be working doing less than their share and less than at hey might do if they were working alone. Such effects are referred to as social loafing reductions in motivation and effort when individuals work collectively in a group compared to when they work individually. In an interesting experiment. Latane and his associates asked groups of male students to clap or cheer as loudly as possible at specific times, either alone or in groups of two four or six. It was observed that the magnitude of the sound made by each person decreased sharply as the group size increased. In other words, each participant put less effort as the group size increased.

Social loafing is a quite common phenomenon. Studies have revealed that social loafing may occur due to several reasons: I) group members may feel less responsible for the task being performed and exert less effort, II) motivation of members may decrease because they realize that their contributions cannot be evaluated on individual basis so why work hard, and III) when they find the task monotonous particularly in such situations where they work with people whom they do not know well or do not respect.

Social loafing can be reduced by: I) making the effort of each person identifiable, II) by increasing group members commitment to successful task performance (pressures towards working hard), III) increasing the apparent importance or value of a task, IV) making people feel that their contribution to the task is unique, and V) by strengthening group cohesiveness which increases the concern for group outcomes.

Risk Taking: Groups perform a variety of tasks including decision-making. As you know, decision making involves combining and integrating the available information in order to choose one course of action out of the several available ones. Today most of the decisions, are taken by groups. Decisions like choosing sports team enforcing laws, government policies political actions. And making educational and career choices are some examples. It is generally behaved that groups, by pooling the knowledge and expertise of their members. Provide opportunities for sharing different viewpoints, in case of complicated problems, there, the chance is greater, that someone in the group would have the skills to solve the problem and thereby reach better decisions than the individuals making decisions alone? Contrary to the popular belief, research has shown that groups are actually more likely to adopt extreme positions than individuals making decisions alone. The group lead to polarization of the position taken in decision-making.

How many times you alone have gathered courage to ask the teacher for a free period? May be never. However, as a class you might have done it several times. Similarly, students in a group may take the risk of bunking classes, which normally as individuals they may not. A number of studies have demonstrated that groups have a tendency to take greater risks than individuals do. The standard method for studying this effect consists of two steps. A group of participants is first asked to make individual decisions on a series of problems in which it is possible to take greater or lesser risk. They are then placed in a group situation, and are required to discuss and make group decisions on the same problems. In an experiment, participants were asked to read a series of problems and make choices among the recommendations that differed in the degree of the risk of failure they carried initially the participants made decision on their own.

Q6. How does a group can be formed? / Explain the stages of group formation.

Ans.

These four group development stages are known as forming, storming, norming, and performing as described below and the skills needed to successfully guide a group through these stages are described by clicking here.

Forming

This is the initial stage when the group comes together and members begin to develop their relationship with one another and learn what is expected of them. This is the stage when team building begins and trust starts to develop, Group members will start establishing limits on acceptable behavior through experimentation other members' reactions will determine if a behavior will be repeated. This is also the time when the tasks of the group and the members will be decided.

Storming

During this stage of group development interpersonal conflicts arise and differences of opinion about the group and its geals will surface. If the group is unable to clearly state its purposes and goals or if it cannot agree on shared goals, the group may collapse at this point. It is important to work through the conflict at this time and to establish clear goals. It is necessary for there to be discussion so everyone feels heard and can come to an agreement on the direction the group is to move in.

Norming

Once the group resolves its conflicts, it can now establish patterns of how to get its work done. Expectations of one another are clearly articulated and accepted by members of the group Formal and informal procedures are established in delegating tasks, responding to questions, and in the process by which the group functions. Members of the group come to understand how the group as a whole operates.

Performing

During this final stage of development issues related to roles, expectations, and norms are no longer of major importance The group is now focused on its task, working intentionally and effectively to accomplish its goals. The group will find that it can celebrate its accomplishments and that members will be learning new skills and sharing roles. After a group enters the performing stage, it is unrealistic to expect it to remain there permanently. When new members join or some people leave, there will be a new process of forming, storming, and norming engaged as everyone learns about one another. External events may lead to conflicts within the group. To remain healthy, groups will go through all of these processes in a continuous loop.

Adjourning

Tuckman's final stage, Adjourning, involves the termination of task behaviors and disengagement from relationships A planned conclusion usually includes recognition for participation and achievement and an opportunity for members to say personal goodbyes. Concluding a group can create some apprehension - in effect, a minor crisis. The termination of the group is a regressive movement from giving up control to giving up inclusion in the group. The most effective interventions in this stage are those that facilitate task termination and the disengagement process.

Leadership

Q7. Define leadership. What are the characteristics of a good leader?

Ans. The group leader is of central importance to the morale of the group. By virtue of his special position within the group structure he serves as the primary agent for the determination of group structures, group atmosphere, group goals, group ideology, and group activities, and we have now seen that the level of moral depends intimately upon these various group properties.

Characteristics of good leader:

The specific functions of a leader vary somewhat with the kind of group being led. Thus, a leader functioning in an "authoritative" group may stress certain functions, whereas a leader in a "democratic" group may stress others. However, whatever the nature of the group, all leaders must partake to some degree of the functions of executive, planner, policy maker expert, external group representative, controller of internal relationships, purveyor of rewards and punishments.

The various characteristics of a good leader are:

Leader of executive

Leader of planner

The leader as policy maker

The leader as expert

The leader as external group representative

The leader as controller of internal relationships

The leader as pursuer of rewards and punishments

The leader as arbitrator and mediator

The leader as exemplar

The leader as symbol of the group

The leader as surrogate for individual responsibility

The leader as ideologist

The leader as father figure

The leader as scapegoat

Leadership is the process of influencing and supporting others to work enthusiastically towards achieving objectives.

Tannenbaum defines leadership as "interpersonal influence, exercised in situations and directed, through the communication process, towards the attainment of goals."

Katz and Kahn suggest that leadership is the influential increment over and above mechanical complains with the routine directive of the organization.

Thus, leadership is an interpersonal process of directing and influencing the behavior of others towards the attainment of particular goats. It is a personal ability and skill to initiate and guide the efforts of a group.

CHARACTERISTICS OF LEADERSHIP

1. Personal ability: Leadership is basically a personal ability and skill. It is personal power which arises out of knowledge, expertise and personality

2. Followership: Leadership requires followers. It cannot without a group of followers.

3. Influencing behavior: Leadership involves the power of influence. It involves an attempt to influence another group member.

4. Interpersonal relationship: Leadership involves group behavior. It is interaction between a leader and one or more followers. It is a reciprocal relationship.

5. Mutual goals: Leadership involves a common of interest between the leader and his followers. It exists for the realization of common goals.

6. Its essence is performance: Leadership depends on doing. Most people agree that leadership is not a personality trait but doing something-guiding, directing, influencing

. 7. Exemplary conduct: Leaders not only tell but also influence by their behavior. They put example in their actions before the subordinates.

8. Leadership is situational: It assumes that leaders are the product of given situations. Leader emerges out of situation.

9. Assumption of responsibility: The leader assumes full responsibility for all actions of his followers. He remains responsible in all situations.

10. Importance of communication: Leadership is established through the communication process. Communication affects the behavior and

performance of followers. The inability to communicate is a serious deficiency in influencing people. Through communication leaders try to influence people's behaviour.

11. All managers are not leaders: Managers are appointed and have legitimate power that allows them to reward and punish. In contrast, leaders may either be appointed or emerge from within a group. Leaders can influence others beyond the actions dictated by formal authority. They have personal capabilities to influence others.

However, not all leaders necessarily hold managerial positions.

12. Leadership may be formal or in informal: Mangers who influence the behavior of their assigned groups are the formal leaders of organizations. Their ability to influence is founded upon the formal authority inherent in their positions. Within the organization, informal groups develop, and within those groups informal leaders who influence the behavior of other group members are the informal leaders.

13.Four-faceted concept: Leadership involves four elements- leader, followers, organization and the environment

These affect one another in determining appropriate leadership behavior,

14. Press: Leadership is a process engaged in by certain individuals. It is an ongoing activity in an organization,

Its outcome is some form of goal accomplishment

15. Other features:

(a) Leadership exists in different forms and at all levels of organization.

(b) It creates work environment in which people can do their best work.

(c) It is the exercise of authority and the making of decisions

(d) It is closely interconnected with motivation. Through motivation, a leader can understand better what

people want and why they act as they do

(e) It involves an unequal distribution of power between leaders and group members.

(f) It should not be confused with aggressiveness and enthusiasm.

(g) It is more emotional, than intellectual or rational Transactional leader: Motivate followers by appealing to their own self-interest, Motivate by the exchange process. Encourage Leader to adapt their style and behavior to meet expectations of followers. EX: business owners exchange status and wages for the work effort of the employee. Focuses on the accomplishment of tasks & good worker relationships in exchange for desirable rewards "If I do this for you... what can you do for me?"}

Q8. Differentiate between transactional and transformational leadership.

Ans.

Transactional vs. transformational leadership

Transactional and transformational are the two modes of leadership that tend to be compared the most, James MacGregor Burns distinguished between transactional leaders and transformational by explaining that transactional leader are leaders who exchange tangible rewards for the work and loyalty of followers. Transformational leaders are leaders who engage with followers, focus on higher order intrinsic needs, and raise consciousness about the significance of specific outcomes and new ways in which those outcomes might be achieved. Transactional leaders tend to be more passive as transformational leaders demonstrate active behaviors that include providing a sense of mission.

Transactional

1. Leadership is responsive
2. Works within the organizational culture implementing new ideas
3. Employees achieve objectives through rewards and punishments set by leader ideals
4. Motivates followers by appealing to their own self interest

Transformational

1.Leadership is proactive
2. Works to change the organizational culture by
3. Employees achieve objectives through higher and moral values
4. Motivates followers by encouraging them to put group interests first

PPP

JOB ANALYSIS

Q9. Define job analysis. What are the methods of job analysis?

Ans. A knowledge of job analysis if a fundamental prerequisite for an intelligent attract upon all personnel problems in any organization. It is important to note that man Industrial-Organizational psychology practitioners prefer to use the term work analysis instead of job analysis. Job analysis focuses on certain tasks and skills that can be transferred from one job to another. The first step in fitting men to job & in maintaining fitness of work, is to make a comprehensive study of occupational activities and requirements

The procedure for obtaining such information is known as job analysis, defined as the scientific study and statement of all the facts about the job which reveal its content and the modifying factors which surround it." It involves a "determination of the essential elements in the job and the qualification of the worker should have for its successful performance." Job analysis involves a detailed description of the component tasks performed on a job. The purpose of job analysis is to describe in specific terms the nature of the component tasks performed by workers on a particular job. A job analysis includes information about the tools or equipment used, the operations performed, the education and training required, the wages paid, and any enquire aspects of the job such as safety hazards.

Job analysis can be classified into four types with respect to purpose:

i) Job analysis for the purpose of improving working methods and processes.

ii) Job analysis for the purpose of protecting health and safety.

iii) Job analysis to be used as a basis for train employees, member of the personnel staff other individually who may be assigned to serve as job analysists on a temporary basis.

Methods of Job Analysis:

There are many different methods which may be used to obtain data for a job analysis. Marsh (1964) has listed nine techniques, each with it won special advantages.

i) Questionnaire Method: This method is usually used to obtain information about occupations via mail survey. The job incumbent is asked to provide data about himself and his job in his own words. The method is good for people who write easily but not so good collecting data from low-level workers who leave little facility for self-expression. Also, it is often a very time-consuming and laborious process to analysis the data obtained in this manner. Job analysis questionnaire may of two types - unstructured and structured questionnaire may be of three types-Task inventories, Position

Analysis Questionnaire (PAQ) and Functional Job Analysis (FJA),

Task inventories consist of job oriented work-activities items, whereas the Position Analysis Questionnaire (PAQ) and Function Job Analysis (FJA) consist of worker-oriented work activity items.

a) Tast Inventories : Task inventories are required to as job analysis typically consists of lists of the tasks pertinent to some occupational area, such as health services or automobile mechanics. the basic data for individual jobs are expressed in terms of quantitative terms, the results of the analysis can be used for various statistical analyses.

b) Position Analysis Questionnaire (PAQ): A questionnaire that lists more Worker-oriented job elements can be used more broadly, because it tends to cover more generalized worker behavioury. On such questionnaire is the Position Analysis Questionnaire (PAQ)

c) Functional Job Analysis (FUA): As on phase of its job analysis program, the U.S. Employment service provides for the analysis of jobs in terms of what are referred to as worker functions (also called functional job analysis or FJA). Worker functions are activities that identify worker relationships to data, people and things. Each function depicts a broad action that summaries what the worker does in relation to data, people or things.

ii) Individual Interview Method: Here representative job incumbents are selected for extensive intervening- usually outside of the actual job situation. The interview is usually structured and the results of a number of interviews are combined into a single job analysis. Then technique is obviously cumbersome, costly and time consuming but a very

complete picture of the job can be obtained with this method.

iii) Observation Interview Method: The observational interview actually takes place sight of the job. The interviewer observes and questions the worker in an attempt to get complete job description data. Like the individual interview, it is a show and costly method which may also interfere with normal work operations. However, it generally produces a good and complete job description

iv) Group Interview Method: The group interview is similar to the individual interview except that a number of jobs incumbents are interviewed simultaneously in the group approach. Under the guidance of the interviewer, the interviewers recall and discus their work activities. The interviewer then combines their comments into a single job description. The advantage over the individual method is the saving the in the time obtained by the group method.

v) Technical Conference Method: These experts are usually supervisors who leave extensive knowledge of the job in question. They meet with the job analyst and attempt to satisfy all the characteristics of the job.

vi) Work Participation Method: With this procedure the job analyst actually performs the job himself. By doing the work himself he is thus able to obtain first-hand information about the characteristics of the job under investigation. The technique is fairly effective for simple jobs, but complex jobs usually requires that the job analyst be extensively trained prior to his session of work activity. The method is time consuming and costly.

vii) Check list Method: This technique requires the worker to check the tasks he performs from a long list of possible task statements. However, in order to prepare the check list, extensive preliminary work is required in collecting appropriate task statements. Which check lists are easy for the incumbent to respond to, they do not provide an integrated picture of the job in question. They are easily administered to long groups and easy to tabulate.

viii) Diary Method: Here job incumbents are required to record their daily activities each day using some type of log book or diary. The method is good in that is systematically gathering a great deal of information, but it can also take a great deal of tone on the part of the worker if the recording forms are not simple.

ix) Critical Incident Method: This involves the collection of a series of statements of job behavior, based upon direct observation or memory, about good and poor job performance. In the usual use of this method, hundreds or thousands of incidents are collected from incumbents, fellow workers, former incumbents, supervisory, and others, using individual or group interviews, questionnaire, diaries, or other means. Such incidents can provide information about critical aspects of the job, but the method does not provide an integrated picture of the entire task.

The critical incidents technique focuses or specific actions that lead to desirable or undesirable can sequence on the job.

PPP

Q10. Write a short note on Occupational hazards.

Ans.

Occupational safety and health are an area concerned with protecting the safety. Health and welfare of the people engaged in work or employment. The goals of occupational safety and health programs include so foster a safe and healthy work environment. OSH may also protect co – workers, family members, employers, customers and many others who might be affected by the workplace environment.

Occupational safety and health can be important for moral, legal and financial reasons. All organization has a duty of care to ensure, that employees and any other person who may be affected by the companies under-Taking remain safe at all times. Moral obligations would involve the protection of employees' lives and health.

Falls are a common cause of occupational injuries and fatalities, especially in construction extraction, Transportation, health care and building cleaning and maintenance.

Machines are common face in many industries, including manufacturing mining, construction and Agri-culture and can be dangerous to workers. Many mechanics involve moving parts, sharp edges, hot surfaces and other hazard with the potential to crush, burn, cut, shear, stab. Various safety measure exists to minimize these hazards, including lock out-target procedures for machine maintenance and roll over protection system for vehicles.

Biological Hazards: - Bacteria, virus, fungi, Mold Blood- borne Pathogens, Tuberculosis.

Biological hazards also knowns as biohazard, refer to biological substances that pose a threat to the health of living organisms, primarily that of humans. This can include medical waste or samples of a microorganism virus or toxin (from a biological Source) that can affect human health. It can also include substance harmful to animals. The term and its associated symbolize generally used as a warning, so that those potentially exposed to the substances will know to take precaution.

Biological agents that are capable of causing disease are known as pathogens. People who work with animals of plants, or in health and child care are most at risk for bio logical hazards. People who work with ventilation system, municipal sanitation or sewage operations are also at increased risk.

Chemical Hazards: - Acids, Heavy Metals, Lead, Petroleum

The use or chemicals has increased dramatically due to the economic development in various sectors including industry, agriculture and transport. As a consequence, children are exposed to a large number of chemicals of both natural and man-made origin. Exposure occurs through the air they breathe, the water they drink or bath, the food that they eat and even the soil they touch, they are exposed virtually wherever they are at home, in the school, on the playground and during transport.

Flammability: - Flammable substances are those that readily catch fire and burn in air. A flammable liquid does not burn itself; it is the vapours from the liquid that burn.

Reactivity: - Reactive chemical hazards invariably involve the release of energy cheat in relatively high quantities or at a rapid rate. If the heat evolved in a reaction, then the reaction rate can increase and cause explosion.

Psychological and Social issues: - Work – related stress, whose causal factors include excessive working time or over work, bullying, which may include emotional and verbal abuse, sexual harassment, mobbing, burnout, violence from outside the organisation, exposure to unhealthy elements during meetings with business associates stress occurs in a wide range or work circumstances but is often made worse when employees fell, they have little support from supervisors and colleagues. Pressure perceives as acceptable by on individual, may even keep workers alert, motivated able to work and learn depending on the available resources and personal characteristics. However, when that pressure becomes excessive or unmanageable it will lead to stress.

Ergonomic hazards: - Ergonomic hazards refer to work place conditions that pose the risk of injury to the musculoskeletal system of the worker. Examples of musculoskeletal injuries include tennis elbow or carpal tunnel syndrome. Ergonomic Hazards include repetitive and forceful movements, vibration, temperature extremes and awkward postures that arise from improper work methods and improperly designed work stations, tools and equipment.

Ergonomic hazards impact employers and workers and their families. Poor workplace design, awkward body posture, and other ergonomic hazards contribute to a staggering number of cumulative disorders. It can affect hands, wrists, elbows, shoulders, lower back and cervical spine Ares, and even structures involved tendons, muscle bones, nerves, and blood vessels.

PPP

CONFLICTS

Q11. Define organizational conflict. Discuss the causes of conflict.

Ans. Organizational conflict, or workplace conflict, is a state of discord caused by the actual or perceived opposition of needs, values and interests between people working together. Conflict takes many forms in organizations. There is the inevitable clash between formal authority and power and those individuals and groups affected. There are disputes over how revenues should be divided, how the work should be done and how long and hard people should work. There are jurisdictional disagreements among individuals, departments, and between unions and management.

· Causes of conflict: The conflict comprises a series of human affective states such as: anxiety, hostility, resistance, open aggression, as well as the types of opposition and antagonistic interaction, including competition. On the other hand, where at least two persons interact, there is an adequate environment for the emergence and development of conflicts. Some important causes of conflict are given below:

1. Personalities: Organizational strife is sometimes traced to "personalities." This is one person differing with another based simply on how he or she feels about that person.

2. Sensitivity/hurt: This occurs when a person, because of low self-esteem, insecurity, or other factors in his or her personal life, sometimes feels attacked by perceived criticism or other interpersonal directness.

3. Differences in perceptions and values: Most conflict results from the varying ways different people view the world. These incongruent views are traceable to differences in upbringing, culture, race, experience, education, occupation, SOCIO economic class, and other environmental factors.

4. Differences over facts: A fact is a piece of data that can be quantified or an event that can be documented. Arguments over facts typically need not last very long since they are verifiable. But a statement like,' It is a fact that you are insensitive to my feelings." is neither documentable nor quantifiable, and so is actually a difference in perception.

5. Differences over goals and priorities: An argument about whether a bank should focus more resources on international banking or on community banking is a disagreement over goals. Another example would be whether or not to increase the amount of advanced professional training given to tellers.

6. Differences over methods: Two sides may have similar goals but disagree on how to achieve them. For example, how should advance teller training is conducted?

7. Competition for scarce resources: Two managers might argue over who has the greater need for an assistant, whose budget should be in- creased more, or how to allocate recently purchased computers.

8. Competition for supremacy: This occurs when one person seeks to outdo or out- shine another person. You might see it when two employees compete for a promotion or for comparative power in your organization. Depending on personalities. this type of conflict can be very subtle sometimes.

9. Misunderstanding: The majority of what looks like interpersonal conflict is actually communication breakdown Communication, if not attended to with care, is as likely to succeed. And when it does. a listener's incorrect inferences about a speaker's intent often create inter- personal conflict.

10. Unfulfilled expectations: Many of the causes listed above contribute to one person not fulfilling the expectations of another. unfulfilled expectations are the ultimate cause of divorce, firings, and other forms of relational breakdown.

The major reason that expectations go unfulfilled is that they are unreasonable, inappropriate, too numerous, or unstated.

11. Lack of communication or wrong communication that leads to the emergence of some misunderstandings. In such cases, the only solution for a conflict is the cooperation which allows each party to find the position and the arguments of the other party

12. Competition regarding insufficient resources - the limited character of organizational to such resources may generate competitions that might turn into conflicts, the insufficiency of resources has the capacity to transform masked or slow conflicts into open and acute conflicts; also, the more limited are the resources, the higher is the conflict potential.

13.Difference of power status and culture in the situations in which the parties have a significant difference in power, status and culture.

Q12. How conflict can be dissolved?

Ans. Conflict Resolution: Individuals vary in the way that they handle conflicts. There are five common styles of handling conflicts. Those styles can be mapped onto a grid that shows the varying degree of cooperation and assertiveness each style entails Let us look at each in turn

1. Competing: assertive, uncooperative, and power-oriented. This person pursues his or her own concerns at the expense of others

2. Collaborating: assertive, cooperative. This person attempts to work with the other person to find a solution that fully satisfies both parties. Collaborating might take the form of exploring a disagreement to learn from each other's insights, or collaborating to solve an interpersonal problem,

3. Compromising: intermediate in assertiveness and cooperativeness. This person tries to find a mutually acceptable solution that partially satisfies both parties. Compromising might mean splitting the difference, exchanging concessions, or seeking a fast, middle-ground solution

4. Avoiding: Unassertive, uncooperative. This person does not immediate pursue his concerns or the concerns of the other party. This person avoids the conflict.

5. Accommodating: Unassertive, cooperating. This is the opposite of a competing. They neglect their own concerns to satisfy the concerns of the other person. Accommodating might take the form of selfless generosity, yielding to another's point of view, or obeying another person's order when you don't want to.

ꝒꝒꝒ

Job Satisfaction

Q13. What are the factors affecting job satisfaction?

Ans. Job satisfaction or employee satisfaction has been defined in many different ways. Some believe it is simply how content an individual is with his or her job, in other words, whether or not they like the job or individual aspects or facets of jobs, such as nature of work or supervision. Others believe it is not so simplistic as this definition suggests and instead that multidimensional psychological responses to one's job are involved. Researchers have also noted that job satisfaction measures vary in the extent to which they measure feelings about the job (affective job satisfaction) or cognitions about the job (cognitive job satisfaction)

According to Abrahan A. Korman, there are two types of factors which determine the job satisfaction of an employee. These are: 1) Organisational Factors2) Personal Factors

Organizational Factors :

1.Occupational level. The higher the level of the job, the greater is the satisfaction of the individual. This is because higher level jobs carry greater prestige and self control.

2. Job Content : Greater the variation in job content and the less repetitiveness with which the tasks must be performed, the greater is the satisfaction of the individual involved

3.Considerate Leadership- People like to be treated with consideration. Hence considerate leadership results in job satisfaction than inconsiderate leadership

4. Pay and Promotional Opportunities- All other things being equal these two variables are positively related to job satisfaction i.e, if pay and promotional opportunities are increased it'll result in an increase in job satisfaction

5. Working Conditions- Working for eight hours or more can be really tolerable if you have a great and entertaining crew working along with you. Further, if you receive the right working conditions, such as lighting, space, and other such factors, it will only increase your level of job satisfaction. In short, you will want to go to work if your organization provides you with a good workplace communication and encouraging environment.

6. Respect from Co-Workers- Employees seek to be treated with respect by those they work with. A hostile work environment with rude or unpleasant co-workers, is one that usually has lower job satisfaction Managers need to step in and mediate conflicts before they escalate into more serious problems requiring disciplinary action? Employees may need to be reminded what behaviours are considered inappropriate when interacting with co-workers.

7. Relationship with Supervisors- Effective managers know that their employees need recognition and praise for their efforts and accomplishments. Employees also need to know, their supervisors door is always open for them to discuss any concerns they have that are affecting their ability to do their jobs effectively and impeding their satisfaction at the office.

8. Opportunity for Advancement-Emplovees are more satisfied with their current job if they see a path available to move up the ranks in the company and be given more responsibility and along with it higher compensation. Many companies encourage employees to acquire more advanced skills that will lead to the chance of promotion.

9 Workload and Stress Level- Dealing with a workload that is far too heavy and deadlines that are impossible to reach can cause job satisfaction to erode for even the most dedicated emplovee. Falling short of deadlines results in conflict between emplovees and supervisors and raises the stress level of the workplace.

10. Financial Rewards- Job satisfaction is impacted by an employees views about the fairness of the company wage scale as well as the current compensation she may be receiving. Opportunities to earn special incentives, such as bonuses, extra paid time off or vacations, also bring excitement and higher job satisfaction to the workplace.

Personal Factors :

1. Personality Job Fit - Individuals should be assigned the job that suits their interest. Recently it has been seen that MBA graduates are satisfied with their job if they get the job related to the "specialization" they have

chosen during the MBA degree

2. Work itself- One of the key findings from research is the open expression of fulfilment in workplace to gain fulfilment in their work is a powerful motivator. To be fulfilled, people need to value their day-to-day work activities. People need to have a sense of accomplishment or pleasure from the work itself.

3. Educational Level- With occupational level there is a negative relationship between the educational level and job satisfaction. The higher the education, the higher the reference group which the individual looks to for guidance to evaluate his job rewards. Well-educated individuals know the scope expectations and dept of their jobs

4. Role Perceptions- Different individuals hold different perceptions about their role. Job satisfaction is determined by this factor also. The more accurate the role perception of an individual, the greater his satisfaction.

5. Gender- One might predict gender to be the case, generally low occupational aspiration of women. Women are less satisfied with their jobs in workplaces where family friendly work environment are not available.

6. Career development- The Employee is more satisfied with the job : Experience within a specific field of interest. Success at each stage of development, educational attainment with each incremental stage.

Other Factors :

1. Achievement- Personal Achievement, Social Achievement, introduce of rewards, Need For Influence, advancement, Recognition.

2. Desires for- personal career development improvement in ones own life standards better education & prospects for children improving ones own work performance.

3. Job satisfaction is closely affected by the amount of rewards that an individual derives from his job, the level of performance is closely affected by the basis for attainment of rewards. Positive relationship between performance and reward.

4. Employees are satisfied with their current job if they see a path available to move up the ranks in the company and be given more responsibility. Many companies encourage employees to acquire more advanced skills that will lead to the chance of promotion. Companies often pay the cost of tuition for employees training courses.

5. Another major factor determining job satisfaction is that recognizes the efforts and work of employees. Appreciating one's work or providing better opportunities will motivate and encourage him to contribute more to

the firm.

PPP

TRAINING

Q14. What is the need of training in organization?

Ans. 1. Increase in efficiency: Training plays an active role in increasing efficiency of employees in an organization. Training increases skills for doing a job in a better way. Though an employee can learn many things while he is put on a job. He can do much better if he learns how to do the job. This becomes more important specially in the context of changing technology because the old method of working may not be relevant. In such a case, training is required even to maintain minimum level of output. For example, working on automatic machine requires skills different than the required to handle manually operated machine. Raw employees cannot handle such a machine. Similar changes are taking place in managerial jobs also.

2. Increase in Morale of Employees: Training increases morale of employees. Morale is a mental condition of an individual or group which determines the willingness to co-operate. Training increases employee morale by relating their skills with their job requirements. Possession of skills necessary to perform a job well often tends to meet such human needs as security and ego satisfaction. Trained employees can see the jobs in more meaningful ways because they are able to relate their skills with jobs.

3. Better Human Relations: Training attempts to increase the quality of human relations in an organization . Growing complexity of organizations has led to various human problems like alienation, inter personal and intergroup problems. Many of these problems can be overcome by suitable human rotations training. Many of these problems can be overcome by suitable human relations training. Many techniques have been developed through which people can be trained and developed to tackle many techniques have been developed through which people can be trained and developed to tackle many problems of social and psychological nature.

4. Reduced Supervision: Trained employees require less supervision. They require more autonomy and freedom. Such autonomy and freedom can be given if the employees are trained properly to handle their jobs without the help of supervision. With reduced supervision, a manager can increase his span of management. This may result in lesser number of intermediate levels in the organization which can serve much cost to the

organization.

5. Increased organizational viability and flexibility: Trained people are necessary to maintain, organizational ability and flexibility relates to survival of the organization during bad days, and flexibility relates to sustain its effectiveness despite the loss of its key personnel and making short-term adjustment with the existing personnel. Such adjustment is possible if the organization has trained people who can occupy the positions vacated by key personnel.

Q15. What are techniques of training?

Ans. On the job training: On the Job Training (OJT) is the most common form of training for any person in the organization. The basic theme of OJT is 'to learn by doing itself'. The trainee learns while he is actually engaged in doing job. This engagement may be on a specific job or there may be job rotation, that is changing the jobs over the period of time. For operatives, who are changed in routine and repetitive job, OJT is the most important tool.

Demonstration: In this method of training, the trainer describes and displays something when he trains the operatives. The usual process is to perform the activity by the trainer in front of the trainees and to explain the various steps involved in the completion of a job. This method can be combined with lectures, and group discussion so as to avoid any ambiguity. The financial costs is one of the drawback of this method.

Lectures: This is traditionally the most formal method of instruction, and usually consists of verbal explanation or description of the subject matter with or without illustration. It is also called chalk and talk method. As a strategy, many it has advantages for the trainer and several purposes, including:

It can used to give an overall view of the subject matter in a short time.

The presentation of new technique and procedures, of which the trainees can have no

Previous knowledge.

Discussion Method: To receive full benefit from the discussion, the trainee should have some preview familiarity with the subject matter. They could be familiar with the subject matter as a result of Outside reading, prior navy training and experience, or civilian training and experience. To help make the class discussion a success, arrange the classroom in such a manner that you are a part of the group. Use the discussion method only when classes are small enough to allow everyone a chance to take part. Computer Bases training: Computer Based Training is a process of learning that is not executed in the traditional manner one would find in the educational environment. Rather than the conventional classroom and instructor or processor setting.

Computer based training: for example, change management tools involves learning using software installed in computers. The student is, in effect, trained by the computer. Often, this method of learning can be much more effective than the practice of teaching and learning in classrooms- because the student, if working alone, can set his or her own speed of learning. As such, the student that is a quick learner can forge ahead at a pace that an average student would not able to handle. On the other hand, for those that take a little more time than the average student to process and learn new information, computer-based training would be ideal, as they can go at their own stride, not full behind and not keep any other students behind schedule.

Case Study: Case study is one of the most frequently used pedagogical tools in management education and development case method of learning has the following objectives:

The description of real business situation to acquaint the learner with the principles and practices obtained in work setting.

Demonstration of various types of goals, problems, facts, conditions conflicts and personalities obtained in organizational settings.

Development of decision making ability and

Development of independent thinking but cooperative approach to work in team situations.

A case is a description of a situation involving problems to be solved. However, the case may not have as compete information about the problem. The amount of detail required would make the case too long to read and too detailed to analyze.

In-basket technique:

In-basket exercise is a simulation technique designed around the 'income mail' of a manager. A variety of situations is presented in this exercise which would usually be dealt by a manager in his typical working day. One method of this exercise is to present mail of various types to a trainee whose reactions on these are noted. A slight variation in this method may be in the form of incident method. In this method, the trainee is given certain incidents and his reactions are noted down. Some trainees may even play surprise roles which interrupt the manager and give him two or more simultaneous problems more like real on the job pressures. Through the feedback of his behavior the trainee comes to know his behavioral pattern and tries to overcome the one which is not productive or functional. Thus, he can learn techniques of giving priorities to various problems faced by him.

Role Paying: Role playing helps the trainees to develop better perspective in performing their jobs because they may see the jobs from different angles. It also develops sensitivity among trainees which is quite helpful in maintaining better human relations. This training method provides immediate feedback about one's role during the training, session which helps him in developing better understanding. However, role playing training is not quite suitable at higher management level.

Coaching / understudy: Coaching is a learning through on-the-job experience. A manager can learn when he is put on a specific job. He can develop skills for doing the job in a better way over the period of time. However, he can learn better if he is given some guidance either in the form of coaching or understudy. Coaching involves direct personal instructions and guidance usually with demonstration and continuous critical evaluation and correction. In understudy method, the trainee works normally as assistant under the direction and supervision of a person.

The coaching method offers certain advantages. If provides an opportunity to a trainee to develop himself. It provides quick feedback. Coaching system has certain drawbacks. One of the main drawbacks is that trainer's styles of working, which may not necessarily be suitable percolate in the trainee.

However, Coaching can be an effective management tool if followed properly. To be effective, coaching demands that the superior renders assistance when the trainee and have patience to develop the trainee. Decenzo and Robbins observe that, "coaching will work well if the coach provides a good model with whom the trainee can identify, if both can be open with each other, if the coach accepts this responsibility fully and if he provides the trainee with recognition of his improvement and suitable rewards.

Job Rotation: Job rotation or channel method of development, involves movement of a manager from one job to another job, from one plan to another plan on a planned basis. Such movement may be for a period ranging from 6 moths to2 years before a person is established in a particular job or department. In this case, the movement is not meant for transfer but is meant for learning the interdependence of various jobs so that the trainee can look at his job in broader perspective.

The advantage of this method is that managers may develop broader horizon and prospective of a generalist than narrower horizon of a specialist.

It may create confusion in the mind of a trainee and he may not be able to understand the rationale of job rotation if not properly counselled. This may affect his performance as well as that of others with whom he works.

Job Instruction Training: Job Instruction Training (JIT), also known as "Training through step-by-step", involves listing of all necessary steps involved in the job performance with a sequential arrangement of all steps. These steps show what is to be done, how to be done and why to be done. JIT involves the following steps

Providing Job information to the trainees by emphasizing its importance, general description of the job and duties and responsibility involved.

Positioning the trainees at work place and explaining them the various steps involved in job performance and the reasons for these steps.

Allowing the trainees to try out work performance on the basis of the steps involved and correcting the errors committed by them.

Incurring the trainees to ask questions about the job performance, and satisfying them with further explanations.

Simulation Training: Simulated method of training involves the duplication of organizational situations in a learning environment. It is a mock-up of real thing. Though there are different methods of training under simulated situations and each of these involves a particular procedure, simulated learning involves the following:

In simulation, essential characteristics of a real-life situation are presented in abstracted form as whole characteristics are difficult to be simulated.

Participants in the training programmers are required to do according to the situation prescribed and to see the problem from the perspective of various roles given in the situations.

The role of the instructor is quite restricted to allow the trainees to participate fully.

After the exercise is over, the instructor provides the feedback to the participants to evaluate themselves and to strengthen themselves by overcoming their weak points.

It is not possible to simulate the real life exactly in the learning situations.

Vestibule training: The concept of vestibule school/training centre is that people will learn and develop skills while working in the situations similar to what they will face after they are put on the actual job. Vestibule training consists of two parts. First, there is lecture method which is conducted in class rooms meant for this purpose. The lecture method focuses on theoretical framework and principles involved in the job performance. Second, there is a practical exercise based on the theoretical aspects in a workshop which is similar to the shopfloor in production department.

Vestibule training offers various advantages:

Trainees feel more freedom for experimentation as they are away from the actual work place. They do not have the psychological fear of being criticized from supervisors and co-workers.

This method of training can be adopted only when there are large number of trainees because it requires additional investment for creating training facilities. This method is suitable for those employees who are required certain specific technical skills before they are engaged in actual operations.

Apprenticeship: Apprenticeship as a method of training in crafts, trades, and technical areas is one of the oldest and the most commonly used method specially when proficiency in a job is the result of a relatively long period of training. The areas in which apprenticeship training is offered are numerous from the job or a draftsman, machinist, printer, tool maker, engraver, electrician etc. In this method, a major part of the training time is spent on the productive job. In India, the Apprentices Act, 1961 (amended in 1973) makes it obligatory on the part of all employers in the specified industries to place apprentices in the designated trades in standard laid down. The advantage is that the organization can build a pool of technically trained personnel with much higher loyalty to it.

Syndicate: Syndicate method of development has been introduced by administrative staff college at Henley-on-Thomas. Syndicate refers to a group of trainees and involves the analysis of a problem by different groups with each group consisting of 8-10 members. Each group works on the problems on the basis of brief and background papers provided by the resource person. After the preliminary exercise, a group presents its ideas on the issues involved along other groups. After the presentation of ideas, these are evaluated by group members with the help of the resource person and group members evaluate where they have lacked. Such exercise is repeated so as to enable the participants to look at the problems in right perspective. The syndicate method is quite helpful in developing analytical skills in the participants and their approach for understanding others, if conducted properly.

Sensitivity Training: Sensitivity training is a small group interaction process in the unstructured from which requires people to become sensitive to others, feelings in order to develop reasonable group activity. The objectives of sensitivity training are as follows:

To make participants increasingly aware, of, and sensitive to the emotional reactions and expressions in themselves and others.

To develop achievement of behavioral effectiveness in participants.

To increase the ability of participants to perceive and to learn from, the consequences of their actions through attention to their own and other's feelings.

It may contribute positively if handled properly, it may damage if handle improperly. For example, those who criticize sensitivity training offer the following reasons:

Many participants of sensitivity training have reported a feeling of humiliation, manipulation, decline in self-confidence and psychological damage.

It incites anxiety with many, negative impacts like causing the people to be highly frustrated, unsettled and upset.

www.ingramcontent.com/pod-product-compliance
Ingram Content Group UK Ltd.
Pitfield, Milton Keynes, MK11 3LW, UK
UKHW022027190726
13853UKWH00005B/2150